EUTHANASIA

In memory of George Garnel Graber,
and in gratitude for the love and support of Virginia Fort Graber,
and Charles W. and Rosemary Olma Thomasma

EUTHANASIA
TOWARD AN ETHICAL SOCIAL POLICY

David C. Thomasma
and
Glenn C. Graber

CONTINUUM • NEW YORK

1990

The Continuum Publishing Company
370 Lexington Avenue, New York, N.Y. 10017

© 1990 by David C. Thomasma and Glenn C. Graber

Printed in the United States of America

Library of Congress Cataloging-in-Publication Data

Thomasma, David C., 1939–
    Euthanasia : toward an ethical social policy / David C. Thomasma and Glenn C. Graber.
    ISBN 0-8264-0470-7
    1. Euthanasia. 2. Medical ethics. I. Graber, Glenn C.
II. Title
R726.T48 1990
179'.7–dc20   90-30987
                                          CIP

Contents

ACKNOWLEDGEMENTS

We wish to thank Doris Kulpa, senior secretary of the Loyola Medical Humanities Program, for her gracious help in bringing this manuscript to press, and Jeff Bulger, graduate assistant in the Philosophy Department at the University of Tennessee, for his assistance. Karin Dean, administrative secretary of the Medical Humanities Program, helped make arrangements. For this we are grateful as well.

Much of the editing of the text took place at the Holiday Inn Papermill Rd. in Knoxville, Tenn. We want to thank the staff of the motel for their support, especially Hazel Mikels, who always made sure our meals there were served with the highest regard for our needs.

Thanks to the *American College of Surgeons Bulletin* for permission to use portions of D. Thomasma, "The Range of Euthanasia," *American College of Surgeons Bulletin* 73, no. 8 (August 1988): 4–13; to *New World Outlook* for portions of "High Technology and Dying," *New World Outlook* 46, no. 8 (June 1986): 256–258; to *Seminars in Oncology Nursing* for permission to use a part of "Ethics and Professional Practice in Oncology," *Seminars in Oncology Nursing* 5, no. 2 (May 1989): 89–94; and to *New Catholic World* for portions of "When Healing Involves Risk to Life: Risky Medical Procedures and Experimentation," *New Catholic World* 230 (July–August 1987): 163–167.

PREFACE

In this study, we discuss the range of euthanasia in several senses of the term "range." We examine a wide variety of cases — many drawn from our own clinical observation, others from the medical ethics literature — that involve options that have the effect of shortening life. Most of these cases are collected in Appendix I, but they are discussed in appropriate places throughout the volume. By means of these cases, we consider the whole range of actions (including omissions) that are sometimes categorized under the label "euthanasia." Also, we examine these issues from the viewpoints of the several "players" in the euthanasia drama: in particular, the patient (especially in Chapters Two and Three), the family (especially in Chapter Four), physicians and other health professionals (especially in Chapter Five), and society at large (especially in Chapter Six). At every stage, we acknowledge the diversity ("range") of opinions about these matters that have been represented in recent discussion. Our attempt has been to listen to every viewpoint, and, where we disagree, to explain the basis of our position in terms that could be agreed upon by all parties and in careful step-by-step argument. Even if some parties to the debates in this area disagree with us in the end, we hope we will have at least succeeded in isolating more carefully than has been done in the past the points at issue.

The authors are both veterans of many hours of wrestling with these issues in the clinical medical setting as well as the classroom and seminar room. Both serve on Hospital Ethics Committees and consultation services, where issues of limiting treatment arise frequently. Both have also discussed these matters with groups of health care professionals, humanities students, and citizens groups. These are issues of significant concern to all these groups — as is shown by discussions of these issues in both the professional and lay literature, as well as by court cases and legislation in this area in recent years. In our judgment, this general social debate is a healthy way to air the reasoning on both sides of the question and to work toward a social resolution of the thorny issues of the appropriate limits to life-sustaining efforts. We will suggest some legislative and social policies in the final chapter.

We consider this book to be suitable either for individual reflection or for group discussion in college or medical school seminars, or by citizens groups who are interested in digging into these issues. Our argument on the background issues is contained in Chapters Two and Three. We then examine the conclusions of those chapters from the point of view of the family, medical profession, and society in Chapters Four, Five, and Six respectively. In each case, we have described what we see as the main problem areas and developed the basic argument from Chapters Two and Three in a way that deals with the issues raised. In the final chapter, we offer a general framework for dealing with terminal care, as well as some legislative suggestions.

Chapter One

THE RANGE OF EUTHANASIA

The idea of active euthanasia is very old.[1] It was recommended by Plato, Aristotle, and Luther, among many others.[2] Nonetheless, active euthanasia is legally proscribed and morally suspect in the United States today, as it is in most countries. The only legally valid ways of ending life at present are abortion, capital punishment, war, and suicide.[3] The situation will no doubt change over the next several years, as increasing discussion of "mercy killing" lays bare some of the major problems facing its opponents.[4] Indeed, in California, where a referendum permitting physicians to employ active euthanasia to relieve patient suffering was recently proposed, 23 percent of six hundred physicians polled said they had helped at least one person die, and 62 percent approved of a physician doing so; 68 percent were in favor of the referendum. Half of those polled said they would assist a patient in dying if it were legal and the request were rational.[5]

In the Netherlands, the Hoge Raad (Supreme Court) declared in a case of active euthanasia that a physician may legally commit homicide at the victim's request, given certain stringent conditions, including a medical emergency.[6] But physicians rarely encounter rational patients, in intractable pain, with supportive families, giving clear directives about euthanasia. Instead they encounter aging patients, in some suffering, without families, and too confused to give directives. For this reason, Dutch physicians are as reluctant as most of their colleagues to kill patients.[7]

Some problems creating a growing trend toward considering active euthanasia are as follows:

1. Medical technology itself has created a crisis in dying that older generations could not have foreseen. No one seems to have seen the shadow of protracted dying behind all the promises of longevity. Do we not have an obligation to direct this technology to good human ends?[8]

2. If persons suffer more pain and psychological discomfort as a consequence of the success of past medical interventions (e.g., controlling infection in burn patients)[9] do we not have a responsibility to address the results of this success?[10] As Kenneth Vaux observes: "If biomedical acts of life extension become acts of death prolongation, we may force some patients to outlive their deaths, and we may ultimately repudiate the primary life-saving and merciful ethic itself."[11]

3. If, from time to time, control of pain and suffering proves fruitless, does not the quality of mercy and compassion compel us to accede to a patient's heartrending request for active euthanasia?[12]

4. Is there any moral difference between omission and commission, if our motive is to help a patient die? Are we not just splitting hairs by arguing that omission permits the "natural course of the disease" to take the person's life, while commission actively intervenes to kill the patient?[13] Is the distinction between active and passive euthanasia clearly applicable in clinical practice?[14]

5. If, as the courts have now consistently affirmed, patients have a constitutional right to determine their own medical care, could the right to privacy and the common law right of self-determination sustain a right to die?[15]

These questions are addressed throughout the rest of the book. We first turn to a discussion of the range of euthanasia that is currently practiced in the United States.[16]

DEFINITION OF EUTHANASIA

Euthanasia comes from the Greek for "good" or "merciful" death. It is "the art of painlessly putting to death persons suffering from incurable conditions or diseases."[17] Current usage requires the distinction to be made between active and passive euthanasia, although some prefer a distinction between positive and passive euthanasia.[18] Active euthanasia is an intentional act that causes death. Passive euthanasia is an intentional act to avoid prolonging the dying process.[19] Euthanasia itself can be distinguished from murder on the basis of motive. Murder would be killing someone for reasons other than kindness.

The difference between active and passive forms of euthanasia cannot be sustained on the basis of motive alone. A merciful motive cannot sustain a homicide, for example. Both forms of euthanasia aim at the same end, a merciful death. Rather, the difference lies in the nature of the act itself. Active euthanasia brings about a kind death through direct intervention. The act performed directly kills the patient. Passive euthanasia, by contrast, is the withholding or withdrawing of life-prolonging and life-sustaining technologies. Death is brought about by the underlying disease or assault on the body. This disease or assault was initially sufficient to kill the patient, but our technology and medical skills arrested that process. Withholding or withdrawing such treatment means that the dying process continues unabated.

In any discussion of euthanasia, therefore, death is not considered to be an enemy. Rather it is considered to be a friend for the patient, whose life itself has now become a burden. Thus, the goal of medicine, usually so clearly articulated as the preservation of life, should now be changed. Medicine should aim at reconstructing life sufficiently to sustain other values. As Engelhardt notes: "One must remember that one prolongs the length of life so that certain values can be realised, not for the mere prolongation itself."[20] These other values include human relationships, working, recreation, study, contributing to society, and the like. When these human values (as defined by the patient) can no longer be sustained because of the physical condition of the patient, then a decision should be made for euthanasia on the basis of the patient's or surrogate's request. One challenge created by the case of "It's Over, Debbie" published in *The Journal of the American Medical Association*[21] (reprinted as Case 1, p. 208) is whether the option for euthanasia should be active or passive.[22]

The deepest challenge, however, arises in a clash of values. On the one side is the ancient injunction of Hippocratic ethics, that physicians should help, or at least do no harm. In this ethic, a physician may not actively kill patients.[23] On the other side is the growing sense that real harm in the form of terminal suffering does come to patients as a result of the application of current medical and surgical interventions.[24] As a consequence, guidelines for actively terminating the suffering of such patients have been proposed by such groups as the Hemlock Society, following Dutch physician-inaugurated guidelines.[25]

The following discussion uncovers a wider range of options than is usually considered when one encapsulates the choices into the general categories of active and passive euthanasia. As each is presented, a brief critique is offered.

THE RANGE OF EUTHANASIA

Perhaps the most noteworthy feature of modern medical and surgical practice is the clinical blurring of the distinction between active and passive euthanasia. Sometimes physicians and surgeons get involved in what are called "gray areas" that muddy even further the duties and obligations we have toward the dying. Also families in desperation take matters into their own hands, apparently finding little or no support in society. Thus a broad range of controversial euthanasia practices appears. A sketch of some different forms of euthanasia demonstrates this point. This sketch proceeds from clearly active to clearly passive forms of euthanasia.

State-sanctioned killing. Some state-sanctioned killing occurs during war, in capital punishment, or during the resisting of arrest for armed robbery. These forms of taking the lives of others cannot be called euthanasia, since the victims do not request a kind death. Nazi termination of the lives of others for eugenic or economic reasons fall into this category as well.[26] Another form of state-sanctioned killing, however, may possibly be called euthanasia. It would be the case of individuals like Gary Gilmore in Utah or like Charles Walker in Illinois, condemned to death by the courts for murder, who request that the sentence be carried out. Walker objected to a stay of execution on April 19, 1988, as the work of "bleeding hearts who should mind their own business."[27] The process of killing such persons in Texas, Illinois, and other states that use death by lethal injection looks strangely like a form of active euthanasia. Although the American Medical Association has strictly prohibited physicians from pushing the buttons to inject such patients, physicians often serve to determine death in these cases and, thereby, already assist at a form of active euthanasia.

Cryonics. A number of people have become enamored of cryonics. At the Alcor Life Extension Foundation Laboratory in Riverside, California, an eighty-three-year-old lady, Dora Kent, had her head surgically removed from her body and frozen in the hopes that someday she could be brought back to life with a new body. She was apparently still alive when the procedure was started. Her son is a believer in cryonics, and supervised the removal of his mother's head. The coroner has classified the death a homicide.[28] If active euthanasia is permitted, and a record were kept that Mrs. Kent consented to this procedure, would it also be permitted?

Killing by family members. More and more frequently, one reads about family members who kill their relatives out of love and compassion. (a) Hans Florian on March 8, 1983, shot his wife who was suffering from Alzheimer's disease. He did so because he was older than she and did not want to leave her alone when he died.[29] The grand jury refused to indict him. (b) But Roswell Gilbert, who expressed no remorse over killing Emily, his wife of fifty-one years, is now convicted of murder. He claims he shot her twice in the head because he had to "terminate her suffering."[30] Some think that he was convicted precisely because he did not cry about it on the stand. (c) In England, a thirty-eight-year-old mother was put on probation for feeding her brain-damaged baby Mandrax (a lethal poison) through her feeding tube.[31] (d) Geraldine Sagel tried to kill her retarded dwarf son whom she had cared for in her home for fifty-one years. Her own failing health made her fear that he would fall on the mercy of the world. (e) Nephews, distraught about the decline of their uncle in a nursing home, shot him with a Luger. The motive was to provide the relief of death, presumably based on the previous expressed wishes of the uncle, or his presumed wishes. This is a form of active euthanasia, but health professionals are not involved, unless it is by passively creating the conditions that lead to such impulses.

Selective abortion. Many argue that abortion itself is a form of active euthanasia, because it takes innocent human lives. It does so without the consent of the victim. Selective abortion occurs when, through reproductive technology, more fertilized ova begin to gestate in the womb than a couple intended. The additional tragedy of requesting that two out of four, for example, be aborted so that the others may properly mature, stems from the fact that the couple had had, until the time of this request, fertility difficulties and want children desperately. Some physicians have consented to abort such fetuses for the reasons given,[32] using a euphemism like "thinning the pregnancy."

Active injection. Active euthanasia by injection is sometimes practiced, but is legally proscribed in the United States. It takes two forms.

In the first, the injection is done to "put someone out of her misery." But in this form, the injection is administered without the consent of the patient, or with inadequate consent. Thus, a nightshift nurse, Bobbie Sue Dudley Terrell, got a sixty-five-year sentence for killing four elderly patients through injections and strangulation.[33]

Later in the book, we will discuss the case of four Austrian nurses who did something similar to forty-nine elderly patients. No one supports this kind of action. If caught, health professionals are tried for murder.

In the second form, however, the patient has requested death by injection (or other means) so that he or she may be relieved of pain and suffering. If all other means have been exhausted for improving the condition of the patient, and the pain seems intractable, a number of thinkers and physicians have supported active euthanasia based on the patient's own request and a motive of compassion.[34] Indeed, some thinkers also support infanticide, or positive killing of persons who are in an irreversibly unconscious state.[35] Problems regarding informed consent occur for this position.[36]

Perhaps the greatest argument in favor of active euthanasia is that it is not a form of taking an innocent human life, which is murder, but a loving response to an individual's wishes. After all, what possible meaning can a life of suffering and intractable pain have? Especially if that suffering will not go away, but increase? It is a loving response to our technological patina of care, a patina that brings about increased survival, but sometimes a lower quality of life. Thus, active euthanasia is a way of taking responsibility for our technology, by assuring people who are its subjects that they will not be crucified on a cross of steel operating tables, shunts, and tubes.

The death management policy recommendation in the final chapter recognizes this responsibility, but avoids directly killing the patient. This recognition is important, because opponents of active euthanasia, in rejecting the action, appear to be insensitive to patient suffering.

Assisted suicide. Sometimes a kind death can be brought about by assisting patients to take their own lives. This form of euthanasia walks a narrow line between active and passive. It is not, strictly speaking, active euthanasia, since the physician would not directly administer the agent that kills the patient. However, by providing the agent for the patient, the physician clearly is not practicing passive euthanasia either. Thus, a surgeon, having operated on a patient with melanoma, and later caring for the patient during the advanced and terminal stages of the disease, may prescribe sufficient pain control medication to kill the patient, and then say: "If things get too bad, take all of this at once." By doing this, the surgeon demonstrates responsibility for reducing pain and suffering of the patient but leaves the action to the patient. Many would argue that such an action betrays complicity in murder. Others would view this as a good compromise as compared to actively killing the patient. We will examine a more recent proposal by Wanzer et al. that favors assisted suicide in Chapter Five.

Court-ordered removal of life-sustaining treatment. Some physicians and hospitals have argued that a court-order prohibiting them from providing fundamental "ordinary means," such as nasogastric feeding tubes, gastrostomies, or even intravenous fluids and nutrition, is tantamount to requiring them to assist at the suicide of patients. Actually, this is a misnomer. Patients who wish to exercise their right of self-determination or privacy and decide whether or not to accept medical interventions are not by that fact committing suicide, nor are their physicians who help them carry out their wishes assisting at their suicides. The reasons are complex. But central to them is the point that the disease the patient suffers is itself the cause of death, not an act of commission or omission on the part of the patient or physician. Deferring death does not make a life for most people.[37] Persons have a constitutional right to refuse life-sustaining treatment.[38]

Organ donation. All organ donation is authorized to benefit others by surrogate decision-makers. Current standards require that the patient, who can no longer participate in this decision, be brain-dead. Nonetheless, American surgeons participated in a case in which the organs of a Canadian-born anencephalic infant were taken to benefit another infant, after which the respirator on which the anencephalic was maintained was turned off (see Case 2, p. 210). This constitutes a form of active euthanasia, since an anencephalic is strictly speaking neither brain-dead, nor brain-absent. Loma Linda surgeons also attempted to keep twelve anencephalics alive on respirators for the same purpose.[39] It is difficult to draw a conclusion about this category of euthanasia, since anencephalics may not truly be persons,[40] lacking as they do the sufficient physiological brain structure; and therefore taking their lives may not constitute active euthanasia.

What if persons could state in their living will that if they ever become permanently comatose or are in a permanent vegetative state, they would want any organs and tissues (like eyes and skin, perhaps) taken from them and then be taken off life-support technology? Can persons donate organs even if they are not brain-dead at the time of harvesting?[41] This is not currently possible under the law, but the requests of families, on behalf of loved ones in such states after accidents, have started to appear in the clinical setting.

Double-effect euthanasia. Often physicians are faced with an intervention that has more than one effect. An example would be the administration of increased doses of morphine to control pain with the knowledge that such massive doses will decrease respiration such that the patient dies. There are even subsets of these cases.

1. The standard example is increasing the intravenous morphine dosage to control suffering while simultaneously accepting the second effect, which is a side effect, of depressing the respirations and killing the patient. Many ethicists hold that this action is good and warranted, because one wills only the first effect (pain control) and not the second (the death of the patient). But others wonder why the motive would make any difference if the result is the same. Why would it be wrong if the physician willed both results, or, as perhaps in the Debbie case, primarily willed the second effect (death of the patient) rather than the first (control of pain)?

2. These questions are brought home when considered alongside a second subset of the double-effect cases, one in which the physician caring for a cardiovascular patient who has now suffered a massive stroke and is comatose, agrees to the family's request that the respirator be removed from the patient. It is removed, and he administers a large shot of morphine shortly thereafter to insure that the patient does not suffer agonal gasping during her dying moments. Perhaps this goal is mixed with compassion for the family as well, since they might suffer from guilt if they witnessed their loved one gasping for breath while dying. Here the motive is to provide a kind death by removing life-sustaining treatment (again at the patient's request through her surrogates), and the cause of death is the underlying disease process. Even though this cause of death is assisted by the morphine or other pain-control medication, it seems that the motive was to reduce suffering, not directly to cause death.

3. How does this case differ from a similar one in which the surgeon, faced with the same conditions, decides to administer the injection before taking the patient off the respirator? (Case 3, p. 211). This would be to insure that agonal gasping would be kept to a minimum. No doubt, however, the injection itself would be a primary cause of death. If one objected to this third instance, but not to the second or first, would that not just be a case of "splitting hairs"? What conceivable difference would it make whether the shot was given before or after the respirator were taken off the patient, since the ultimate goal in both cases is to help the patient die a comfortable death?

Transferring to die. Physicians sometimes transfer patients as a means of providing euthanasia. Their motive is that the patient die during the transfer. Often this occurs by transferring from intensive care to intermediate or ordinary care wings, or by transferring the patient to a less technologically intensive hospital. This method is actually one that restricts access to high technology interventions that would only prolong the dying process. It is an explicit euthanasia goal to transfer patients to hospices.

Tragic choices. No one holds physicians responsible for the difficult and tragic choices involved in some people's diseases. A young patient may be brought to the emergency room with severe abdominal pain. She is operated on for intestinal blockage, but it is found during surgery that her intestines have died as a result of aortic blockage, something rarely seen at her age. The surgeons can remove all intestines, put her on hyperalimentation for a short time, and permit her to speak with her family before her nutritional status is completely compromised, and she dies; or they can sew her up and never permit her to awaken from anesthesiology. Both "arms" of the action lead to death. There is nothing that can be done. Which choice leads to the lesser harm during the dying process?

Withholding and withdrawing. While virtually everyone agrees that withholding or withdrawing extraordinary means during the dying process is a form of passive euthanasia that is acceptable, not everyone agrees about what constitutes extraordinary means. Because the distinction between ordinary and extraordinary has taken on a normative character not originally intended (ordinary = obligatory; extraordinary = optional), most ethicists and the courts as well have stressed the proportion between the intervention and the outcome.[42] The plan should be to reduce burdens and increase benefits. What should be considered extraordinary is anything that adds to the burden of the patient during the dying process.

For this reason, Do Not Resuscitate orders have become common.[43] The case of an elderly patient for whom DNR orders were issued without her involvement (which would have been impossible) or that of any surrogate in the emergency room of a hospital, for example, led to a legislative initiative about DNR orders that eventually produced a monumental state policy governing institutional actions in this regard.[44] A similar study and proposal was developed by the New York State Task Force on Life and the Law regarding appointment of a health care agent regarding life-sustaining treatment.[45]

By contrast, the case of Shirley Dinnerstein (Case 4, p. 212) in Massachusetts led to a decision that did not require an extensive policy governing institutions. In a previous decision about Joseph Saikewickz, the Massachusetts Supreme Court had required involvement of a judge in making withholding and withdrawing decisions about incompetent patients. In *Dinnerstein*, the family and physician concurred that a DNR order was appropriate. The Court in this case judged that it is not necessary to check with judges and that institutions need not require this.

More common than thought previously, deaths of renal dialysis patients occur because the dialysis was simply stopped.[46] The A.M.A. statement on withdrawing fluids and nutrition also reflects the ethic of not unduly prolonging dying.[47]

Social euthanasia. Over 37 million people in the United States cannot gain access to health care because they are uninsured or underinsured. If we continue each day to ignore this problem, are we not just practicing a form of social euthanasia of the passive sort? By restricting access, we are condemning many persons to death who might otherwise benefit from interventions readily available for those who are able to pay. But this form of passive euthanasia does not count as voluntary euthanasia, since it neglects the wishes of patients. As such it comes dangerously close to the eugenics and euthanasia projects of Nazi Germany and Stalin's Russia, in which millions of people were murdered for flimsy social goals.

Some system is needed to provide access to the 37 million citizens without health care at present. The bias built into the current system denies access to blacks, homosexuals, the poor, and other broad classes of people. The system may not be driven just by economics, but also by inbuilt prejudice against these groups. The reality is that certain human lives are more valued than others in contemporary society. Thus, as John Golenski avers:

> In certain areas of the country, if you're diagnosed with AIDS and anybody supposes that you are a homosexual, you are not going to be as aggressively treated as you would be if you had presumably come down with the disease through a blood transfusion.[48]

A kind of explicit ageism also directs the current health care system.[49] Many physicians themselves are now calling for a Canadian-type health care system in the United States to provide access without, it is hoped, increasing health care spending.[50]

CONCLUSION

Discussion of active euthanasia should therefore continue. Problems do exist in prolonging suffering.[51] These problems must be thoroughly discussed by our health professional societies and by society at large.[52] The reason is that if patients do request active euthanasia, the physician is put on the spot. He or she must make some response to patient needs. The discussion should move beyond proposed guidelines to protect patient wishes, however, to a discussion of professional and social consequences. As Drs. Gaylin, Kass, Pellegrino, and Siegler say, "If physicians become killers or are merely licensed to kill, the profession — and, therewith, each physician — will never again be worthy of trust and respect as healer and comforter and protector of life in all its frailty."[53] An additional concern is that in Nazi Germany, physicians began taking lives and were not prosecuted for it.[54] Soon active euthanasia was legalized in medical and nursing facilities.[55] Will the same actions in Dutch and other Western societies lead to the same eventuality?[56]

Yet patients seem to support active euthanasia by their physicians more than physicians themselves do, perhaps countervailing the concerns about patients being able to continue trusting physicians.[57] In a Roper Poll, 62 percent of Americans support doctors who allow patients to die, but opinions on active euthanasia were not asked as a separate question.[58] There is a real concern, expressed by Robert Baker, that if physicians do not respond to suffering patients, instead leaving them "howling like dogs," then society should not entrust them with the power of mercy killing. They would have lost all sensitivity to the very meaning of mercy.[59] Offering an alternative like death management may satisfy both physicians and patients alike.

NOTES

1. D. J. Pounder, M. Prokopec, G. L. Pretty, "A Probable Case of Euthanasia Amongst Prehistoric Aborigines at Roonka, South Australia," *Forensic Science International* 23 (1983), 99–108.

2. J. Weinfeld, "Active Voluntary Euthanasia — Should It Be Legalized?" *Medicine and Law* 4 (1985), 101–111.

3. Daniel Maguire, "Death: Legal and Illegal," *Atlantic Monthly* 233 (February 1974), 72–85.

4. D. Clarke, "Euthanasia and the Law," in John Monagle and David Thomasma, eds., *Medical Ethics: A Guide for Health Professionals* (Rockville, Md.: Aspen Publishers, 1988), pp. 217–213.

5. Joan Beck, "Californians May Be Invited to Vote on a Right to Die," *Chicago Tribune*, April 21, 1988, sec. 1, 23.

6. Hoge Raad (Supreme Court), November 27, 1984, nederlandse Jurisprudentie = NJ 1985, No. 106; H.-J. Scholten, "Court Decision: Justification of Active Euthanasia," *Medicine and Law* 5 (1986), 169–172.

7. Greg Pence, "Do Not Go Slowly into That Dark Night: Mercy Killing in Holland," *American Journal of Medicine* 84 (1988), 139–141.

8. Jon Van, " 'Debbie' Case Helps Euthanasia Cause," *Chicago Tribune*, March 20, 1988, sec. 1, 8.

9. I. Pondelicek and R. Koenigova, "The Problem of Euthanasia and Dysthanasia in Burns," *Burns* 10 (1983), 61–63.

10. Helga Kuhse, "The Case for Active Voluntary Euthanasia," *Law, Medicine and Health Care* 14 (1986), 145–148.

11. Kenneth Vaux, "Debbie's Dying: Mercy Killing and the Good Death," *Journal of the American Medical Association* 259 (1988), 2140–2141.

12. Charles Clark, "Letters," *Journal of the American Medical Association* 259 (1988), 2095.

13. Joseph Fletcher, "Medical Resistance to the Right to Die," *Journal of the American Geriatrics Society* 35 (1987), 679–682.

14. Phillip Montague, "The Morality of Active and Passive Euthanasia," *Ethics in Science and Medicine* 5 (1978), 39–45; James Rachels, "Active and Passive Euthanasia," *New England Journal of Medicine* 292 (1975), 78–80.

15. S. Wolhandler, "Voluntary Active Euthanasia for the Terminally Ill and the Constitutional Right to Privacy," *Cornell Law Review* 69 (1984), 363–383.

16. George Lundberg, "Editorial: 'It's Over Debbie' and the Euthanasia Debate," *Journal of the American Medical Association* 259 (1988), 272.

17. Raanan Gillon, "Acts and Omissions: Killing and Letting Die," *British Medical Journal* 292 (1986), 126–127.

18. Bernard Gert and Charles Culver, "Distinguishing Between Active and Passive Euthanasia," *Clinics in Geriatric Medicine* 2 (1986), 29–36; Kevin O'Rourke, "Active and Passive Euthanasia: The Ethical Distinctions," *Hospital Progress* (now *Health Progress*) 57 (November 1976), 68–73, 100.

19. James Rachels, "Killing and Starving to Death," *Philosophy* 54 (1979), 159–171; James Rachels, "Euthanasia, Killing and Letting Die," pp. 146–163 in John Ladd, ed., *Ethical Issues Relating to Life and Death* (New York: Oxford University Press, 1979); Philippa Foot, "Euthanasia," *Philosophy and Public Affairs* 6 (1977), 85–112.

20. H. Tristram Engelhardt, Jr, "The Counsels of Finitude: Death Inside Out," *The Hastings Center Report* 4 (1974), 119.

21. Anonymous, "It's Over, Debbie: A Piece of My Mind," *Journal of the American Medical Association* 259 (1988), 272.

22. Charles Krauthammer, "The 'Death' of 'Debbie,'" *Washington Post*, February 26, 1988; Victor Cohn, "Tales of Two Dying Patients: In One Case, the End Was Painful; In Another, Drugs Eased the Way," *Washington Post Health*, March 1, 1988, p. 15; Joseph Cardinal Bernadin, "Action in 'Debbie' Case Was Immoral," *Chicago Tribune*, March 10, 1988, sec. 1, 20.

23. R. Barry, "Killer-Doctor," *Chicago Tribune*, February 14, 1988, sec. C, 2; Jon Van, "'It's Over Debbie' and a Doctor Takes a Life," *Chicago Tribune*, January 31, 1988, sec. 1, 1; Isabel Wilkerson, "Essay on Mercy Killing Reflects Conflict on Ethics for Physicians and Journalists," *New York Times*, February 23, 1988, sec. A, 26, 1; Mark Siegler, "The A.M.A. Euthanasia Fiasco," *New York Times*, February 26, 1988, sec. A, 35, 1.

24. A. Woozley, "Euthanasia and the Principle of Harm," pp. 93–100 in Donnie J. Self, ed., *Philosophy and Public Policy* (Norfolk, Va.: Teagle and Little, 1977).

25. Don C. Shaw, "When Patients Should Be Helped to Die," *Chicago Tribune*, February 20, 1988, sec. 1, 9.

26. Robert Jay Lifton, *The Nazi Doctors: Medical Killing and the Psychology of Genocide* (New York: Basic Books, 1986).

27. "Judge Stays Execution of Walker," *Chicago Tribune*, April 20, 1988, sec. 2, 1.

28. "Attempt at Cryonics is Called a Homicide," *Chicago Tribune*, February 25, 1988, sec. 1, 8.

29. George F. Will, "When Is Killing Not a Crime?" *Washington Post*, April 14, 1983, sec. A, 23.

30. "Man Convicted of Killing Wife Who Begged to Die," *New York Times*, May 10, 1985, sec. A, 16.

31. Legal Correspondent, "Mercy Killing and the Law," *British Medical Journal* (November 27, 1976), 1333–1334.

32. Gina Kolata, "New Dilemma: Selective Abortion," *Chicago Tribune*, January 26, 1988, sec. 1, 10.

33. "Nurse Gets 65-year Sentence for Killing 4 Elderly Patients," *Chicago Tribune*, February 25, 1988, sec. I, 4.

34. W. Royce Clark, "The Example of Christ and Voluntary Active Euthanasia," *Journal of Religion and Health* 25 (1986), 264–277; Helga Kuhse, "'Letting Die' Is Not in the Patient's Best Interests: A Case for Active Euthanasia," *Medical Journal of Australia* 142 (1985), 610–613.

35. James Rachels, "Commentary: Active Euthanasia with Parental Consent," *Hastings Center Report* 9 (1979), 19–20; Helga Kuhse, "Death by Non-feeding: Not in the Baby's Best Interests," *Journal of Medical Humanities and Bioethics* 7 (1986), 79–90; Carson Strong, "Positive Killing and the Irreversibly Unconscious Patient," *Bioethics Quarterly* 3 (1981), 190–205.

36. Billie Shepperdson, "Abortion and Euthanasia of Down's Syndrome Children — The Parent's View," *Journal of Medical Ethics* 9 (1983), 152–157; John Fletcher, "Abortion, Euthanasia, and Care of Defective Newborns," *New England Journal of Medicine* 292 (1975), 75–78; H. Lauter and J.-E.

Meyer, "Mercy Killing without Consent: Historical Comments on a Controversial Issue," *Acta Psychiat. Scand.* 65 (1982), 134–141.

37. A. Quindlen, "Deferring Death Does Not Make a Life," *Chicago Tribune*, October 23, 1987, sec. 5, 1.

38. Rasa Gustaitis, "Right to Refuse Life-sustaining Treatment," *Pediatrics* 81 (1988), 317–321; E. Emanuel, "Review of the Ethical and Legal Aspects of Terminating Medical Care," *American Journal of Medicine* 84 (1988), 291–301.

39. "Doomed Fetus to Be Organ Donor," *Chicago Tribune*, December 9, 1987, sec. 1, 11.

40. David C. Thomasma, "Corpo e persona," *Kos* 5, no. 42 (March 1989), 6–7, 10–11, 14 and 15.

41. David Thomasma, "Making Treatment Decisions for Permanently Unconscious Patients: The Ethical Perspective," pp. 192–204 in John Monagle and David Thomasma, eds., *Medical Ethics: A Guide for Health Professionals* (Rockville, Md.: Aspen Publishers, 1988).

42. John Edward Ruark, Thomas A. Raffin, and the Stanford University Medical Center Committee on Ethics, "Initiating and Withdrawing Life Support," *New England Journal of Medicine* 318 (January 27, 1988), 25–30.

43. Jack E. Zimmerman, William A. Knaus, Steven M. Sharpe, et al., "The Use and Implications of Do Not Resuscitate Orders in Intensive Care Units," *Journal of the American Medical Association* 255 (January 17, 1986), 351–360.

44. New York State Task Force on Life and the Law, "Do-Not-Resuscitate Orders: Proposed Legislation and Report by the New York State Task Force on Life and the Law" (New York, N.Y.: New York State Task Force on Life and the Law, April 1986).

45. New York State Task Force on Life and the Law, "Life-Sustaining Treatment: Making Decisions and Appointing a Health Care Agent" (New York, N.Y.: New York State Task Force on Life and the Law, September 1987).

46. Steven Neu and Carl M. Kjellstrand, "Stopping Long-term Dialysis," *New England Journal of Medicine* 314 (1986), 14–19.

47. Kevin O'Rourke, "The A.M.A. Statement on Tube Feeding: An Ethical Analysis," *America*, November 22, 1986, 321–324.

48. "System Needed to Guarantee Access to Health Care in USA," *Medical Ethics Advisor* 5, no. 7 (July 1989), 1.

49. David C. Thomasma, "Moving the Aged into the House of the Dead: A Critique of Ageist Social Policy," *Journal of the American Geriatrics Society* 37 (1989), 169–172.

50. Michael Weinstein, "At the Annual Session: Views on Access to Care," *The American College of Physicians Observer* 9, no. 6 (June 1989), 1, 20–21.

51. Diane Davis, "Letters," *Journal of the American Medical Association* 259 (1988), 2097; Susan D. Wilson, "Letters," *Journal of the American Medical Association* 259 (1988), 2097.

52. David C. Thomasma, "Letters," *Journal of the American Medical Association* 259 (1988), 2098.

53. Willard Gaylin, Leon Kass, Edmund Pellegrino, Mark Siegler, "Commentaries: Doctors Must Not Kill," *Journal of the American Medical Association* 259 (1988), 2139.

54. J. Boozer, "Children of Hippocrates: Doctors in Nazi Germany," *Annals of the Academy of Political and Social Science* 450 (1980), 83–97.

55. G. Aly and K. H. Roth, "The Legalization of Mercy Killings in Medical and Nursing Institutions in Nazi Germany from 1938 until 1941," *International Journal of Law and Psychiatry* 7 (1984), 145–163.

56. R. Barry, "Killer-Doctor," *Chicago Tribune*, February 14, 1988, sec. C, 2.

57. George Lundberg, "Editorial: 'It's Over Debbie' and the Euthanasia Debate," *Journal of the American Medical Association* 259 (1988), 2142; Kenneth Vaux, "If We Can Bar the Door to Death, Can't We Also Open It?" *Chicago Tribune*, February 10, 1988, sec. 1, 23; Don C. Shaw, "When Patients Should be Helped to Die," *Chicago Tribune*, February 20, 1988, sec. 1, 9; Robert H. Cantwell, "Dignity in Death: Letter," *Chicago Tribune*, April 21, 1988, sec. 1, 22.

58. Jim Spencer, "Euthanasia Gains Favor," *Chicago Tribune*, July 17, 1986, sec. 5, 2.

59. Robert Baker, "On Euthanasia," pp. 5–28 in James M. Humber and Robert F. Almeder, eds., *Biomedical Ethics Reviews* (Clifton, N.J.: Humana Press, 1983).

Chapter Two

JUSTIFIED AND UNJUSTIFIED EUTHANASIA

The issue of the moral propriety of euthanasia is complex, in part because of the wide range of acts (and omissions) that are classified under this label. In order to examine the core ethical issues systematically, we will begin by looking at a pair of paradigm cases — one of active killing that is clearly *un*justified, the other of withholding extraordinary treatment that we shall argue *is* clearly justified. After probing into the ethical issues involved in these two cases, we will introduce extensions from it in various ways — including, in Chapter Three (p. 69), consideration of active euthanasia.

PARADIGM CASES

"Murder Most Foul!" the tabloid headline screamed. Bobby Bright, a teenage boy who was an honor student, a star athlete, and popular with both fellow students and teachers at his high school, was brutally murdered at the convenience store where he worked in the evenings by a small-time hood with a "Saturday Night Special." Following store policies, Bobby had given the hood all the money in the cash register (less than $100) without resistance. Nor did he resist when the hood tied him up and locked him in a storage room to delay his notifying police. But, after leaving the store, the hood returned and pumped six bullets into Bobby as he lay helplessly tied up on the floor. Bobby did not die immediately. He lived for several hours before he was discovered and just long enough afterwards to tell officials through his excruciating pain that he had begged the robber not to kill him and that the assailant had said as he fired: "I hate your guts. You have had all the breaks, and I have never had any. This will make us even!"

This is a paradigm case of a "bad death." A victim who has promising life prospects before him and who has every desire to live is killed in a painful way in an act of malice. This is the sort of case we have in mind when we speak of the wrongfulness of killing, and there can be no doubt that such an act is horrendously wrong.

But it does not follow from the wrongness of this case that *every* case of contributing to the death of another person is morally wrong. Contrast the case above with Case 5, p. 213, the story of a physician in the final stages of a terminal illness who is hospitalized in a foreign country. In Scene 2 of Case 5, the patient is in excruciating pain, and he requests that he be allowed to die if he should have another cardiac arrest. Surely it would be wrong to impose life-sustaining measures on him against his wishes.

What, precisely, makes the difference between these two cases? Clearly, Bobby Bright's death is involuntary and the other would be voluntary. Bobby is healthy; the physician-patient is gravely ill. Most important, Bobby is vibrant and alive; the physician-patient is in pain and has no real future before him. There are many other differences that may change the moral character of an act in their lives. Table 1 summarizes key points of comparison relevant to our present debate.

The task of this chapter is to examine the moral import of the various points of difference between these two cases. In the process (in later sections of the chapter), we will examine a range of cases intermediate between these two extremes and try to determine precisely when life-prolonging measures are morally optional and/or when life-shortening measures are morally acceptable.

Is death always a bad thing? The first issue we must consider is the *value* of life and death (i.e., item 6 in Table 1). Some theorists would maintain that life is *always* a value, no matter how negative the person's quality of life. This view is called "vitalism." But this claim does not bear analysis. Consider the patient in Scene 2 of Case 5. True, he is conscious and thus he is capable of some experiences that are of value: memories, moments of association with his caregivers, opportunities to manifest courage in the face of suffering and other admirable traits, moments of pleasure from music, literature, fine (hospital?) food, and the like. The value of these must not be discounted. They and other such possibilities in Bobby Bright's case are precisely what lead us to regard Bobby's death as a *tragedy*. But surely it is not possible to fault the judgment of the patient in Case 5 that these valuable experiences are not worth the cost to him in pain and thus that he would be "better off dead." Even if we would not

TABLE 1

Case 5	Bobby Bright
1. terminal illness	1. victim healthy
2. irreversible	2. continuation of good health expected
3. death is imminent	3. normal life expectancy
4. intractable pain	4. victim not initially in pain
5. patient requests to forego proposed treatment	5. victim begs not to be killed
6. this request (#5) is based on a judgment that he would be "better off dead"	6. this request (#5) is based on a judgment that life continues to have value for him
7. the patient's request (#5) is coherent with his or her fundamental values ("in character")	7. the victim's request (#5) is coherent with his or her fundamental values ("in character")
8. family and caregivers share these fundamental values	8. family and caregivers share these fundamental values
9. these values are rationally defensible	9. these values are rationally defensible
10. continued treatment is a burden to *others* (family, significant others, caregivers)	10. continuing to sustain the victim's life would bring a net benefit to *others* (family, significant others, caregivers)
11. what is being requested is to *withhold* a treatment	11. a direct death-dealing measure
12. what is to be done is an *omission*, not a positive action	12. a positive action
13. the treatment in question is an *extraordinary* measure (i.e., no reasonable hope of benefit, excessively painful, expensive, or burdensome)	13. life-sustaining measures would be ordinary measures (notably, refraining from killing the victim).
14. the consequences of the proposed action (omission) would *not* involve pain, suffering, indignity, or other burden for the victim.	14. the consequences of the proposed action would involve pain, suffering, indignity, and/or other burdens for the victim.
15. the intention of the agent is to avoid prolonging the dying process, *not* to kill the patient	15. the intention of the agent is to kill the victim
16. compassion is the predominant motive prompting everybody	16. malice is the sole motive prompting the agent
17. the underlying illness will be the *cause of death*	17. the aggressive action will be the *cause of death*

make the same judgment if we were in a parallel situation, we cannot deny his right to make this judgment in his own case. Add to this the consideration that his death is imminent, and it seems wholly reasonable to agree with his calculation that it would be a *net loss* to extend his life by a few hours or days.

Given his state of life in Scene 3 of the case — after his second (and third, etc.) resuscitations, nothing of value *to him* was added by this three-week extension of life. Bare life, devoid of possibilities for worthwhile *states* of life, appears to be neither valuable nor disvaluable. What gives value to life is the opportunity it offers to experience meaning; and when this is no longer present, life has lost its quality or value. Furthermore, in a situation in which disvaluable states predominate and are virtually certain to do so for the remainder of life, it is reasonable for the person to judge that he or she would be better off dead. This judgment is most acceptable when made by the person himself/herself, for others cannot be sure of the fundamental values the patient would apply in this measurement. Furthermore, the judgment must always be made exclusively *from the point of view of the patient himself/herself.*

Of course, the patient's judgment is only reasonable to the extent that it is based on a realistic appraisal of the facts — and uncertainties — of the case. In the case at hand, the patient's background as a physician warrants a presumption that the decision is well-informed. However, even here further exploration by caregivers is justified to insure that his medical experience includes familiarity with the technologies and procedures he faces. A dermatologist, for example, may not have had much experience with an intensive care unit. In other cases, this need is even more urgent. Case 9, p. 218, illustrates the problem. This patient's initial refusal of treatment stems, in large measure, from misunderstanding about the nature of intensive care technology. Once she was given an opportunity to ventilate her fears and to have her questions answered, she consented to treatment.

It does not change our judgment here that caregivers found value in caring for this doctor-patient through the three weeks just before he finally died. This may indicate the value of this period of his life *for them*, but it does not alter the conclusion that it was valueless *for him* (cf. Case 12, p. 221). Conversely, the fact that it is extremely troublesome for the caregivers to maintain another patient in a state of life that she finds of value does not warrant saying that she would be better off dead. *They* might be better off if she were dead, but *she* would not be (as in Case 13, p. 222).

The principle of nonmaleficence. The attempts to prolong this physician-patient's life in Scene 3 were *cruel*, since they were likely to cause pain to the patient (item 4 of Table 1, p. 18) and suffering to family and caregivers (item 10).[1] There is a general moral obligation not to cause, promote, or prolong pain and suffering, expressed in the principle of nonmaleficence; and this would dictate a Do Not Resuscitate order in Scene 2. "At least doing no harm" is considered the negative side, a minimalist principle actually, of a more positive and embracing duty of beneficence.[2]

The principle of respect for autonomy. To try to prolong this physician-patient's life would be to repudiate his explicit request to *forego* the intervention (item 5); and there is a general moral obligation to honor a person's wishes, expressed in the principle of respect for autonomy. This obligation applies especially, though not exclusively, to thoughtfully considered and emphatic wishes, as were issued in this case. Thus this, too, dictates a Do Not Resuscitate order.

An appeal to the patient's "right to life" is often employed to support preserving life at all costs. However, it is characteristic of rights that the possessor has the option whether to claim them or to waive them. We can regard the patient's request not to be resuscitated as a limited waiver of his right to life. (There are thorny problems in philosophical analyses of rights, which are not the principal subject of this book.[3])

The principle of realism or medical indications. Attempting to prolong his life would be futile, even if we tried, since his condition is irreversible (Table 1, item 2) and death is imminent (item 3). This, too, dictates against making the attempt. A strong case can be made (as will be discussed in Chapter Five) that physicians have no responsibility to institute futile or medically contraindicated treatment.[4] Often the hospital medical staff by-laws contain a phrase to this effect, protecting physicians and patients from unwarranted requests.

Other considerations. In addition, other features of the case support the decision that would hasten death. We are not speaking here of a positive, aggressive action that causes the patient's death, but rather of withholding an intervention (item 11) and an omission (item 12). Moreover, the proposed intervention is one that could plausibly be labelled extraordinary (item 13). Furthermore, the intentions and motives of all parties are morally acceptable (item 15).

All in all, the second resuscitation of the physician-patient and subsequent life-support measures must be regarded as inappropriate. A Do Not Resuscitate order would have been the more appropriate response to the situation in Scene 2. By contrast, it was quite appropriate that every effort was made to save Bobby Bright.

Objections. If there were any moral wrong at this point, it would be rooted in the general moral rule that prohibits taking another's life. However, this prohibition does not apply in the type of case we are discussing at present. The obligation to refrain from taking another person's life stems, in turn, from that person's right to life; but the physician-patient in Case 5 has waived this right by explicitly requesting not to be resuscitated. In effect he has transferred or delegated his own authority to end his life to the person or persons whom he has asked to carry out his wishes.

Rights — Inalienable and Alienable. Some people (including the authors of our own Declaration of Independence and the political theorists who inspired them) maintain that the right to life is an "inalienable" right — that is, one that cannot be transferred or delegated to another person. If they are correct about this, then the defense of euthanasia that we are offering based on the principle of respect for autonomy collapses.

Now, we would not deny that *some* rights are inalienable. No person can submit themselves to slavery, for example, by transferring to another person their right to liberty. Nor can any person "alienate" her right to seek redress in the courts. Further, we would agree that the right to life is not transferable in all possible ways or in all circumstances. A person could not give you the right to kill her in exchange for the payment of a sum of money to her family, for example.

In contrast, it seems clear that the right to the pursuit of happiness — the third purportedly inalienable right specified in the Declaration of Independence — is transferable in a wide variety of circumstances. When one takes traditional vows of marriage, for example, one gives up the right to pursue sexual satisfaction with partners other than one's spouse. (Some of the personalized marriage contracts developed by couples in recent years do not include this feature.) When one takes on the responsibilities of parenthood (in the course of the pursuit of a certain kind of pleasure, be it noted), one gives up the right henceforth to pursue happiness in ways that would interfere with these responsibilities. One ought not "junk" the wife and kids and run out West.

What makes the difference between those circumstances in which a given right is transferable or alienable and those in which it is not?

Many theorists maintain that this is due to some special character of the right itself. However, a more plausible account is to see it as a function of the moral obligations that apply to the possessor of the right.

For example, a property right is ordinarily transferable at will. We can sell any item of property we own — or we can even give it away, if we want to. Some thinkers argue that we ought to be able to sell our own organs. At any rate, we can have them donated for us by our survivors. This suggests that one kind of property we "own" is our own body, since we can transfer at least portions of it to others.

But suppose that a certain item was given or sold to a certain person on the basis of a firm promise that he would not dispose of it. (This sort of thing might happen with a family heirloom given to him by his parents, or with a piece of real estate sold to him by a person who wanted to keep it out of the hands of some third party.) The recipient has a moral obligation to honor the promise he has made. Thus, in these circumstances, his property right is not transferable — and what this means is that he would be doing something morally wrong if he attempted to transfer it.

The claims above about the transferability or lack thereof of the right to life, liberty, and the pursuit of happiness can be explained and defended in these terms. We not only have a right to liberty; each of us has also a very strong moral obligation to protect (and, we would contend, to exercise) our personal liberty or autonomy. This obligation is rooted in the intrinsic value of liberty, the challenge of acting morally in the full exercise of personhood, and in liberty's importance as a condition of achieving other things of value. A Kantian would root it in honoring in ourselves the dignity of a rational being. There is even a theological requirement for believers to shape and test what is good for themselves, to develop their own character, and to stamp their lives with their values. It is because of this obligation that we cannot sell ourselves into slavery, because then we lose the morally significant feature of human life — i.e., freedom to pursue and test the good.

In contrast, there is no direct moral obligation to pursue happiness for oneself (probably because we are only too willing to do this without being prodded by moral duty, or because a religious belief impels us to sacrifice our own happiness for the good of another). As a consequence, there are practically no limits to the alienability of this right.

To return to the right to life: It would be inalienable in all circumstances only if there were an absolute moral obligation to refrain from taking one's own life. But people in dire situations like those of Case 5 are clearly outside the realm within which such a duty applies. Family members do not have a moral right to demand that a person endure this sort of painful existence against his will, and God (given divine benevolence) would surely not make such a demand. It follows, then, that the right to life is transferable in the sort of circumstances we are considering and thus that there is nothing wrong in such a patient requesting not to be resuscitated.

It is advisable to supplement the case we have presented with an examination of some criticisms that might be levelled against it.

"The reason it is wrong to kill a person is that God commands us not to." A full-scale analysis of the theology of life and death is beyond the scope of this study. However, some common-sense response to this objection is called for. In the first place, we assume that the way God is supposed to tell us of God's command on this point is either (a) through Scripture or (b) by means of personal conscience. However, (a) a careful reading of scriptural texts does not support the claim that killing is prohibited under all circumstances. Killing seems to be enjoined on some occasions, at least in the Old Testament. Thus an appeal to Scripture does not support the claim that it is always wrong to kill a person "no matter what." Furthermore, (b) both personal conscience (ours, at least) and the most plausible understanding of divine benevolence suggest that God would allow us to assist patients in ending their suffering in the circumstances of Scene 2 of Case 5. It would be an act of extreme cruelty to force a patient in this condition to continue to endure it. Thus it seems justified, even on this basis, to help end a life in these circumstances.

"To kill a person intentionally is murder, and murder is always wrong." This view of the matter is incorporated into most existing systems of statutory law; and thus one risks criminal prosecution by actively assisting a suicide, even in the sort of hopeless and painful situation of Case 5. But refraining from a futile attempt at resuscitation, as in Case 5, would not be considered in the same way, under the law, as active killing or assisting suicide. Refraining from using technological interventions is usually seen as acting from the duty not to prolong dying,[5] such that the person dies from the underlying disease process. Active intervention, such as the murder in the Bobby Bright case, clearly does not fit this same description and thus is properly classified as murder. But what of assisting the Case 5 patient more actively? We will discuss this in Chapter Three below.

"The reason it is wrong to let a person die is that you harm that person in doing so." It seems obvious from the start that this charge

does not apply in Case 5. We have just said that it would be an act
of cruelty to force a patient in this situation to remain alive. How,
then, could it be a harm to end his life?

It will be worthwhile to go beyond this intuitive reaction and explore this objection a bit to see just what is wrong with it. Such
an inquiry can advance our understanding of the nature of harm in
general and the harm of death in particular.

In the ordinary case, one does harm to a person by killing him even
if the act is unexpected and painless. This harm can be analyzed as
a species of robbery — depriving him of existence in the future.

The difference between the ordinary case and Case 5 is that in
Case 5 the future existence of the person is not of positive value
to him. Indeed, we would be sparing him a great deal of pain
and suffering by ending his life. Thus, it would seem that we
would be doing him a favor by killing him, rather like (although
on a much grander scale) a robber who stole someone's garbage
and thus saved that person the trouble of carrying it to the city
dump.

However, there are two problems with this response to the objection as it stands.

1. In addition to preventing future pain, we would also be depriving the person of whatever positive values might have been available
to him (for example, continued association with his caregivers). Thus,
to that extent, we *would* be doing him a harm.

However, the physician-patient in Case 5 must have thought that
he would be better off dead, or else he would not have requested to
die. And if his judgment is correct, then the amount of good that we
do by ending his life outweighs the harm. Therefore, although our
act of helping him to end his life does bring some measure of harm
to him, its net result is beneficial.

2. This argument makes use of the analogy of stealing someone's
garbage, and it is possible to challenge the argument by casting doubt
on the analogy. The problem is, of course, that it is morally wrong
to steal someone's garbage.[6] First, the thief might look through the
contents of the garbage in order to gain information about the person
(as some enterprising newspaper reporters did with the garbage at
Henry Kissinger's home a few years ago when he was secretary of
state), and this would violate the person's right to privacy. Second,
it is a violation of the person's property rights to deprive him of his
garbage against his wishes, even if no further wrongful use is made
of it. It is *his* garbage, after all. Property rights do not depend on the
value of the property. Even if the garbage is of no value at all to its

owner, he has grounds for objecting to having someone take it from him without his permission.

The proper response here is to point out that the patients we are talking about have given their permission to having someone act to end their life. Further, the violation of the right to privacy is a separate issue, over and above any wrong involved in stealing the garbage. It would clearly be wrong for an agent to violate someone's privacy in the course of euthanasia, but this can be avoided, and so it does not entail that there is anything wrong with euthanasia on request in itself (given the level of analysis we have reached so far). Hence the problems with the analogy of stealing garbage do not infect our argument. The closest analogy to Case 5 is actually the official garbage collectors who remove our garbage upon our request.[7] Surely there is neither harm nor moral wrong in their action — assuming that they do not violate our privacy by examining the contents.

"The reason it is wrong to kill a person is that human life is sacred." The chief problem here is to determine precisely what it means to say that human life is "sacred."[8]

1. The term has religious connotations that would seem to link it to the objection regarding God's command (p. 23 above). But we have already dealt with that. Religious arguments about the value of human life have their basis in theological issues that are beyond the scope of this study. However, whatever their foundation, they must be explicated in the terms we are dealing with here — i.e., in terms of either values, obligations, or rights; and thus they are subject to the weighting arguments we are developing in the present section.

2. An alternative to a divine-command reading of this principle is to interpret it as another way of saying that every human being has a right to life. But we have already dealt with this, too. This principle is one foundation of our case *for* euthanasia in Case 5.

3. The only other alternative we can think of is to interpret it as equivalent to the claim that human life is an *absolute value*, something always worth preserving no matter what the cost. But surely this claim is false. Taken literally, it entails that any quantity of human life — even a fraction of a second — outweighs any quantity of any other value and, further, that this is true no matter what the quality of that life. Losing one's life to defend freedom would seem to be ruled out following this argument. Further, it follows that it would be reasonable to ask every person in the world to contribute all their possessions beyond the bare minimum required for the survival of themselves and their dependents in order to provide a fraction of a second of life to a person in excruciating pain who was asking to

die. This value judgment seems obviously mistaken. It is the reason vitalism, in its absolute mode, must be rejected by any reasonable person.

In a somewhat less extreme form, this claim entails that no one is ever better off dead. The value of life itself would counterbalance any amount of disvalue to be expected within that life. But we have seen a convincing counter-example on this point in the description of Case 5. Other cases also show this point, e.g., the trapped pilot in terrible pain in *Alive*,[9] who begged to be shot.

"The reason it is wrong to kill a person is that you thereby treat her as an object, a mere means to an end; whereas human beings should be treated as ends in themselves." This is the position of the influential philosopher Immanuel Kant.[10] Here again, part of the problem is to figure out precisely what is meant.

1. One possibility is to interpret the notion of an "end in itself" as equivalent to a claim of absolute value. But we have dealt with this just above.

2. A more plausible interpretation is this: To treat someone as an end is to respect the ends or goals that she has set for herself. Thus we should never impose anything on a person against her will. We may even have a positive obligation to do what we can to help her further her goals. To do otherwise implies that she is not important; and, in the extreme case, it may amount to treating her in the way we would treat an inanimate object — as nothing more than a means to our goals.

The most dramatic cases of this would be ones in which the person is treated exactly as one would treat an inanimate object. Our own children, for example, do not hesitate to step on us when we are sitting or lying on the floor in order to reach objects that would otherwise be too high for them. (We forgive them, because they are very young and do not know better; but we fervently hope they will learn better before they reach a size that would make this practice harmful to us.) In slapstick comedies, one person will sometimes duck behind another to avoid the cream pie that has been thrown at him.

Only slightly removed from physically treating a person as an object is the act of getting someone to do what you want by means of deceit or coercion. Here the agent knows that the other person has no desire to do the thing in question. (If she did, neither deceit nor coercion would be required in order to get her to do it. The most that would be needed would be a polite request.) But the agent does not let her unwillingness stop him from getting what he wants. He "uses" her, by appealing to goals that she does have — the desire not to be harmed, in cases of coercion; a variety of other goals, in cases of deceit.

It should be pointed out that the agent would still be using her as a means if he got her to do the thing by means of a polite request. However, in this case, he would not be using her *merely* as a means. By offering her the chance to decline the request, he acknowledges respect for her wishes and thus treats her as an end as well as a means. Kant sees nothing wrong in this sort of action, in most cases. (Nor do we.)

Surely we would all agree that the sort of action Kant condemns is indeed morally wrong. However, this does not challenge our conclusions in Case 5, since there the patient himself has set death as his goal. It appears that the action which would treat him as a means would be to fail to help him to achieve this goal.

However, Kant would not be satisfied to let the matter rest here. He himself was strongly opposed to suicide, and thus he would not approve of assisted suicide or euthanasia on request. His objection to suicide is that it involves treating *oneself* as a means to the goal of relief from pain or some other ulterior goal. And it is just as wrong to treat oneself merely as a means as it is to do this to another person.

The first problem for Kant's argument is that this description does not fit all cases of suicide. Some suicides have no ulterior motive beyond that of simply ending their life.[11] For example, an individual may be exercising intense freedom in committing suicide, as Sartre saw. However, Kant's description does fit the situation in Case 5, so we can take little comfort from this flaw in his argument. It does not help us to escape whatever ethical force there may be in the case.

The deeper problem for Kant is the difficulty of making sense of the notion of treating oneself merely as a means and of showing what is wrong with this. Now there is a certain similarity between the patterns of action we have described as treating another person merely as a means and what goes on within the thinking of the person in Case 5, but the resemblance is only on the surface.

Undoubtedly, the patient in Case 5 still has some "will to live." Thus life is one of his goals. However, he has determined that it would be better for him to sacrifice this goal in order to avoid the pain he would have to endure if he continued to live. Notice that this particular goal is itself being treated in a way somewhat similar to that in which we act when we treat another person merely as a means. The goal of life is not being acted upon; instead it is overridden in favor of another goal of the person — freedom from pain. Now when this sort of thing is done with the goals of one *person* in favor of the ends or goals of *another person*, we say the former person is being treated merely as a means.

But we cannot say anything similar to this in relation to two goals within the thought of a single person. For one thing, there is no way to avoid treating one or the other of these desires in this way. If the person decides to continue to live, she will frustrate her desire for freedom from pain; and, if she dies, she will frustrate her desire to live. This is the tragedy that arises when a person has two goals that are in direct conflict — a situation that arises often in life, and in moral choice. Yet surely it is essential that she make a choice in favor of one or the other of these goals. To do nothing is to choose one or the other of them by default. Thus there can be nothing morally wrong in the choice itself.

The problem must be, then, that suicide is the *wrong* choice. For the physician-patient in Case 5 to frustrate his desire to end the pain is not to treat himself merely as a means; but to frustrate his desire to live *is* to treat himself merely as a means. This difference cannot be a function of the strength of the desires in question, since he appears to desire freedom from pain more strongly than life — else why would he have requested to die? The crucial factor must be something in the content of the choice. Thus, at the basis of Kant's objection to suicide is the claim that the value of life is greater in itself than the value of freedom from pain or any other goal that might persuade one to suicide. But this is simply another version of the claim that human life is an absolute value. The notion that we rejected in the first interpretation of Kant's argument has been smuggled into it again through the back door. And, once this is recognized, the argument loses much of its force.

"It might be morally justified to kill a person in the circumstances of Case 5 if we could be absolutely sure that all the specified conditions were met. But we can never be sure. It is always possible that we have made a mistake somewhere, and thus that one or more of the conditions are not satisfied." We regard the retreat to this sort of objection as a significant victory for our case. The previous objections are all attempts to show that our position is mistaken in principle, claiming that euthanasia would be wrong even if all the conditions in Table 1 (p. 18) were known to be satisfied. The present objection does not go this far. It grants that our argument is valid in theory; what it denies is that we could ever be justified in putting the theory into practice, since we can never be sure that the requisite conditions are satisfied in a particular case.[12]

This objection contains an important grain of truth. Surely it would *not* be morally justified to allow a patient to die if there were serious doubt about whether the conditions of Table 1 were satisfied — for example, if there were a real question as to whether he had requested to die or whether his pain could be relieved by medication. This sort of doubt is what is troublesome about Case 14: Walter Arnold, a combative elderly patient with multiple organ failures and a steadily deteriorating condition, is ambivalent about his wishes. At times, he expresses the desire to discontinue dialysis; at other times (and especially in the presence of his youngest son), he indicates the wish to continue it. The only appropriate responses to this sort of uncertainty are (a) to sustain the patient while (b) investigating further. In a somewhat different way, this is what is done in the case we call "The Hotel Guest" (Case 15) — a man found unconscious on the floor of his hotel room. He is stabilized and maintained until reversible causes of his collapse are ruled out and attempts can be made to locate family or friends to take part in the decision to limit treatment.

This factor serves to limit the range of cases in which euthanasia is justified, and we will discuss it at some length below when we turn our attention to extensions of this situation. However, it is possible to carry this point too far. It is unreasonable to place significant weight on possibilities that are remote. The only contingencies that need to be taken into account in our decisions are those that are genuinely likely to occur. If no attempt at all has been made to relieve the pain with medication, or if a class of generally effective medications has been overlooked, then there are real grounds for doubt as to whether the pain is intractable. However, if every known kind of pain-killing drug has been tried and found to be ineffective, then it is unreasonable to hesitate on the possibility that a totally new kind of medication might be discovered tomorrow that would be effective. The chances of this are so remote as to be negligible.

There are times when we can be sufficiently certain that the conditions for Case 5 in Table 1 are met to be justified in acting to assist the patient in ending his life. Uncertainties about prognosis were removed after a few days in the case of the hotel guest (Case 15) and thus a further decision was made to withhold antibiotics. In Case 14, it is less clear that the uncertainty has been resolved in Scene 2 when further information about Mr. Arnold's abiding wishes is uncovered. The present objection serves as a useful reminder that we ought to exercise extreme caution in making this judgment; but it does not show that we cannot ever be warranted in making it.

"The reason it is wrong to kill a person in these circumstances is that somebody might do the same thing — or worse — to you." This objection can be interpreted in two very different ways: (1) as an expression of the Golden Rule, or (2) as a limited version of what has been called variously "the Slippery Slope Argument," "the Wedge Argument" and "the Argument of the Camel's Nose." We will consider each of these in turn.

1. Some form of the Golden Rule has been enunciated in almost every culture sufficiently advanced to develop a system of morality. However, useful as it can be within its proper domain, even this principle can be carried too far. Stated without restrictions, it can serve as an invitation to impose our own personal value choices on other people. Even reasonable values can be applied wrongfully on this basis. It would be a misapplication of the Golden Rule for a person to work to outlaw the eating of snails just because she would not want an opportunity to eat them herself.

The appeal to the Golden Rule in the objection being considered at present involves this same sort of mistake. It is addressed to those who are sure they would *not* want euthanasia for themselves, and it makes this the basis for denying it to others who *do* want it. But surely this step is not morally justified.[13]*

Remember that one of the conditions specified for Case 5 is that the patient explicitly requests to die (see item 5 in Table 1, p. 18). It might improve the case for the Golden Rule to some extent if this condition were taken into account in applying it. Thus the question to ask is *not*, "Would you want to be killed if you had a terminal illness?" but rather, "Assuming that you had a terminal illness *and requested to die*, would you want your request to be granted?"

But there can be problems with the Golden Rule even under these restrictions. Someone might have certain personal values at present that are strongly contrary to euthanasia — for example, a desire to exhibit courage and endurance of suffering; and this might lead her to reply that she would *not* want a future request to die to be granted, since she can only assume that she would have lapsed into irrationality or cowardice before making such a request. Now we have no objection to her adopting this policy in her own case, but surely any

---

*Of course, some oppose euthanasia not merely because they find it distasteful and do not want it for themselves, but because they judge that no one ought to want it for themselves. Their view is that it is morally objectionable, not merely distasteful or personally offensive. We have critically examined the central ethical arguments against euthanasia, which support such a claim, throughout this section.

principle that would allow her to impose the policy on others who do not share these values is morally objectionable.[14]*

One possible exception to this conclusion stems, not from the Golden Rule itself, but from the service orientation of the caregiver-patient relationship. Insofar as it does not violate the caregiver's conscience, she is expected to honor the patient's values. Thus a patient who finds oral medications extremely objectionable might be treated instead with an injection, if this is equally effective medically. However, the patient who demands general anesthesia for a minor surgical procedure might be denied his wish if the physician judges that the risks of general anesthesia are too great to justify the slight reduction of anxiety its use might promote. The case of the Trans-fused Cat (Case 13, p. 222) raises similar issues, which we will discuss in some detail in Chapter Five below, in connection with other issues about caretakers' responsibilities.

In general, the Golden Rule has a limited usefulness. It can serve to point out certain fairly obvious moral wrongs in a context of shared values. (To a small child: "Stop biting people. How would you like it if people bit you?" This is, of course, even more effective if accompanied by a demonstration!) But it can by no means provide the basis for the whole of morality.

2. The second interpretation of this objection is like the previous objection (p. 28 above) in focusing on a danger involved in putting our theory into practice. It does not deny that euthanasia is morally justified in the narrow set of circumstances specified in Case 5, but maintains that it will not be possible in practice to restrict it to that domain. We will discuss these situations at length in Chapter Six below, when we discuss societal issues.

Conclusion. Thus far, we have defended the limited claim that *one* form of euthanasia (i.e., a DNR order) would be morally justified in *one* specific set of circumstances — i.e., those described in the paradigm case and outlined in Table 1 (p. 18). This does not mean, of course, that *all* forms of euthanasia are justified in *all* circumstances. We turn now to examine variations on Case 5 in Table 1 in order to determine how far this justification extends, as well as ferreting out more information about the moral principles upon which it is based. It may be necessary to reconsider some of the objections just

---

*Remember, we are not talking about allegiance to moral rules here, but about a personal policy that is meant to be the *source* from which moral rules are generated. Our critique of *rules* against ending life in these situations is found in earlier sections of this chapter.

discussed as we examine the issues in other situations, since some of our replies were based on specific features of Table 1.

We can identify different situations by systematically varying the circumstances in Table 1. The ideal analysis would probably be to attempt to consider all possible variations of each feature in Table 1 and all possible combinations of these variations, but this would be unworkable. Instead, we shall concentrate on those variations that appear to be most morally significant. The remainder of this chapter will be devoted to examination of such variations in the individual case. Others more relevant to family relationships, caregiver relationships, and general societal issues will be discussed in Chapters Four, Five, and Six respectively.

WHEN DEATH IS NOT IMMINENT

Our initial case dealt with a patient in the final stages of a terminal illness who has only a few days, at most, to live. Now suppose, instead, that we are dealing with a patient with a diagnosis of a terminal condition such that, with intensive therapy, the patient could probably be kept alive and conscious for several months before he dies. This is the situation of William Meissner in Case 16. All likely therapies have failed, and it seems clear that his tumor will continue to progress despite all attempts to arrest it. The only questions are how long this will take, whether pain control can be effective during this period, and how much effective consciousness can be maintained. Mr. Meissner requests active euthanasia, but let us postpone consideration of this element until Chapter Three.* If we focus instead on the physician's offer to discontinue chemotherapy and to withhold antibiotics if infection develops, we have a situation parallel to Case 5 in all respects other than the time dimension (item 3), as schematized in Table 2.

Would this difference in the length of time the patient has to live alter the moral justifiability of assisting him in ending his life?

Nonmaleficence. In at least one respect, the case for euthanasia in the present situation is even more compelling than in Case 5. If there is reason to act in Case 5 to spare the patient from a few days of pain and anguish, then surely there is even stronger reason for action here where it is weeks or months of suffering that is involved. There is a general moral obligation to do what we can to relieve pain and suffering (one aspect of the duty of beneficence), which supplements the

---

*We will take this up in Chapter Three below (pp. 50ff.).

TABLE 2

Case 16: DNR and Withholding Antibiotics

1. terminal illness
2. irreversible
3. death within weeks or months
4. intractable pain
5. patient requests to forego proposed treatment
6. this request is based on a judgment that he would be "better off dead"
7. the patient's request is coherent with his/her fundamental values ("in character")
8. family and caregivers share these fundamental values
9. these values are rationally defensible
10. continued treatment is a burden to *others* (family, significant others, caregivers)
11. what is being requested is to *withhold* a treatment
12. what is to be done is an *omission*, not a positive action
13. the treatment in question is an *extraordinary* measure (i.e., no reasonable hope of benefit, excessively painful, expensive, or otherwise burdensome)
14. the consequences of the proposed action (omission) would *not* involve pain, suffering, indignity, or other burden for the patient
15. the intention of the agent is to avoid prolonging the dying process, *not* to kill the patient
16. compassion is the predominant motive prompting everybody
17. the underlying illness will be the *cause of death*

duty created by the patient's request to die. The same factor also supports this request itself by helping to create the sort of circumstances in which it is legitimate for one to transfer his right to life.

Of course, Mr. Meissner's remaining weeks or months will not be an unbroken pattern of gloom. He may encounter some things of positive value; periods of relief from or moderation of the pain, good qualities of character that are developed or expressed in response to the pain (e.g., courage on his own part, sympathy and concern for his plight on the part of those around him), and worthwhile experiences that are possible in spite of the pain (e.g., fond memories, association with family and friends, the opportunity to say good-bye to loved ones). To assist him in ending his life would have the effect of depriving him of these things and thus, to this extent, it would be a harm toward him. These positive prospects also count against the legitimacy of his waiving or transferring his right to life. They also are factors in a concern about honoring a patient's request for active euthanasia.

Conflict of duties. Thus those whom he asks to help him end his life are caught in a conflict of duties: on one side there is the duty not to cause harm, which dictates against ending his life; and on the other side there is the duty to relieve pain and suffering plus a duty that is created by his request for assistance, and both of these favor ending his life. The way to resolve this conflict is to determine the relative strengths of the duties on each side of the issue and to follow the path of stronger duty.

There can be no formula for determining the weight or stringency of duties. In some cases, we have quantifiable elements that can be comparatively weighed. For example, it may be possible to quantify the severity and duration of the patient's pain. Suffering is harder to quantify,[15] and it is still more problematic to attempt to quantify the value of such positive experiences as moments of personal association with family, friends, and caregivers. Furthermore, elements such as the patient's request to be allowed to die cannot be quantified. We might measure the vehemence of this request, but (as we shall see just below, p. 35) the prima facie duty to honor this request stems from the mere *fact* that the patient made it.

In weighting and comparing conflicting prima facie duties, we accept the dictum Sir David Ross adapted from Aristotle: "the decision rests with perception."[16] We need not accept the entirety of Ross's moral epistemology to employ this as a *practical* guide. This means that those closest to the case, Mr. Meissner, his family, and the doctors, with adequate analysis of both facts and duties involved, would be best able to weight them properly.

Even elements that might be quantified are not properly compared in purely quantitative terms. Let us turn to one of the chief reasons why we cannot do so.

"Causing harm." We cannot properly assess the strength of the duty not to cause harm unless we take into account certain points about it, including especially its relationship to certain other moral principles. These points are frequently not acknowledged, for example, in references to the principle "*primum non nocere*" (which is commonly translated as: "First, do no harm").

Among the distinctions we contend have moral import are those between *intrinsic, intended,* and *incidental* effects of actions, and between (merely) *causing* harm and *inflicting* harm. These notions can be roughly characterized as follows:*

---

*For an extended analysis of these distinctions, see Appendix II, pp. 282–295.

The *intrinsic* effects of an action are those stated or directly implied in our description or characterization of the action. For example, if one sets out to eat a hearty meal, it is an intrinsic effect of her action that she eats a meal.

The *intended* effects of an action are those that figure into the agent's goals in acting. For example, if one sets out to eat a hearty meal in order to become healthier, good health is one intended effect of his action.

The *incidental* effects of an action are those neither directly implied in its characterization nor part of the goal in acting. For example, if one sets out to eat a hearty meal in order to improve health, the need to wash dishes afterwards is an incidental effect of her acting in this way.

●

One can be said to *inflict* harm if (a) the harmful effect is either an intrinsic or intended effect of his action **and** (b) the harm is brought about by a positive action (in contrast to a negative act or omission).

One would be said (merely) to *cause* the harm if either (a) the harmful effect is an incidental effect of her action **or** (b) it results from a negative action or omission rather than a positive action.

In Case 16 , the harm of depriving Mr. Meissner of valuable future experiences is not inflicted on him; rather it is an (unintended or incidental) essential aspect of the attempt to bring to him a substantial benefit (i.e., relief from intolerable pain and suffering through the passive euthanasia measures the physician proposes). Although there may be a point to saying that we ought not harm him in this way, such action is morally justified in the final analysis because of the pressing importance of the particular benefit involved and its causal inseparability from the harm.[17]

Patient's request. The conclusion we have reached to this point follows strictly from weighing the duty not to bring about harm and comparing it to the duty to relieve pain and suffering. No reference has been made to the duty arising from his request for assistance in ending his life. The same sort of comparison between the harms and the benefits that figured in our argument in the paradigm case in the first part of this chapter also serves to show that he is justified in waiving or transferring his right to life; and this, in turn, strengthens the duty arising from his request. When the weight of this duty is added in, the moral warrant for passive euthanasia in this case is even more firmly established.

Other features of the case. Several other features of this situation give rise to moral issues that we should examine. For one thing, a prognosis of death is bound to be less definite here. When death is imminent, the physical basis of the prognosis will be manifest; the disease process will have reached an advanced stage, and the patient will already be severely debilitated. It will be clear to any knowledgeable observer that death is imminent. However, here matters will be much less clear-cut. The disease may have few overt symptoms. To the casual observer, the patient may appear relatively robust. More to the point, the best data available about the nature of the disease process and the general physical condition of the patient will contain too many variables and too many unknowns to allow absolute certainty in any prediction about the future course of the disease. Spontaneous remissions, although infrequent, sometimes occur, even at this stage of development of a tumor.

As long as these uncertainties leave open a substantial possibility that the patient might escape both intense suffering and death from the disease, then surely it would not be morally right to help her end her life. An action as drastic as this must not be undertaken unless the evidence upon which the decision is based is extremely strong. It is not so in our case.

It would be a mistake, however, to take these points as adequate reason for refraining from euthanasia in all instances. Even though the margin of error is increased, in some instances the prognosis will still be supported by a compelling weight of evidence. Hence there will be a sound basis for action. It would be cruel to the person who asks for our help in ending his life for us to refuse because of a remote possibility of error in the prognosis (especially if the patient has considered this possibility and still requests that his life be ended).

An argument against stopping to which we object is illustrated clearly in the following passage:

Miracles — I use the term to signify phenomena that we simply can't explain — do occur.... There is hardly a surgeon of any experience who hasn't on at least one occasion given a patient up for dead only to find that the patient makes a complete recovery — one that is unexplainable, in terms of scientific knowledge.

   Is there any wonder that in the face of such experiences a surgeon is reluctant to "pull the plug"? Is it any wonder that he hesitates to "play God"?[18]

If we translate the emotional appeal of this passage into an argument, it amounts to the following: a physician ought *never* to assist a patient in ending his life, because nearly every physician will make a mistaken prognosis of fatality at least *once* in his lifetime. Of course, we must regret the loss of that one life that might have been restored to healthy status; but this must be weighed against the amount of suffering that would be caused to the many patients whose lives would be prolonged needlessly — and we must not forget that we would be refusing explicit requests for assistance in all cases. It is far from clear that the wait for that one "miracle" is worth this cost (see Case 17, p. 227). This seems also to be a concern of the brother of Mr. B., who awaited a miracle as well (Case 18, p. 228).

Another argument that carries greater force here than with regard to our paradigm case of the "physician in an overseas hospital" is the possibility that a cure of Mr. Meissner's malady might be developed in time to rescue him. This possibility should certainly be investigated; but, unless there is a definite indication that a research breakthrough is near at hand, this should not be a source of hesitation about acting to assist the patient in ending his life.

Nowadays innovative therapies do not burst upon the scene suddenly, taking the medical community by surprise. Each step in the development of a new therapeutic substance or technique is well-charted through scientific publications. Further, the amount of testing required in order to authorize general use of a new therapy takes a substantial amount of time after it first shows promise of being helpful. A new drug, for example, cannot be used even experimentally for therapeutic purposes until the completion of extensive animal studies and nontherapeutic tests on humans to establish safe dosage levels and to study possible side effects, with the possible exception of current practices on AIDS interventions that have not yet been sufficiently tested.[19]

WHEN THE CONDITION IS NOT TERMINAL

Let us move one step further away from the paradigm. Suppose now that we are dealing with a patient whose condition is not inevitably terminal, but rather such that it leads to severe impairment of function and involves a long period of intense and intractable pain, as well as other states of life regarded as intolerable by the patient. Case 19, the story of a young man we call "Donald C.,"*who was

---

*This name is assigned to Dax Cowart by the *Hastings Center Report*, originally to protect confidentiality. However, since that time, Mr. Cowart has made a video that describes in interviews his present life, and has waived his confidentiality rights. We

severely burned, and wanted to die, is a dramatic example of such a
situation.[20] The features of this case are set out in Table 3.

TABLE 3

Case 19: Donald C.

1. severe disability
2. irreversible
3. life expectancy shortened, but not greatly
4. intractable pain
5. patient requests to forego proposed treatment
6. this request is based on a judgment that he would be "better off dead"
7. the patient's request is coherent with his/her fundamental values ("in character")
8. family and caregivers *do not* share these fundamental values
9. these values are rationally defensible (?)
10. continued treatment is a burden to *others* (family, significant others, caregivers)
11. what is being requested is to *withhold* a treatment (i.e., another in a series of surgical procedures and/or another in a series of treatments to prevent infection)
12. what is to be done is an *omission*, not a positive action
13. the treatment in question is regarded by the patient as an *extraordinary* measure (i.e., no reasonable hope of benefit, excessively painful, expensive, or otherwise burdensome); caregivers regard it as an ordinary measure
14. the consequences of the proposed action (omission) *would* involve pain, suffering, indignity, or other burden for the patient
15. the intention of the agent would be to honor the wishes of the patient, *not* directly to kill the patient
16. compassion is the predominant motive prompting everybody
17. the underlying illness will be the *cause of death*

Is there rational warrant for Donald's judgment that he would be
better off dead? (Cf. items 6–9 in Table 3.) The key points to guide
this judgment are the following: (a) It is a mistake to focus on general
claims about capabilities. Rather we must base our judgment on a
realistic appraisal of his present preferences and those he is actually
likely to have in the future. (b) We must also take into account his
personal ideals and personal integrity. If the pattern of preferences
that is likely to develop violates his present standards for the kind
of person one should be, this may be reason to say that he would
be better off dead, even if we could be sure that he would be happy

---

will continue to use "Donald C." throughout the text, following the initiative of the
Hastings Center Report.

in his future life (i.e., that his later and newly developed preferences would be satisfied).

There are strong indications in Donald's case that his judgment that he would be better off dead is rationally justified. It is clear that he has thought the issue through with care. He does not fail to acknowledge the positive values that would be available to him. It is just that he concludes that they are not worth the cost in pain, incapacity, and disfigurement. His requests to die are not hesitant or ambiguous, but rather emphatic and repeated. He expresses the same wish at moments when he is relatively free from pain, as well as at the moments of most severe pain. (You may confirm our analysis of Donald's situation for yourself, if you wish. An interview with the patient is available on video tape.[21])

Yet we must not discount the possibility that Donald's judgment is based on a mistaken assessment of his own values and prospects. This was the conclusion of the psychiatrist who examined Donald. He conceded that death was Donald's conscious wish; but he sensed that the key value influencing Donald's thinking was, not a desire to avoid pain, incapacity, and disfigurement, but rather a desperate desire to neutralize his current status of total dependence on others by gaining personal control over his own life.[22] Further, the psychiatrist pointed out that this value could be made available to Donald, thus making his life worthwhile on his own terms in spite of the pain, incapacity, and disfigurement.

The psychiatrist's judgment seems to be supported by the subsequent course of events. Donald finally won the legal right to refuse any further therapy; but he did not exercise that right. Once the power of decision was placed in his hands, he gave permission for the next stage of therapy. His stated reason for this decision was that he wanted to remain alive long enough to campaign for the right to die for all patients; but it seems reasonable to interpret his action as confirmation of the psychiatrist's analysis. Once his control over his own life was restored, he found meaning in life and wanted to continue. He has subsequently married, continued his studies, and made a film about his case; but he still reports ambivalent feelings about his choices.

The moral of this story is twofold: (a) it requires sympathetic and sensitive communication with a person to discern his deepest wishes, since often he will not be fully aware of them himself; and (b) an important tool in this process is an analysis of the *values* expressed in the patient's request. Straightforward acknowledgement of a patient's wish to die — on the surface of it, so ethically sensitive to the value of autonomy — may miss the personal engagement truly required by the patient and thus may be in danger of dispatching persons whose values are actually ambiguous though they do not immediately appear to be. (See Cases 6–11, pp. 215–220, for related cases.) We will discuss this situation further in the final chapter, arguing that personal engagement with patients is more crucial than laws permitting voluntary active euthanasia today.

Actually, there is yet a third moral to be drawn from this case, which may provide a basis for answering the challenge presented to a proeuthanasia position by this sort of possibility. It is significant that a thoughtful and sympathetic psychiatrist came to *recognize* that this patient did not really want to die. Thus it is possible (although it may be far from easy, in many cases) to discover the patient's real wishes.

It is incumbent upon the agent who has been asked to assist a patient in ending his life to question in depth whether this request expresses the patient's deepest values (see item 7 in Table 3). This will require, at the very least, an extended series of discussions with the patient focusing on the values that underlie the request and an examination of their far-reaching implications. It is strongly advisable to enlist the help of a sympathetic and skilled psychological professional in this task, when at all possible.

If there is genuine reason to doubt that the request to die is an expression of the patient's deepest values, then it would not be morally right to act on that request. However, this proviso will not rule out euthanasia in all cases. There will be some instances in which a thorough inquiry raises no grounds for doubt, but only serves to confirm the judgment that the patient really wishes to die. The popular film *Whose Life Is It, Anyway?* starring Richard Dreyfus is a case in point. Furthermore, a careful calculation of the disvalues and values in prospect for the patient may convince us that the patient's judgment is rationally and morally justified. In this situation, euthanasia is morally justified; which type of euthanasia is still to be discussed.

Item 8 of Table 3 raises two additional issues that will be postponed for discussion until later chapters: (a) Donald's mother strenuously disagreed with his judgment that he would be "better off dead." We will discuss the family's perspective on euthanasia decisions in Chapter Four (see especially pp. 87f.). (b) The physicians and other caregivers disagreed both with his judgment of his quality of life (item 9), and also with his classification of the treatments as extraordinary measures (item 13). We will discuss the medical perspective on these matters in Chapter Five.

WHEN THE PATIENT IS NOT CONSCIOUS

Suppose that the patient is not conscious, as in Case 20 — the well-known story of Karen Quinlan.

TABLE 4

Case 20: Karen Quinlan

1. persistent vegetative state
2. irreversible
3. life expectancy uncertain
4. no pain because the patient is permanently unconscious
5. patient unable to express present wishes, but earlier indicated desire to forego life-sustaining treatment in a situation like this
6. family members judge that she would be "better off dead"
7. foregoing life-sustaining measures is coherent with her fundamental values ("in character")
8. family share these fundamental values; initial caregivers do *not*
9. these values are rationally defensible
10. continued treatment is a burden to *others* (family, significant others, caregivers)
11. what is being requested is to *withdraw* a treatment already begun
12. what is to be done is a positive action (i.e., turning off a respirator)
13. the treatment in question is regarded by the patient's family as an *extraordinary* measure (i.e., no reasonable hope of benefit, excessively painful, expensive, or otherwise burdensome); initial caregivers regard it as an ordinary measure
14. the consequences of the proposed action (omission) would *not* involve pain, suffering, indignity, or other burden for the patient (as far as we can judge, she is incapable of feeling pain)
15. the intention of the agent would be to honor the wishes of the patient, *not* directly to kill the patient
16. compassion is the predominant motive prompting everybody
17. the underlying medical condition will be the *cause of death*

This will link with the other circumstances we have been discussing in several ways, creating a variety of challenging questions.

If the state of unconsciousness is not permanent, then what we have here is essentially an instance of the same sort dealt with in one of the sections above (depending upon the prognosis), with the only new feature being a temporary relief from pain by natural means. This may alter the details of our calculations of benefits and harms, but it does not affect the general outlines of the patterns of reasoning discussed above in connection with these cases.

But for Karen Quinlan (Case 20), there was a firm prognosis that this state of unconsciousness was permanent. She was described as being in a *persistent* vegetative state." As in other cases, we must allow for the uncertainty of this prognosis.[23] If there is a real possibility that the patient will regain consciousness, then we should invoke the reasoning of the appropriate one of the foregoing cases.

Only if no serious basis can be found for questioning the prognosis of irreversibility do we have a genuinely new sort of situation.

Pain and suffering. The first thing to notice here is that the absence of consciousness automatically means, as well, an absence of pain and suffering on the part of the patient. Or, at least, so it is assumed by most authorities. It is reported that Karen Quinlan would occasionally groan or cry out as if in pain; and some speculated that she might be experiencing some pain at these moments. Balanced against this, it is significant that she did not react at all to normally painful stimuli such as injections. It appears, then, that she did not experience pain in anything like the usual sense; and thus the duty to relieve her pain and suffering no longer applied to support ending her life. But what if, in fact, the "awareness" one has is of being trapped and unable to return to life? This might form the basis of an argument *against* prolonging life on grounds of cruelty.[24]

Nonmaleficence. The argument *against* ending her life on the basis of the duty not to cause harm is also considerably weakened in this situation. Her lack of consciousness made it impossible for her to attain such positive values as developing courage or other admirable traits of character and meaningful association with family and friends even if she remained alive. Death could not harm her further in these respects, since she had already been deprived of these values by loss of consciousness.

Indignities. It does not follow, however, that an irreversibly comatose patient is not subject to *any* benefits and harms. There are values and disvalues that do not "lie in sensation,"[25] and some of these will apply to the comatose patient. Some proponents of euthanasia make a good deal of one group of these that they collect under the labels "dignity" and "indignity." The slogan "death with dignity" refers to a certain ideal for the kind of dying that befits a human being. It includes such features as independence or self-possession, bodily integrity, personal choice or initiative, and courage or self-control. Perhaps most important of all of these is gaining some measure of control over one's dying.

In contrast, the following (all of which are common features of dying in the contemporary clinical setting) are considered to be indignities — and thus harms — to the patient: separation from the familiar and comfortable surroundings of one's home and replacement by the "cold" and frightening clinical environment, debility and dependence, infantilization, incontinence, limits on access by family and friends (i.e., the notorious five- or ten-minute visitation periods in intensive care units), exposure of private parts of one's body, being scrutinized and/or talked about in intimate detail by large numbers of people (i.e., consulting physicians, specialized technicians, students in the various health care professions — even ethicists), invasion of the body with tubes and attachment of wires, reduction to a "vegetable" state of existence, total dependence on machines for life-support, intrusive resuscitation procedures (e.g., tracheostomy).[26] For the conscious patient, these elements are experienced as suffering, even if not pain.

The duty not to cause harm dictates against prolonging a patient's life under conditions such as these. Of course, the strength of this duty will vary with the severity of the disvalue. The duty to relieve pain is more pressing when severe pain is involved than it is in the case of a mild headache; and, similarly, the duty to relieve indignities will be more pressing when the indignity involved is substantial. It would hardly be justified to end a patient's life, for example, in order to prevent having someone on the hospital staff mispronounce her name (although this might be regarded by the patient as an indignity).

There may be other disvalues that are independent of sensation, and they would have to be taken into account in our calculations as well. In general, there is a substantial prima facie reason in favor of euthanasia whenever the sum of negative values outweighs the sum of positive values — or, in other words, when the patient would be "better off dead."

Patient's request. We must also consider how the factor of irreversible unconsciousness affects the duty arising from the patient's request for assistance in ending her life.[27] Three questions arise in this connection: (a) Is the wish to avoid prolongation of an unconscious state sufficient to justify waiving or transferring her right to life? (b) Does the patient's request to have her life ended under these circumstances (which would obviously have to have been made before the onset of the permanent vegetative state) continue to have force after she has lost consciousness irreversibly? (c) Does a general advance directive like "I don't want to be kept alive by machines" apply to specific, technical therapies like nasogastric (i.e., through the nose) feeding tubes or gastrostomies (i.e., tubes surgically implanted through the abdominal wall)? These questions are addressed in Chapter Six (see p. 167) when we talk about the Cruzan and O'Connor cases (Cases 21 and 22 respectively, p. 233).

1. The first of these questions is obviously related to our discussion of indignities just above. If there are genuine disvalues that apply in a comatose state (and we argued that there are), then it must be possible in principle that their sum in a given case might outweigh the positive values available to the patient. Thus, it would be reasonable for the patient considering such a situation to judge that she would be better off dead if she were ever placed in such a condition, and hence there would be justification for her to waive or transfer her right to life in these circumstances.

2. The second of these questions raises two separate issues: first, a point about the nature of rights; and, second, a point about the status of any request made outside the context in which it is to be applied.

On the first point, some philosophers have argued that a certain minimum level of self-consciousness and self-awareness is an essential condition for the possession of any rights.[28] * This claim is usually brought up in connection with the issue of abortion, but it has implications for euthanasia as well — especially in the situation we are now considering, in which the patients are no longer capable of self-consciousness and self-awareness.

Our duty to honor a person's request is rooted in a corresponding right that she possesses (i.e., the right to have reasonable and non-burdensome requests honored). But then it would follow from the view of rights just mentioned that irreversibly comatose patients have no claim upon us to honor their requests.

But surely this conclusion is not acceptable. We generally feel a moral obligation to honor the last requests of a person who has died; and, in the case of requests set out formally in a last will and testament, the law assigns considerable strength to this obligation. It is a peculiar (and distressing) feature of contemporary society that we pay more attention to a person's wishes after he dies than we do while he is still alive but in a comatose state.[29]

It is not clear that duties toward the dead stem from *rights* on their part, however. Any attempt to ascribe rights to the dead faces serious conceptual difficulties. For example, the third of Epicurus's

---

*We do not agree with this analysis of rights; but it would carry us too far afield to explore this issue here, so we will accept it for purposes of argument in this section.

well-known arguments about death points out that "when death is present" there may be no subject who could be said to possess rights. Thus obligations toward the dead may have their foundations elsewhere than in rights — for example, in respect for the person who was but is no longer, or perhaps as a symbolic act of respect for the general social institutions of honoring requests and promises elicited by those requests.*

These same reasons apply to requests made by and promises made to persons who are now comatose. There can be no basis for giving them less consideration than we give the dead. Hence, it is clear that we have an obligation toward them on this basis even if it were not appropriate to say that they have rights in the matter. A person who is unconscious or incompetent is not considered to have lost her authority to control treatment.[30]

On the second point, one part of the problem is to determine whether the patient's request meets the test of realistic appraisal of the facts. At the time she asked that her life not be prolonged in an irreversibly comatose state, she had no first-hand knowledge as to what this state is actually like. Thus it would seem that her request was not rationally justified when she made it, and therefore it need not be honored now.

However, this argument is based on a mistaken view of the requirements of reasonable appraisal of the facts. All that can be required of us here is that we make sound use of all the evidence that is available to us. *None* of us can know first-hand what the state of *irreversible* coma is actually like, and relatively few have first-hand knowledge of any sort of coma. Therefore, we must base our decisions on whatever evidence is available to us: second-hand reports of and scientific theories about what the state is like for the person in it, personal observation (if possible) of the indignities it involves, etc. If this evidence is employed in careful reasoning, then there can be no basis for questioning the rational justification of the conclusion.

How do we know she has not changed her mind on the matter and would withdraw her request if she could communicate? Of course, we cannot know this for certain. But there may be evidence relevant to this judgment — e.g., the degree of firmness with which she origi-

---

*The value of such a symbolic act is that, by honoring requests we have agreed to when it is obvious to all that we cannot be held accountable by the promisee, we both accustom ourselves to honor all promises and also reassure those living persons to whom we make a promise that we will honor it even if they do not check up on us. In short, this symbolic act establishes a basis for trust for the living — an assurance for the currently living that their impact on us will perdure after they die.

nally made the request, whether she repeated it on various occasions, whether it is consistent with other values she held, whether it was written down, etc. In the absence of concrete grounds for suspecting a change of mind, we must assume that none occurred. We do, after all, have one strong piece of evidence to support the view that she wants to die: i.e., her request.

WHEN THE PATIENT IS NOT IN PAIN

Suppose that the patient is conscious, but not in pain. As usual, we are assuming that the remaining features of our paradigm apply, as specified in Table 5.

TABLE 5

1. terminal illness
2. irreversible
3. death within hours or days
4. conscious but free from pain
5. patient requests to forego proposed treatment
6. this request is based on a judgment that he or she would be "better off dead" due to "indignities" of continued treatment
7. the patient's request is coherent with his or her fundamental values ("in character")
8. family and caregivers share these fundamental values
9. these values are rationally defensible
10. continued treatment is a burden to *others* (family, significant others, caregivers)
11. what is being requested is to *withhold* a treatment
12. what is to be done is an *omission*, not a positive action
13. the treatment in question is an *extraordinary* measure (i.e., no reasonable hope of benefit, excessively painful, expensive, or otherwise burdensome)
14. the consequences of the proposed action (omission) would *not* involve pain, suffering, indignity, or other burden for the patient
15. the intention of the agent would be to honor the wishes of the patient, *not* to kill the patient
16. compassion is the predominant motive prompting everybody
17. the underlying illness will be the *cause of death*

Note particularly that the patient is in the final stages (item 3) of a terminal condition (item 1), that he specifically requests to die (item 5), and that his judgment that he would be better off dead (item 6) is shared by family, friends, and caregivers (item 8). Could there be justification for ending his life in these circumstances?

The key question here is whether it would be possible for the disvalues other than pain (e.g., the indignities listed above, p. 42) to outweigh the positive values available to the conscious patient. It seems clear to us that this *would* be possible and hence that euthanasia would be justified in some instances of this sort. However, the conclusion in each specific instance must depend on a careful and thorough comparative weighing of the positive and negative values, the degree of uncertainty in the prediction that they will occur and persist, and the issue of whether the patient's request to die reflects his most fundamental values.

CONCLUSION

Having examined the paradigm cases of justified intervention to save a life (Bobby Bright) and unjustified euthanasia, with variations in between, we now turn to the more difficult questions involving voluntary and involuntary euthanasia.

NOTES

1. Susan Braithwaite and David C. Thomasma, "New Guidelines on Foregoing Life-Sustaining Treatment in Incompetent Patients: An Anti-Cruelty Policy," *Annals of Internal Medicine* 104 (1986), 711–715.

2. Edmund D. Pellegrino and David C. Thomasma, *For the Patient's Good: The Restoration of Beneficence in Health Care* (New York: Oxford University Press, 1988).

3. See Joel Feinberg, *Social Philosophy* (Englewood Cliffs, N.J.: Prentice-Hall, 1973); David Lyons, ed., *Rights* (Belmont, Calif.: Wadsworth, 1979).

4. Micetich and Thomasma unpublished; David C. Thomasma, "Philosophical Reflections on a Rational Treatment Plan," *Journal of Medicine and Philosophy* 11 (1986), 157–165.

5. See Paul Ramsey, *Ethics at the Edges of Life* (New Haven: Yale University Press, 1978), p. 297.

6. A recent Supreme Court ruling held that it is not *legally* wrong to seize and search one's garbage, but we would contend that the moral assessment we defend here is unaffected by this legal ruling.

7. See Chapter Four for a discussion of the implications of this analogy for the role of health professionals.

8. David C. Thomasma, *An Apology for the Value of Human Life*, Chapter 1; Owesi Temkin, William K. Frankena, Sanford H. Kadish, *Respect for Life in Medicine, Philosophy, and the Law* (Baltimore: Johns Hopkins University Press, 1977).

9. Piers Paul Reid, *Alive: The Story of the Andes Survivors* (Philadelphia: Lippincott, 1974).

10. Immanuel Kant, *Foundations of the Metaphysics of Morals*, translated, with an introduction, by Lewis White Beck (Indianapolis: Bobbs-Merrill, 1959).

11. Glenn C. Graber, "The Rationality of Suicide," in Samuel E. Wallace and Alben Eser, eds., *Suicide and Euthanasia: The Rights of Personhood* (Knoxville: University of Tennessee Press, 1981), pp. 51–65.

12. Glenn C. Graber and David C. Thomasma, *Theory and Practice in Medical Ethics* (New York: Continuum, 1989).

13. John Stuart Mill sets out the reasoning here at length in connection with the issue of meat-eating. See his *On Liberty*, Chapter IV.

14. Even the philosopher R. M. Hare, who attempts to base his ethical theory on a formalized version of the Golden Rule, admits that this can happen. See his discussion of the "conscientious Nazi" in *Freedom and Reason* (London: Oxford University Press, 1963), pp. 158–177. It seems to us that Hare overstates the fruitfulness of the Golden Rule in other contexts as well; but we will not go into this subject here.

15. For reasons we will explain at length in Chapter Six.

16. *The Right and The Good* (Oxford: Clarendon Press, 1930), p. 42.

17. Glenn C. Graber, "Some Questions about Double Effect," *Ethics in Science and Medicine* 6, no. 1 (January 1979), pp. 65–84.

18. William A. Nolen, *The Making of a Surgeon* (New York: Pocket Books, 1972), p. 216.

19. The Food and Drug Administration has recently developed a "fast-track" approval process for drugs relating to tragic and catastrophic diseases such as AIDS. However, even here it is unrealistic to expect a dramatic curative drug to burst on the scene without prior notice in scientific publications — and, often, in the public media.

20. An entire book has recently appeared, devoted to the issues raised by this case. See Lonnie D. Kliever, *Dax's Case: Essays in Medical Ethics and Human Meaning* (Dallas, Tex.: Southern Methodist University Press, 1989).

21. This videotape can be obtained from the Library of Clinical Psychiatric Syndromes, Department of Psychiatry, University of Texas Medical Branch, Galveston, TX 77550. See also the film *Dax's Case*, produced by Concern for Dying. We must warn readers, however, that viewing this tape is a difficult emotional experience for sensitive souls.

22. Robert B. White, "Comment," *Hastings Center Report* 5, no. 3 (June 1975), 9–10.

23. There are some reports of returning from a permanent vegetative state. One such was Sgt. Mack.

24. See the vivid description by a woman who slipped into a diabetic coma of how that condition felt to her in Kim Painter, "Life Catches Up with an '80's Woman," *USA Today*, July 25, 1989, sec. D, 1.

25. See Thomas Nagel, "Death," *Nous* 4, no. 1; reprinted with revisions in James Rachels, ed., 2nd ed. *Moral Problems* (New York: Harper & Row, 1975), p. 406.

26. Eric Cassell calls all of this the "humiliation" of dying. See his "Life as a Work of Art," *Hastings Center Report* 14 (October 1984), 35–37.

27. It is interesting to note that the New Jersey Supreme Court refused to give consideration to reports that Karen had indicated that she would not want to have her life sustained in this sort of situation. They dismissed testimony about these conversations as "hearsay evidence." A decade later, the same court announced in their opinion in the Conroy case that this had been a mistake and they should have given significant weight to these reports. See *In re Conroy* at 1230.

28. See, for example, Michael Tooley, "Abortion and Infanticide," *Philosophy and Public Affairs* 2 (Fall 1972), 37–65, and Ronald Green, "Conferred Rights and the Fetus," *Journal of Religious Ethics* 2, no. 1 (Spring 1974), 55–75.

29. We are grateful to Frank H. Marsh, Jr. for calling this point to our attention.

30. *In re Conroy* at 1229.

Chapter Three _____

UNWILLING AND/OR ACTIVE EUTHANASIA

In the previous chapter, we examined a number of variations on the paradigm case of justified euthanasia. Now we turn to the two most controversial issues of voluntary and involuntary euthanasia, and active and passive euthanasia.

WHEN THE PATIENT DOES NOT REQUEST TO DIE

Could there ever be a moral justification for ending the life of a patient who does not explicitly request to die? The focus here is on item 5 of our case schemas in Tables 1–5 of Chapter Two. As usual, there are several distinct possibilities, each of which must be considered separately. They are listed in Table 6.

TABLE 6

1. *Voluntary Euthanasia:* The patient explicitly requests to die (as in Chapter Two above).

2. *Presumed Voluntary Euthanasia:* The patient never explicitly expressed a wish to die under present circumstances, but there is a solid basis of evidence — in terms of values she did express — for assuming that this is what she would want.

3. *Nonvoluntary Euthanasia:* The patient never expressed his wishes nor offered any solid evidence on the basis of which they might be inferred.

4. *Presumed Involuntary Euthanasia:* The patient never explicitly expressed a wish to be kept alive under present circumstances, but there is substantial evidence for assuming that this is what she would want.

5. *Involuntary Euthanasia:* The patient explicitly requests that his life be sustained under present circumstances.

Voluntary euthanasia. Voluntary Euthanasia is another way of expressing what we discussed in Chapter Two, so we need not go into it at length here. However, it might be helpful to recapitulate the general moral principles that have figured in our argument in favor of voluntary euthanasia in certain circumstances, so that we can determine their force in connection with these other forms of euthanasia.

1. *Right to Life:* Every person has a right to life.

   a. *Avoiding Killing:* It is wrong to end a person's life.

   b. *Waiving Right to Life:* One may waive her right to life or transfer it to another person (but only in circumstances in which she would be better off dead).

2. *Non-Maleficence:* It is wrong to bring harm to persons in any way.

   a. *Comparative Non-Maleficence:* Some ways of bringing harm are *more* wrong than others.

3. *Persons as Ends:* It is wrong to treat persons (including oneself) merely as means.

4. *Beneficence:*

   a. *Positive:* We all have an obligation to promote the good of others.

   b. *Negative:* We all have an obligation to relieve pain, suffering, and other disvaluable states.

5. *Honoring Requests:* Every person has a right to have others honor their reasonable and non-burdensome requests.
      Criteria of reasonableness here include: (a) factual realism, (b) value realism, and (c) the request must express the patient's deepest personal values.

6. *Promise-Keeping:* A person to whom one has made a promise has a right to have that promise kept.

Let us begin with three of these principles that are related to each other and obviously relevant to the present distinctions: the principles of Waiving Right to Life, Honoring Requests, and Promise-Keeping. Recall the role these principles have played in our case for voluntary euthanasia. The principle of Waiving Right to Life serves to make it permissible to bring about a person's death. It neutralizes the general moral prohibition against ending a person's life (stated in the principle of Avoiding Killing, which we have argued to be — together with the principle of Waiving Right to Life — an implication of the principle of Right to Life. The principles of Honoring Requests and Promise-Keeping go further than establishing the permissibility of voluntary euthanasia. Each serves to make it a moral *obligation* when the relevant conditions are met. (In the principle of Promise-Keeping, the relevant conditions include the fact that one has made a promise to assist the patient in this way. Obviously, this principle will have the narrowest range of application of the three.)

Applying these principles to other domains. What, then, will be the role of these principles outside the domain of voluntary euthanasia?

1. At the opposite end of the spectrum — when we are dealing with involuntary euthanasia, the principles of Honoring Requests and Promise-Keeping will each count *against* ending the person's life and the principle of Waiving Right to Life will not apply at all (thus leaving the force of the principle of Avoiding Killing to weigh against ending life).

2. In connection with nonvoluntary euthanasia, all three principles fail to have application (again, leaving the force of the principle of Avoiding Killing weighing against ending life).

3. In connection with either presumed voluntary euthanasia or presumed involuntary euthanasia, the principle of Promise-Keeping will not apply — since no promise can have been made if the issue was never explicitly discussed.

Presumptions. It seems to us, however, that the principle of Honoring Requests will apply in most instances of both kinds of presumption and the principle of Waiving Right to Life will apply in most cases of presumed voluntary euthanasia — although both principles may carry somewhat less weight here than they do when explicit requests or waivers are involved. Both parts of this conclusion follow from a natural and plausible normative doctrine about presumed requests in general. Suppose, for example, that a small boy from the neighborhood drops by as you are baking cookies and he casts an obvious longing gaze at the cookies but does not explicitly request one. It would be reasonable to assume that he wants a cookie but that something prevents him from coming right out and asking for it (shyness, perhaps, or maybe orders from his parents to wait until such things are offered). It seems to us that his longing gaze is tantamount to a request for a cookie. (His parents would probably agree with this assessment, and thus they might well reprimand him for acting in this way: "You should not request treats; and you should not gaze longingly at them or drop hints about them, either.") Now surely you have some obligation to give this little boy a cookie if you have one to spare. This presumed request has as much claim to be honored as an explicit request.

The analogue to this situation with regard to euthanasia is the (quite common) situation in which the patient has given definite indications of her wishes in the context of abstract discussions of the issue ("I shudder when I think of Karen Quinlan being kept alive. Why do they do things like that to people? We would be much kinder toward a pet." Or "I shudder when I think they turned off the respirator. How can they do that to a person? It is still a life they are ending even if she is hopelessly unconscious.") At the same time, however, she has been prevented by the emotional and social barriers surrounding talk about one's own death from coming right out and making an explicit request.[1] (Further, in most such cases the family will have been prevented by these same barriers from asking directly for an expression of her wishes in her own case.) It seems to us that these indications of her views can be regarded as tantamount to an explicit request and should be honored as such.[2]

A qualification must be attached to this conclusion. There will, of course, be some degree of uncertainty in the interpretation of any such oblique indications of her wishes. Hinting and abstract discussion can never be quite as clear-cut as a direct request. This is what leads to the weakening of the force of these principles in the contexts of presumed requests. To the degree that the presumption is uncertain, the principle or principles built upon it must be regarded as tentative. Thus, in possible instances of presumed voluntary euthanasia in which there is considerable uncertainty, it would not be morally justified to end the patient's life. But there will be some instances in which the indications of the patient's wishes are clear enough to warrant euthanasia. Similarly, cases that are classified as presumed involuntary must be treated as nonvoluntary when there is considerable uncertainty and as tantamount to involuntary when there are strong and definite indications that the patient wishes not to have his life ended under present circumstances.

Nonvoluntary euthanasia. What moral guidelines apply in nonvoluntary cases?

1. We have seen that none of the three principles discussed so far (i.e., Waiving Right to Life, Honoring Requests, Promise-Keeping) play any role here.

2. The general moral prohibition against ending a person's life (what we have called the principle of Avoiding Killing will dictate *against* euthanasia, as will the principle of Nonmaleficence (since

we have agreed previously that ending a person's life causes some measure of harm to that person).

3. On the other hand, other applications of the principle of Non-maleficence and the principle of Beneficence will weigh in favor of euthanasia, since death will also bring some benefit to her.

4. Further, it makes a difference that the good effects (i.e., relieving the patient of the harm of pain, etc.) will generally be the intended effects of euthanasia, whereas the harm brought about by ending the life will be unavoidable incidental effects.

5. Clearly if this were *not* so — if, for example, one's goal in ending the patient's life were to deprive her of continued association with her family, in an act of revenge toward either her or them, or if the aim were to reduce the burden on society (as in euthanasia programs in Nazi Germany or in Stalinist Russia) — then it would clearly *not* be morally justified. This sort of case would also violate the principle of Persons as Ends.

6. However, we must be careful not to put too much weight on the distinction between intended and incidental effects. If the amount of harm caused to her by ending her life greatly outweighed the benefits to her (suppose, for example, that she is experiencing a great deal of pain at present but that the condition is a temporary one and she will be restored to perfect health in a week's time), then surely the act would not be morally justified even if the benefits were intended and the harm incidental.

7. Our conclusion is that euthanasia is morally justified in the absence of any explicit request by the patient or any definite indication of her wishes if (a) a careful assessment of her condition makes it clearly reasonable to judge that she would be substantially better off dead and (b) the intended effect of the action is to relieve her pain, suffering or other disvaluable state. As we have indicated earlier, we mean for the judgment in (a) to be made from the patient's viewpoint and in terms of her own personal values (insofar as they can be known).

8. The viewpoint of others who are affected by the decision must also be taken into account here. However, rather than bringing in this issue at this point, we prefer to deal with it in connection with involuntary euthanasia — to which we now turn.

Involuntary euthanasia. In the case of involuntary euthanasia, quite a number of our principles dictate against ending the patient's life: i.e., Avoiding Killing, Nonmaleficence, Persons as Ends, Beneficence (if the patient would be aware of what we are doing), Honoring

Requests and Promise-Keeping (if we have made a promise). Could there ever be a moral justification for involuntary euthanasia in the face of this strong weight of opposition? Consider, as examples, Case 23 ("Edward Faulkner") and Case 24 ("Mr. McIntyre's Last-Minute Request"), p. 235.

1. In Case 23, Edward Faulkner is a seriously ill but mentally alert ninety-year-old who repeatedly and explicitly requests aggressive life-sustaining treatment. His wife makes similar requests. The chief question here is the soundness of the physician's judgment that the patient would be better off dead. The patient's wife clearly does not agree with this assessment, and it appears that the patient himself did not, either. Suppose however that, in a given case, a careful and realistic assessment of the patient's situation in terms of his own deepest personal values leads us to judge that he would really be better off dead (cf. Case 12, p. 221). This judgment seems plausible in Case 24, the case of a severely disabled twenty-eight-year-old who has made a carefully deliberated decision to discontinue dialysis but then requests its reinstitution at the last minute. Mr. McIntyre's own previous judgment that he would be better off dead was persuasive to his family and caregivers, and thus it carries a great deal of weight in our assessment of his situation. And yet, after dialysis has been discontinued at his request, Mr. McIntyre then requests that his life be sustained. Here we have a conflict between his (latest) explicit request and his own genuine best interests. The question is, then, which of these we ought to follow.

Clearly we would have to say that his request to be put back on dialysis was not rationally justified. And, since the principle of Honoring Requests includes the specification that it is *reasonable* requests that ought to be honored, its force seems to be neutralized. Further, to honor his request would cause him the harm of prolonging his suffering and/or other disvaluable state; and thus the principles of Nonmaleficence and Beneficence would weigh against honoring his request. This analysis demonstrates why the principle of autonomy, if taken as an absolute in medical ethics, cannot assist us very much in broaching the questions of honoring requests.[3]

These principles favoring ending the patient's life must be balanced against the opposing principles that were indicated above. The force of opposition to euthanasia on the basis of the principle of Nonmaleficence would seem to be more than neutralized by the judgment that he would be better off dead. Sustaining his life would cause *more* harm to him than ending it. The principle of Promise-Keeping would carry a great deal of weight — especially if an explicit promise had been made that dialysis would be reinstituted at any time he requested it.[4] But the principle of Promise-Keeping would not apply at all in the absence of such an explicit promise (and none appears to have been made in Case 24); and its weight would be neutralized if the conditions of the promise contained the qualification that the request to be honored must be reasonable. (This sort of qualification probably should be included in any general promise made in advance.)[5]

The decisive principles in Mr. McIntyre's situation seem to be the principle of Avoiding Killing and Persons as Ends. The principle of Avoiding Killing creates a presumption against ending a person's life in the absence of an explicit request to do so. The principle of Persons as Ends would also weigh against denying the person's explicit request in order to realize his genuine best interests, because to do this would be to treat the person's capacities for moral agency (by means of which he expressed the request) as a means — to his own best interests.

We conclude that it would not be justified to ignore the patient's explicit request and end his life if his request is at all reasonable. The best approach would be to lead him to rethink his situation (in a caring and supportive atmosphere, needless to say) and thus convince him by rational considerations that he would be better off dead and that he ought to change his request.

The question we are left with in Case 24, then, is whether Mr. McIntyre's request is (a) autonomous and (b) reasonable. There are considerable grounds for doubts on both points in this case. Given the firmness of his initial decision, it seems most plausible to interpret this reversal as a "failure of nerve" rather than a genuine change of mind. Thus, the appropriate response is to seek to calm his fears. Furthermore, given the effects of going without dialysis, we cannot be sure a priori that he is thinking clearly at all. And, the physical effects of having foregone dialysis make it problematic to reinstitute it at this stage. Organ damage may be irreversible at this point. (See the reversal of consideration in Case 25, p. 237).

2. Suppose that a given person requests that her life be sustained, yet it is clear that certain *other* people would be better off if she were dead. Could there ever be moral justification for denying her request on this basis?

Obviously it is important to consider who these other people are and in what way they would be better off as a result of her death, as well as the amount of benefit and harm that her death would cause to her. We will discuss these matters in some detail when we take up euthanasia and the family in the next chapter. For now, let us consider some fairly extreme examples.

A. The patient is conscious and relatively free from pain. The chief benefit to others as a result of ending her life would be the satisfaction it would cause to a person who has strong feelings of hatred toward her.

Surely it would be wrong to end her life in this case.

B. The patient is irreversibly comatose and has only a few days, at most, to live. To sustain her life this long would require use of some scarce medical resource (e.g., the last remaining dose of a certain drug or the last available mechanical respirator, or the last bed in the ICU) that is also urgently needed by another patient who also wants to live and who has a real chance for a long and satisfying life if aided through the present crisis.

In this case, surely it is justified to deny our patient's prior request to have her life sustained. Both patients have a right to life, to have their requests honored, etc. Thus these factors will neutralize each other, and the final decision must be made on the basis of which alternative would bring the greatest benefit and least harm.[6]

C. The patient wavers between coma and semi-consciousness in which she neither can communicate with others nor show signs of recognition of people, place, etc. She could be maintained in this state for weeks or months before dying, but only by expensive measures that would be financially ruinous for the family.

It seems to us that in this case her prior request to have her life sustained under these circumstances is nullified by the burden it imposes upon the family. Further, the weight of her right to life is diminished by the low quality of life available to her; and, finally, the scales are tipped in favor of ending her life by consideration of the harmful burden the alternative would cause to her family.

Someone might object to this conclusion on the grounds that the society as a whole could (and should) remove this burden from the family by means of a program of financing this sort of therapy through general taxation. We are sympathetic with this sort of proposal in general, and we agree that it might make a difference in certain cases of this type; but it will not solve the problem in all cases. The same issue will arise at the level of burdening social resources. We, for example, would not be willing to pay half our income in taxes to pay the costs of therapy for one such patient or to reduce the temperatures in our house to 45 degrees (which would present not merely an inconvenience, but a threat to the health of our families) in order to divert electricity for the machines required to sustain this sort of life.

The difficult question, obviously, is to determine the precise limits of moral justifiability on the continuum stretching from case A through case C to case B. No abstract general rule can be formulated to specify this. Decisions must be made in the concrete case, on the basis of a serious and thoughtful attempt to enumerate all the relevant moral principles and to compare the weights of the duties on each side of the issue.[7] We will discuss these issues further in Chapters Four and Six.

COMPARISON OF DEATH MANAGEMENT MEASURES

Throughout the previous discussion, we have deliberately restricted the means by which the person's life would be ended to "passive" measures. It is now time to examine a wider range of possibilities. Table 7 shows possible measures distilled from our discussion in Chapter One, with some examples of each.

TABLE 7

1. *Treat with ordinary measures, but withhold extraordinary or heroic measures,* e.g., heart-lung transplant, or highly experimental drug known to be extremely painful or damaging to some major organ

2. *Decline to initiate treatment,* that is, one that would normally be labelled as ordinary, such as cardiopulmonary resuscitation (CPR), or antibiotics when pneumonia develops

3. *Stop ongoing treatment,* that is, one that would normally be labelled as ordinary, such as nutrition, insulin, or mechanical respirator

4. *Give the patient means to kill himself,* e.g., (a) place the respirator so the switch is within his reach and instruct him how to turn it off, (b) place a fatal dose of morphine within his reach, (c) place a fatal dose of cyanide within his reach

5. *Take an action that indirectly brings about the death of the patient,* e.g., inject a dose of morphine that is sufficient to relieve this patient's pain fully, although you know (or, at least, strongly suspect) that this amount will prove fatal. We call this "double-effect euthanasia."

6. *Take an action that directly causes the death of the patient,* e.g., inject curare

---

The question is whether there are important moral differences between the actions on this list.

Extraordinary/ordinary measures distinction. Traditional moral theology teaches that it is morally permissible (although not generally morally required) to withhold extraordinary or heroic measures (i.e., item 1, Table 7; see also item 13 in the case specifications in Tables 1–5), but that any of the other actions on the list (with the possible exception of item 5, as will be discussed below, p. 66) are absolutely prohibited. This view is expressed firmly in the following statement by Pope Pius XII:

[1] man (and whoever is entrusted with the task of taking care of his fellowman) has the right and the duty in case of serious illness to take the necessary treatment for the preservation of life and health. . . . [2] But normally one is held to use only ordinary means — according to circumstances of persons, places, times and culture — that is to say, means that do not involve any grave burden for oneself or another. A more strict obligation would be too burdensome for most men. . . . [3] On the other hand, one is not forbidden to take more than the strictly necessary steps to preserve life and health, as long as he does not fail in some more serious duty.[8]

The logical structure of this position is compatible, up to a point, with the argument we have been presenting. Each of us has a duty to do what is necessary to preserve life and health, but this is not an absolute duty.* If a situation arises in which fulfilling this duty would involve a "grave burden for oneself or another," then the duty has reached its limit and we are not here required to act on it (although we may still be permitted to do so).

1. One primary difficulty with this position lies in determining precisely where to draw the line between ordinary and extraordinary means. The criterion offered by Pope Pius XII is extremely vague. The criterion is made somewhat more specific in the definition most often employed by Catholic moral theologians. According to this account:

ordinary measures = "all medicines, treatments, and operations, which offer a reasonable hope of benefit and which can be obtained and used without excessive expense, pain, or other inconvenience."

extraordinary measures = "those which cannot be obtained or used without excessive expense, pain, or other inconvenience, or which, if used, would not offer a reasonable hope of benefit."[9]

This is still far from precise. Just *how much* expense, pain, etc. is "excessive"? What is, and what is not, properly included under the heading of "inconvenience"? What are the limits beyond which the hope of benefit ceases to be "reasonable"?[10] It is, of course, impossible to answer these questions definitively in the abstract.

---

*This is the point in our argument where a vitalist disagrees with us and apparently would have to do so with Pope Pius XII as well.

However, it would be a serious mistake to reject this criterion completely because of its vagueness. After all, we are dealing with complex and thorny issues; and thus we should not expect our tools of analysis to be simple and clearcut.[11] It may be possible to come to rational agreement about the answers to these questions in specific cases even if we cannot do so in general terms; and, if so, this criterion may be a useful aid to decision-making despite its vagueness.

Given the present state of the art, heart-lung transplantation is an obvious example of an extraordinary measure. This procedure may extend the recipient's life for a short period of time, but there can be little hope for long-term benefit. Furthermore, the surgery and related therapy involve considerable pain, as well as the tragically complementary "inconveniences" of a danger of rejection of the transplanted organ, on the one hand, or, on the other hand, the danger of life-threatening infection as a result of the immuno-suppressant drugs used to prevent rejection. Surely one is not morally required to endure a burden such as this.

Similarly, one is not obligated to accept an extremely painful or debilitating experimental therapy, for which there is little basis for hope of effectiveness. Of course, if the patient is willing to undergo such measures (whether in hopes that they might prove beneficial to him or from an interest in contributing to the discovery of knowledge that will help others in the future), then he has every right to do so.

2. Where we find ourselves in disagreement with this stated position is in the refusal to go beyond withholding extraordinary measures, in some cases, in order to bring about death. Up to this point, we have looked primarily at only one component of the view: that the duty to take the necessary treatment for the preservation of life and health is suspended when the treatment required classifies as extraordinary. But it is often also maintained that the duty to take treatment holds absolutely up to the point where the necessary measures become heroic. No other element is sufficient to override the duty to preserve life. It is this element of the view with which we disagree. We contend that the duty to preserve life is a prima facie obligation in all respects and thus when it is clear that the patient is or will be in a state of such extreme pain or other disvalue that life itself becomes a grave burden, there may be moral warrant for any and all of the sorts of actions on our list, including perhaps (in the most extreme cases) direct killing.

(a) Consider the issue of whether to administer an antibiotic when pneumonia or other massive infection develops in a patient who is already near death from other causes. The last stages of the life of

Karen Quinlan (Case 20, p. 230) illustrate this situation,[12] which is schematized in Table 8.

TABLE 8

Case 20: Karen Quinlan's Final Days

1. persistent vegetative state
2. irreversible
3. life expectancy uncertain
4. no pain because the patient is permanently unconscious
5. patient unable to express present wishes, but earlier indicated desire to forego life-sustaining treatment in a situation like this
6. family members judge that she would be "better off dead"
7. foregoing life-sustaining measures is coherent with her fundamental values ("in character")
8. family and caregivers at this stage share these fundamental values
9. these values are rationally defensible
10. continued treatment is a burden to *others* (family, significant others, caregivers)
11. what is being requested is to *withhold* a treatment (i.e., antibiotics)
12. what is to be done is an *omission*, not a positive action
13. the treatment in question is an *ordinary* measure (i.e., relatively inexpensive, nonpainful, promises benefit for the specific intercurrent infection which now threatens her life)
14. the consequences of the proposed action (omission) would *not* involve pain, suffering, indignity, or other burden for the patient (as far as we can judge, she is incapable of feeling pain)
15. the intention of the agent would be to honor the wishes of the patient, *not* to kill the patient
16. compassion is the predominant motive prompting everybody
17. the *cause of death* will be the intercurrent infection, which could be successfully treated with antibiotics

---

Note especially items 13 and 17. As indicated in item 13, we classify this, on the list above, as declining to initiate ordinary treatment (i.e., under item 2 in Table 7, p. 58) because the use of the antibiotic would be relatively inexpensive, painless, and convenient, and it offers reasonable hope of achieving the limited benefit that is intended — curing the infection. However, this treatment would also have the indirect (and, presumably, incidental) effect of prolonging the patient's suffering and/or other disvaluable state by postponing her death from the unrelated primary threat. We would argue that the duty to prevent suffering here overrides the duty to preserve life, and hence it seems to us that it would be fully justified to withhold

the antibiotic and allow the infection to end her life rather than forcing her family (and perhaps her as well, if she experiences pain) to
continue to endure their suffering until her primary condition reaches
the critical point at which her survival comes to depend upon heroic
measures (refer also at this point to Case 26, p. 239).

Some ethicists deal with this case by extending the category of
heroic means to include this sort of treatment, on the grounds that
it does not offer any prospect of improving the patient's overall
situation.[13] The burden is considered extreme compared to the benefits. We have no real quarrel with this proposal, but it is important
to recognize that it involves a significant departure from a morality
of strict adherence to principles in the direction of consequentialist
reasoning. It cannot be denied that the antibiotic offers reasonable
hope of the specific benefit of curing the intercurrent infection. Further, surely this benefit will be the intended effect of administering the
drug. Thus the basis of classifying this as an extraordinary measure
must be a calculation of the sum total of all the values and disvalues
that result in the long run — those that are incidental to the action as
well as those intended by means of it and those intrinsic to it.

In addition to the theoretical difficulty that this pattern of reasoning is at odds with some central principles of traditionalist theories,
there is the practical problem that it has implications that carry further than we suspect ethicists like Ramsey are willing to go.

(b) For example, this same pattern of argument leads to the conclusion that it is morally justified to stop ongoing treatment of such
an obviously ordinary kind as nutrition. If a terminal patient is in
extreme pain, then to continue to support his life through nourishment has the (incidental) effect of prolonging his suffering — without counterbalancing benefit in terms of his overall condition[14] (cf.
Case 27 and Case 28, p. 240).

(c) But, further, if it is justified to bring about death by withholding nutrition when the patient is in pain, why would it not be equally
justified to withhold nutrition at an earlier time in anticipation that
the patient will suffer if kept alive? A consequentialist calculation of
the positive and negative values to be expected for the patient would
lead to the conclusion that here, too, nutrition would not provide a
net benefit to him. Hence if an action is classified as an extraordinary
measure (or, as some prefer to put it, a "useless ordinary measure") in
terms of the *net* benefit to the patient, withholding nutrition would
be justified.

We strongly doubt that traditionalist moral theologians would be
willing to endorse this conclusion, but we do not see how they can

avoid it once they take the first step in extending the category of heroic measures as described in (a) above. Since we *are* willing to go this far, we are not inclined to bother looking for a way in which they might extricate themselves from this difficulty. (It might be pointed out that, in earlier discussions in this and the previous chapter, we have already barricaded a number of possible escape-routes they might attempt to employ — such as, for example, an appeal to the uncertainty of such a prognosis.)

For our own part, we would much prefer to avoid consequentialist reasoning of this sort by admitting from the start that the duty to preserve life is a prima facie duty. The latter is the pattern of argument we have been employing throughout this chapter. The arguments by means of which we would defend withholding nutrition in anticipation of a painful terminal state follow our line of argument in Chapter Two ("When Death Is Not Imminent," p. 32).

Withholding/withdrawing distinction. The foregoing discussion establishes that there is not a crucial normative difference between 2 and 3 on our list of ways of bringing about death in Table 7 (p. 58). There might still be some question, however, about the step from item 2 to item 3. To many minds, there seem to be important differences between declining to initiate treatment and stopping treatment once it is begun.[15] However, although we do not deny that these differences have *some* moral significance, we think it can be shown that they are not crucial in the context of euthanasia.

1. In the first place, the conceptual basis of the distinction between withholding and withdrawing treatment is not as well-established as one might imagine. Suppose, for example, that a resuscitation team were to decide, in a given case, to use manual resuscitation techniques but not to employ an electrical defibrillator or drugs that stimulate heart activity. If we focus on the whole series of resuscitation techniques that are normally used together, we would say that they had stopped ongoing treatment at a certain stage; but, if we consider each separate technique as a distinct treatment, then we would say that they declined at a certain point to initiate further treatment. And there is no solid basis for ruling that either one of these descriptions is correct and the other mistaken. But, then, what would be the mistake in regarding each separate instance of exerting pressure on the patient's chest or each separate squeeze on the breathing bag as a distinct treatment? If we view things in this way, then to suspend either of these activities would be labelled as declining to initiate a treatment rather than stopping ongoing treatment.[16]

At the other extreme, the whole series of things done to the patient in the course of his hospitalization could be viewed as a single course of treatment. Surgery to remove an inflamed appendix is, in a sense, a continuation of the attempt to combat the infection with antibiotics; and thus to decline to perform the surgery could be viewed as stopping ongoing treatment.

2. Nevertheless, we do make the distinction between declining to initiate treatment and stopping ongoing treatment; and, further, there is fairly widespread agreement about how to classify a specific act in certain cases. Therefore, we ought to examine the moral import of this distinction.

We agree that there is a moral difference here. By starting a given treatment we create hopes or expectations in the mind of the patient and/or his family for its continuation and success. If, for example, a wife arrives at the hospital emergency room in an ambulance carrying her husband whose heart has ceased to beat as a result of a heart attack, she will probably not be surprised if he is declared dead and no attempt is made to resuscitate. (She will, no doubt, be dismayed by his death; but she is bound to have realized that this is a possible — even probable — outcome.) However, if resuscitation measures are initiated, then she will undoubtedly begin to take hope that he might survive; and, when attempts to revive him are abandoned, the disappointment of this hope will add to the measure of her dismay about his death. Similarly, a patient who is undergoing a course of chemotherapy for cancer will have formed certain hopes and expectations with regard to this treatment, and these will be disappointed if the course of treatment is suspended.*

The upshot is, then, that stopping ongoing treatment brings about a somewhat greater measure of harm (i.e., the disappointment of these hopes and expectations) than failure to initiate therapy. This bears on clinical decisions in two ways: It serves as a reason *against* stopping ongoing treatment even when all realistic hope for its success has vanished (in order to avoid disappointing these expectations); and it serves as a reason *in favor* of declining to initiate therapy when the prospects for success are slim (in order to avoid raising these hopes and expectations).†

However, we must not overestimate the strength of these considerations. They cannot serve as the basis for a general policy or presumption that it is better, when in doubt, to decline to initiate ther-

---

*For further analysis of expectations, see the example of Bert and Ernie, pp. 289f.
†See note 15 for an example of this reasoning.

apy rather than to start it and have to stop it later. The meaningful life which will result if the treatment succeeds is far more important than the disappointment which will follow if it is tried and fails. Hence it is worthwhile to initiate treatment whenever there is any significant possibility that it could be successful.

Further, this factor cannot serve as the basis for an absolute rule against stopping ongoing therapy. If the patient is (or will be) in a state of considerable pain or other disvalue, then it may be *more* cruel to prolong his agony by continuing treatment than it would be to disappoint his and others' expectations by stopping the therapy and thereby allowing him to die.[17] Thus there is no absolute barrier to the step from item 2 to item 3 on our list of ways of bringing about death. There is moral justification for stopping ongoing therapy as well as for declining to initiate treatment.[18]

3. Many medical ethicists insist there is *no* moral difference between 2 and 3.[19] In our judgment, this claim is too strong, for reasons we have just given. An additional differentiating factor — the emotional impact on caregivers — will be addressed in Chapter Five.

Assisted suicide. Item 4 in Table 7 is the one that most clearly fits the label "assisted suicide" (although some thinkers would view it as appropriate to describe most of the other patterns of action on the list in these terms, if they are carried out in response to an explicit request of the patient). Later we will discuss Wanzer et al. on this point.

Suppose that the patient is capable of carrying out his own death, but still requests our assistance. Is there a moral justification and/or a moral obligation to grant this request?

1. We see no serious difficulty in showing, in terms of the same principles outlined on p. 51, that we would be morally justified in assisting. The patient is transferring his right to life to the agent by his request. This neutralizes the general prohibition against taking another person's life. Further, we can see no basis for claiming a general prohibition against rendering assistance in this sort of situation. (It might be wrong to do too much for one's children, for example, since this might prevent them from developing independent capacities. But this sort of reason can hardly apply in the situation of assisted suicide.)

2. On the issue of whether we would be morally *obligated* to act on such a request, we must balance (a) the benefit our assistance would bring to the patient against (b) the burden this would place upon the agent (including the immediate mental anguish, the likely strength and duration of feelings of guilt, any conflict with his personal in-

tegrity, the risk of criminal prosecution and penalty, etc.). Since there is little reason to believe that the benefit to the patient from our assistance (presumably in terms of relief from his own mental anguish, loneliness, and hesitation in carrying through the act) would be great enough to override the risk of criminal penalties, it would appear that there can be no moral obligation to assist those who can help themselves as long as the legal climate remains as conservative as it is at present. Apart from this, the presence of an obligation to assist would depend on the weight of the specific factors in each individual situation. If the burden on the agent would be slight and the benefit for the patient substantial, it seems to us there would be an obligation to assist. There are other considerations, including religious teaching about the sacredness of human life, that we have not considered in drawing this conclusion, of course. Some of these will be addressed in Chapters Six and Seven.

3. We do want to call attention to one point about this item in Table 7. We cite three examples, which roughly parallel items 3, 4, and 5 respectively on the main list. The same disputes that arise about these items on the larger list may apply to the three examples of assisting suicide. They are likely to make it more difficult to justify active, direct euthanasia.

Indirect euthanasia. Item 5 in Table 7 (p. 58) introduces two new elements: active vs. passive, and direct vs. indirect.

1. In the first place, the action here seems to be an "active" or "positive" cause of the death of the patient, in contrast to the "passive" or "negative" causal relationship involved in the previous items. When pneumonia develops, for example, withholding antibiotics (as in item 2) seems to play a passive or negative role in bringing about the death of the patient. It is the pneumonia that actively causes death. In contrast, when a large dose of pain medication is administered in item 5, it is the chemical action of the drug that is primarily and positively responsible for the patient's death. Certain physiological and biochemical processes within the patient's body also play a crucial role here — i.e., in distributing the chemical agent within the body and giving it effect; but these elements are regarded as subsidiary or passive in relation to the role of the drug. Thus, in this respect, item 5 qualifies as active or positive euthanasia, and items 1–4 should be classified as negative or passive euthanasia.

There is likely to be some dispute about our classification of item 4. (For example, Howard Brody classified this together with our items 5 and 6 as a form of active euthanasia.)[20] It does seem that, e.g., handing the patient a bottle of poison capsules is a positive action in a way that, e.g., withholding antibiotics is not, and thus it might seem natural to classify the former as active euthanasia in order to contrast it with the latter (passive) form of euthanasia.

Virtually all the authors who discuss euthanasia give in to this natural impulse and draw the distinction between active and passive euthanasia on the basis of whether the agent engages in a positive action or a negative action (omission).[21] However, this seems to us a mistaken basis of classification.

The main problem with this approach is that it would make the distinction between active and passive euthanasia cut across the distinctions we have drawn on our list in Table 7. To stop the ongoing support of a mechanical respirator requires a positive action (i.e., pulling the plug, flipping the switch to the "OFF" position, or adjusting the dials to reduce the oxygen level or the number of respirations), whereas stopping insulin therapy merely requires refraining from administering future injections. Hence the former example of stopping ongoing treatment would be classified as active euthanasia, while the latter would be a case of passive euthanasia. Even more paradoxical, stopping ongoing medication administered via an IV bottle would count in the standard view as passive euthanasia when accomplished by failing to replace an IV bottle that has emptied and as active euthanasia when action is taken to disconnect the IV or to stop the flow while the bottle still has some fluid in it.

It makes much more sense to base the distinction between active and passive on the nature of the *causal relationship* between the action (positive or negative) that is undertaken and the resulting death. Withholding a given medication will have the same causal relationship to the patient's death no matter whether it is accomplished by means of a positive action (in mid-bottle) or through an omission. In both cases, it is the disease process in the patient's body that will function as the primary or active cause of death. Hence both cases count as passive euthanasia. Some opponents claim that a person then dies as a result of starvation or dehydration, when in fact they die from their disease, one that includes an inability to eat and drink normally. Usually the death occurs rather soon as a result of underlying causes, since withholding or withdrawing fluids and nutrition leads to a gradual weakening rather than an abrupt death.

In this sense, providing the means for suicide would count as passive euthanasia. It is the action of the patient in making use of these means that functions as the primary or active cause of death. Providing the means plays a subsidiary or passive role here.

2. The second new element introduced by item 5 is the issue of intention. The difference between indirect killing (item 5) and direct killing (item 6) lies in the intentions of the agent (cf. Chapter Two, item 15 in our argument schemas). If the death of the patient is an incidental effect of an action directed toward some other goal (e.g., relief of pain), then the case is an indirect killing (e.g., double-effect euthanasia). In contrast, the case is a direct killing if the death of the patient is the intended effect of the action (or, at least, *one* of the intended effects).

In this respect, item 5 contrasts not only with item 6 but also with all four of the items on our list that we have already discussed. In none of these is the death of the patient characteristically an incidental effect of the action taken. Instead, in most cases the death will be a "chosen means"*to the ultimate goal of relieving the patient's pain or other disvaluable state and/or of granting the patient's wish. The patient's death cannot reasonably be construed as an incidental effect of achieving this goal, as it is in item 5. There the drug that is administered has an independent and direct capacity to relieve pain that will still have effect even if it does not cause death. The measures that fall under items 1–4, however, offer no such independent means of relieving suffering. The only way in which they can provide one release is through death.

It is hard to conceive what justifiable goal other than this there could be for, e.g., withholding antibiotics when pneumonia develops. The death of the patient would be an incidental effect only if the *whole* purpose of withholding antibiotics were some goal independent of the death and the agent were not influenced at all by a desire to provide the patient release from suffering through death. However, it is highly unlikely that this pattern of motivation would ever be exemplified in pure form; and, even if it were, surely the act would be morally unjustified. Goals other than providing release from suffering through death will not be sufficiently weighty to provide justification for bringing about the patient's death as an incidental effect. In the case of measures that are heroic due to placing an excessive burden on the agent, she might be morally justified in withholding them simply in order to avoid being subjected to this undue burden; but we would ordinarily expect concern for the patient's suffering to be a co-ordinate intended effect here, as well (cf. Case 12, p. 221). Thus death will almost always be a "chosen means" in items 1–4.

3. When we come to normative assessment, these two novel ele-

---

*For the full definition of this notion, see Appendix II, p. 284.

ments of item 5 pretty much cancel each other out. There is a stronger causal relationship between the act and the death. Thus if there is a general moral obligation not to cause death, it will apply here with greater force than in the four previous items. However, this will be neutralized (a) in some cases, by the explicit request of the patient to have his life ended and (b) in all cases, by the fact that death is an incidental effect of the action. (See our hierarchy in Appendix II, p. 287, of degrees of seriousness in connection with different ways of bringing about harm for further support for this claim.)

Active euthanasia. The pattern of action in item 6 is what characteristically comes to mind when we speak of "mercy killing" or "active euthanasia."* A great many people — including some who would accept most of the other items on our list in certain cases — are firmly convinced that mercy-killing is absolutely wrong and could never be justified under any circumstances.

Some critics of active euthanasia maintain that there is crucial normative significance in the fact that the agent is the active or positive cause of death in active euthanasia whereas in passive euthanasia it is the disease process that actively or positively causes death. That is the distinction we have drawn as well up to this point. Although there is a grain of truth in this claim, we must not exaggerate its importance.

1. It will be useful here to recall the distinctions between different ways of bringing about harm that we sketched earlier in this chapter.[22] We pointed out there that one would be said (a) *to cause* a harm or injury if it is an incidental effect of her action and (b) *to do* or *to inflict* the harm (or simply *to harm* or *to injure*) if the result is both intended and actively or positively caused. Carrying this classification one step further, we would say that one (c) *willfully causes* or *virtually inflicts* the harm if it is intended and passively or negatively caused.

Parallel distinctions can be drawn with regard to other kinds of effects, although the terminology will be different in places. For example if the result is a benefit rather than a harm, then we would speak of (a) *causing* it when it is an incidental effect, but of (b) *bestowing* the benefit (or simply, of *benefiting* the person) if it is actively caused and intended, and (c) *virtually bestowing* it or (less often, because of

---

*Speaking strictly, only actions of the type in item 6 should be described in these terms, since they are the only ones that both involve active causation (as the terms "killing" and "active" imply) and include the direct intention to bring about a "merciful" or "good" death.

the negative connotations of the adverb "willfully") *willfully causing*
it if the benefit is passively caused and intended.

When death is the effect, there is yet different terminology to mark
these distinctions. (a) When the death is an incidental effect, we
speak of *letting die* or *allowing to die* (or perhaps, of *causing death*).
(b) When the death is brought about intentionally and actively, we call
it *killing*. (c) When it results passively and intentionally, we speak of
willfully allowing to die or *virtually killing*.

Seeing these distinctions should help to clarify some of the terminological confusions that surround attempts to contrast item 6 with
the other items on our list. For instance, Paul Ramsey claims:

> In omission no human agent causes the patient's death, directly or indi-
> rectly. He dies his own death from causes that it is no longer merciful or
> reasonable to fight by means of possible medical interventions. Indeed, it
> is not quite right to say that we only care for the dying by an omission,
> by "doing nothing" directly or indirectly. Instead, we cease doing what
> was once called for and begin to do precisely what is called for now. We
> attend and company with him in this, his very own dying, rendering it as
> comfortable as possible.[23]

Ramsey is here recommending a form of action in which the death
of the patient would be an incidental effect. Ongoing treatment is
stopped (our item 3) or we decline to initiate a new stage of therapy
(our item 2), but he claims that the purpose is not to bring the patient
release from his suffering through death. This, as we have seen, would
make the death an intended effect of the negative action.* Rather the
purpose of withdrawing or withholding treatment is to allow the agent
to devote his energies to "attend and company with" the patient. The
goal of this positive action is to make the patient "as comfortable as
possible" in her dying days and hours, and thus her death itself is
only an incidental effect of the shift of energy away from medical
interventions and to "attending and companying."

However, Ramsey is mistaken when he says that "no human agent
causes the patient's death" in this situation. At the very least, we
would have to say that the agent *causes* death or *allows the patient
to die*, because he engages in a (negative) action (i.e., withdrawing or
withholding therapy) that contributes to the patient's death.[24]

Furthermore, we have serious doubts about the interpretation of
this situation that leads Ramsey to this characterization of it. The
troublesome issue is the identification of the motive for stopping on-

---

*Presumably the reason is that traditional theology prohibited intending or willing
the death of another. This is a subset of the Rule of Avoiding Killing.

going treatment. In the sentence immediately preceding the passage quoted, Ramsey describes the situation as "ceasing to do something that was begun in order to do something that is better because now more fitting." We were trying to express this point of Ramsey's when we said above: "the purpose of withdrawing or withholding therapy is to allow the agent to devote his energies to 'attend and company with' the patient."

The problem with this interpretation is that it presupposes that the two acts specified (i.e., medical therapy and "attending and companying") are mutually exclusive. But surely they are not. Surely it would be possible to "attend and company with" the patient while, at the same time, continuing ongoing medical therapy. We would hope that health care professionals regularly combine these two sorts of actions with regard to all their patients, including those whose illnesses are not fatal.

But if it is possible to do both these things at once, then the need to attend and company with the patient cannot be the real reason for withdrawing medical therapy. There must be another, independent reason for withdrawing treatment. And we would suggest that the motive is to provide the patient release from her suffering or other disvaluable state through death. Ramsey seems to acknowledge this when he speaks of the life-threatening disease process as something "that it is no longer merciful or reasonable to fight by means of possible medical interventions."

Thus the motive that Ramsey tried to sidestep does seem to enter into the decision after all. This means that the death of the patient is an intended effect of withdrawing treatment. Consequently, we must say something stronger than "he allowed the patient to die." Since the intention is expressed in a negative way (i.e., by withdrawing treatment), the appropriate description is that he *willfully allowed her to die*. (We will consider the normative force of this description in a moment.)

The analysis of Ramsey's position also reveals the mistake that is made by the many authors who describe passive euthanasia as "letting die." Since withdrawal of treatment and other forms of passive euthanasia are almost always (if not always) intended to produce death, these acts should also be described as *willfully allowing the patient to die*.

2. These terminological disputes are not merely academic quibbles. They have important implications for assessing the normative moral status of the various actions. We have seen in our discussions of harms throughout this chapter (and more detailed discussion

found in Appendix II) that the way in which one brings about an effect makes a significant difference to the moral quality of the act.

When we turn our attention from harms to beneficial effects, we begin to speak of moral praise and degrees of merit rather than moral blame and degrees of seriousness. Consequently the hierarchy of harms must be turned upside down.

a. Merely *to cause* a benefit to someone is not particularly meritorious, since the beneficial effect did not enter into the person's motive for acting thus and may not even have entered his mind. For example, one may return a book to the library purely in order to avoid a fine, not knowing (or knowing but not caring) that this makes the book available for another to borrow in order to meet a pressing need.

b. *To virtually bestow* or *willfully cause* a benefit is significantly more meritorious, since the realization that the other person will benefit enters into one's motive for acting. For example, a person may start to check a certain book out of the library and then change her mind and refrain from doing so when she remembers that you have a pressing need for the book and will be coming to look for it shortly.

c. Finally, *to bestow* a benefit is ordinarily the most meritorious of all, since it involves not only other-regarding motives but also some expenditure of effort in acting upon these motives. For example, a person may learn of your pressing need for the book and, as a result, take the trouble to phone you with an offer to lend you his personal copy.

However, the principle that actively bestowing a benefit is more meritorious than virtually bestowing it (i.e., causing it in a passive or negative way, but intentionally) must be qualified here, in at least two ways. First, passive causation may sometimes require an expenditure of effort equal to or greater than active causation, and a substantial discrepancy on this score may override differences in merit due to the type of causality involved. Thus, for example, a starving father who refrains from eating in order to leave adequate food to insure the survival of his child exerts far more effort of will than a person who takes ingredients from an abundant supply on hand and bakes a pie for a friend. (To avoid certain complexities, let us assume in both cases that the initial supply of foodstuffs was provided by some third party.) The pie-baker would be described as actively bestowing the benefit of the pie on his friend, whereas the father benefits his child in a passive way that can only be described as willfully causing the benefit or virtually bestowing it. Yet surely the father is far more meritorious than the pie-baker, due to the magnitude of his sacrifice.

Second, the same example illustrates the difference made by a substantial discrepancy in the quantity and/or quality of the benefit involved between the two acts. To virtually bestow a great benefit may be more meritorious than to actively bestow a very slight benefit. The person would do better to leave the book you need in the library for you to check out rather than going to the trouble to read it and report its contents to you if his report is so garbled and inaccurate as to be virtually worthless to you.

In contrast, no amount of discrepancy in either the expenditure of effort involved or the magnitude of the benefit will serve to elevate the category of (merely) causing benefit to a higher degree of merit than either virtually bestowing it or actively bestowing it. Since the effort is directed at some goal other than benefiting you and the benefit was not intended, whatever its amount, its occurrence earns the agent no particular merit. Surely either a person who spotted a dime on the sidewalk and left it there with the motive of brightening the day of the person who next found it (= virtually bestowing), or a person who picks up the check for a friend's cup of coffee (= actively bestowing) would be more meritorious than one whose action, though spiteful in intent, happened to benefit another despite the agent's plans (perhaps someone tore out pages from a book, but that action accidentally helped you focus on just the pages you needed).

3. The time has come to apply the above-made distinctions in order to figure out what normative moral differences there are between the different ways of bringing about death. The critics of active euthanasia maintain that *killing* is significantly more serious than either *willfully allowing to die* or simply *allowing to die*. The question we must now address is whether they are correct about this. We plan to base a large part of our analysis of the relative normative status of different ways of bringing about death directly on these distinctions about different ways of bringing about benefits and harms.

We have maintained throughout this chapter that death involves a mixture of benefit and harm for the person who dies — benefit, insofar as it spares him pain and other disvaluable states, and/or fulfills a wish to die that he has, and/or gives him access to heavenly bliss or other worthwhile states in an afterlife; harm, insofar as it deprives him of values that his life would have contained in the future (had he lived on), and/or violates his wishes, and/or subjects him to negative states in an afterlife.

Further, we have argued that the moral wrong in ending a person's life is to be found in two elements: first (and foremost), that it characteristically violates the patient's right to life; second, that it

brings harm to him. However, this moral wrong is not an absolute
in either element. If the patient explicitly requests to die, then he
thereby waives his right to life or transfers it to the other party; and
thus the first element no longer serves as a reason against ending his
life. Furthermore, the patient's right to life may be overridden if
the measures required to continue his life would place an inordinate
burden on others (see "Involuntary euthanasia," p. 54 above). The
second consideration would be neutralized if the patient's situation
were such that the benefits of death outweigh the harms (i.e., "he
would be better off dead").

Our present contention is that the normative force of the distinctions between different ways of bringing about death is wholly a
function of the relevant principles about benefits, harms, and rights.
This means that there will be no independent hierarchy of degrees
of seriousness among the different ways of bringing about death.
We cannot say that *allowing to die* is intrinsically more or less serious than *killing*. Rather, one particular way of bringing about
death will be more serious than another if it involves a more serious harm or a more serious violation of the victim's right to life,
without countervailing benefit. Compare, for example, the following
two cases:

A. You lie down on your neighbor's sofa to take a nap and suffer a heart
attack while you are sleeping. Your condition is such that, if the person
had noticed immediately when you stopped breathing and had rushed you
to the hospital at once, you could have been revived and would regain
nearly normal functioning. However, the neighbor does not notice and
therefore you die.

B. A neighbor digs a large hole in her front yard — so deep that it requires
a ladder to get out of it. After she has removed the ladder and gone inside
her house, she notices you come by and fall into the hole. With a vile
chuckle, she decides to let you struggle for awhile before helping you get
out. She figures you could not have injured yourself seriously in the fall;
but, in fact, you struck you head against a rock and you are unconscious
and bleeding from nose and mouth. Your condition is such that, if she
had rushed you to the hospital at once, you could have been revived and
would have recovered. Instead, you die before she ventures out of her
house to help you.

Both of these cases would be classified in our schema as *causing
death* or *allowing to die*. Neither agent intended to bring about the
death of the victim, although each contributed to that outcome by
means of a negative action. However, we would give very different
moral assessments of these two actions — holding the agent in case B

to a significant degree morally responsible for the death, whereas the agent in case A would bear little if any responsibility.

The difference between these moral judgments comes, we think, from the location of the respective actions in our hierarchy of ways of bringing about harm. The agent in case A would be described as *causing the harm*. The agent is, *at most*, careless — and even this is too strong a description unless he had prior reason to suspect the possibility of a heart attack or other condition which required observing you closely as you slept. The agent in this case intended neither death nor harm. In contrast, the agent in case B intended harm to you and expressed this intention by refraining from rescuing you from the hole. In other words, she *willfully caused* you the harm of remaining trapped in the hole. The agent did not intend that you die, but her willingness to cause you harm is enough to make her morally responsible for further negative consequences of her action.

In both these cases, the benefits brought to you by death will be so few and small as to be insignificant for all practical purposes. However, it might be worth pointing out that these are all incidental effects in both cases A and B, and hence they would be said in our terminology to be caused or allowed rather than either virtually bestowed or actively bestowed.

An alternative account of the normative difference between these two cases could be based on the rights of the victim in each case. The differentiating factor is not the right to life, however. This right is not infringed in either case. (Some might dispute this conclusion, arguing that the right to life encompasses a right to anything and everything needed to maintain one's life. This seems too strong an interpretation, however, since it would entail that the agent violated your right to life in case A by failing to observe your breathing at every moment.)

There is a difference between the two cases with respect to certain other rights related to the right to life. It is natural to speak of a right to be rescued promptly in case B, but it does not seem at all appropriate to speak of a right to be observed for signs of breathing in case A. If there were a basis for suspecting that your life or health were threatened, we might speak of your having a right to be observed while sleeping (for example, a baby who is susceptible to Sudden Infant Death Syndrome); but this is not the situation in case A.

Now consider these two cases, presented in an influential article by James Rachels:

C. Smith stands to gain a large inheritance if anything should happen to his six-year-old cousin. One evening while the child is taking his bath, Smith sneaks into the bathroom and drowns the child, and then arranges things so that it will look like an accident.

D. Jones also stands to gain if anything should happen to his six-year-old cousin. Like Smith, Jones sneaks in planning to drown the child in his bath. However, just as he enters the bathroom Jones sees the child slip and hit his head and fall face down in the water. Jones is delighted; he stands by, ready to push the child's head back under if it is necessary, but it is not necessary. With only a little thrashing about, the child drowns all by himself, "accidentally," as Jones watches and does nothing.[25]

On our schema, Smith would be said to have *killed* his cousin, while Jones *willfully allowed his cousin to die.* The harmful effects of death (in particular, the cousin's being deprived of his inheritance) are intended in both cases. Smith and Jones differ in the way they achieved their harmful purpose: Smith actively *inflicted* the harm on his cousin; whereas Jones *willfully caused* the harm to his cousin (by refraining from rescuing him). Rachels maintains that there is *no* normative difference between Smith and Jones:

Did either man behave better, from a moral point of view? If the difference between killing and letting die were in itself a morally important matter, one should say that Jones's behavior was less reprehensible than Smith's. But does one really want to say this? I think not.[26]

The principles we have defended in the foregoing lead to a somewhat different conclusion, but not necessarily to a drastic disagreement with Rachels. We have argued that, in general, inflicting harm actively is a more serious wrong than willfully causing harm. Hence, Smith's action is more reprehensible than Jones's. However, Jones's action is serious enough to merit extremely strong condemnation; and the relatively small discrepancy between his action and Smith's may escape notice given the enormity of his crime. Compare the following two situations: Does one really want to say that a person who kills her husband and also carves an obscene word on his chest does something greatly more wrong than one who "merely" kills? Does one really want to say that a person who rescues a small child and also treats her to an ice cream cone is greatly more meritorious than one who risks life and limb to rescue but neglects to offer ice cream? Speaking technically, there is a normative difference between these cases, but one is not inclined to pay it much heed. Subtle normative differences are swallowed up by the extremity of the situation in all these cases. Further, any normative difference there might otherwise be between Smith and Jones is diminished by the fact that Jones is not only *willing* to take the further step of engaging in the sort of positive aggression that Smith carried out, but that he actually did form the intention to act in this way and initiated steps to carry out his intention — to the extent of entering the bathroom and standing ready.

The difference between Smith and Jones can also be accounted for in terms of rights. Smith directly violates his cousin's right to life, whereas Jones violates the right to rescue — a different right but surely one *nearly* as strong as the right to life.[27] In another aspect, there is no normative difference between the two cases. Both cousins have a right to the inheritance, and this right is infringed in each case.

Any benefits that death might bring to either cousin would be incidental effects. There is no indication that either Smith or Jones is motivated to benefit anyone but himself. Hence the benefits are merely caused or allowed in both cases.

Next let us consider the following combination of case, comment, and questions taken from Philippa Foot:[28]

E. We are about to give to a patient who needs it to save his life a massive dose of a certain drug in short supply. There arrive, however, five other patients each of whom could be saved by one-fifth of that dose. We say with regret that we cannot spare our whole supply of the drug for a single patient, just as we should say that we could not spare the whole resources of a ward for one dangerously ill individual when ambulances arrive bringing in the victims of a multiple crash. We feel bound to let one man die rather than many if that is our only choice.

F. Why then do we not feel justified in killing people in the interests of cancer research or to obtain, let us say, spare parts for grafting on to those who need them? We can suppose, similarly, that several dangerously ill people can be saved only if we kill a certain individual and make a serum from his dead body. (These examples are not over fanciful considering present controversies about prolonging the life of mortally ill patients whose eyes or kidneys are to be used for others.)* Why cannot we argue from the case of the scarce drug to that of the body needed for medical purposes?

Before we can answer the question that Foot poses in case F, we must analyze the two situations in terms of the distinctions we have offered.

In case F, the death of the one patient is both directly intended (i.e., an instance of what we called a "chosen means") and actively

*Or the more recent use of fetal tissue in research and possible treatment [D.C.T. and G.C.G.].

brought about. Hence we must describe this case as *killing* one patient in order to save several lives. In case E, in contrast, the death of the one patient is neither directly intended nor actively brought about. This one death is not part of the purpose or goal of the action, nor is it a chosen means to that goal. Rather, it is a regrettable by-product or incidental effect of the decision to allocate the supply of drug to the five patients. Hence we must describe case E as *allowing the one patient to die* in order to save five lives.

The harmful effects of death are not directly intended in either case E or case F. The fact that our action will have the effect of depriving the one patient in each case of future association with family and friends, for example, is no part of our goal in the decision favoring the several patients, nor is it any part of the means by which the several lives are saved in either case. Hence, in both case E and case F we must say that the harm to the one patient is merely *caused* or *allowed*. In neither case is it either willfully caused or actively inflicted.

The beneficial consequences of death are also incidental effects of the action in each case. In neither of the cases is there any indication that the choice of who is to die is made with an eye toward minimizing the pain, suffering, etc. of that patient.

But, if this is true, then Foot's question arises with a vengeance. If case E and case F both fall in the same category in our hierarchy of ways of bringing about harm, then what could be the basis for pronouncing a different normative verdict in the respective cases? As Foot asks: "Why cannot we argue from the case of the scarce drug to that of the body needed for medical purposes?"

In terms of our principles about harms, the normative distinction between the pair of cases we are presently considering would be founded on the amount of harm involved and the points about expectations that we discussed above (see p. 64). In case E, we assume that none of the patients have been led to expect that they will receive the treatment, and we base our decision to favor the five patients on the judgment that to allow five patients to die would involve a greater total harm than allowing the one patient to die. We can see the role this judgment plays in our reasoning by varying the case with respect to it.

E.₁ Suppose that the five patients were each irreversibly comatose and terminally ill and that administering the drug to them would merely prolong their lives in a comatose state, whereas the one patient is conscious and could be restored to robust health and look forward to a long and active life if the whole dose were administered to him.

In this situation, surely we would not hesitate to let the five patients die and save the one. Even if the five patients could be sustained long enough to total more hours of life than could be expected for the one patient, we would stand by this decision on the grounds that more harm is done by depriving the one patient of conscious, active life.

The action in case F is unjustified because the victim would have expectations of continued life, whereas the several dangerously ill patients could not expect normally to have measures this extraordinary taken to save their lives. Hence, in terms of disappointment of expectations, more harm is clearly done to the one patient by killing than would be done to all the potential recipients together by allowing them to die.

Here again we can test the role of this judgment by varying it.

F.₁ Assume that the one patient is mortally ill and explicitly requests that his life be ended in order to save the lives of the other patients.

Then it would be clear that he had no expectations for having his life protected. Further, suppose that the other patients have expectations that they will be benefited in this extraordinary way — perhaps on the basis of an explicit promise the one patient conveyed to them that he would sacrifice himself in this way. In this situation, it is not nearly so clear that it would be unjustified to kill the one patient in order to save the several others.

An even more solid basis for distinguishing between case E and case F is in terms of rights. In case E, no rights of the one patient are violated. His right to life is not directly violated, and there is no basis for saying that he has a right to the medicine. In case F, on the other hand, the one patient's right to life would be directly violated by his being killed.

Now let us look at another pair of cases to further develop the distinction between active and passive euthanasia:

G. The patient is in extreme pain, in the last stages of a terminal illness. She asks to die. The health care professionals are moved by her plea, so when she suffers a cardiac arrest, no attempt is made to resuscitate.

H. The patient is in extreme pain, in the last stages of a terminal illness. He asks to die. The physician is moved by his plea, and, as a result, injects a mortal dose of curare.

This is the pair of cases we are particularly interested in. Case G is an instance of passive euthanasia or willfully allowing the patient to die, and case H is an instance of active euthanasia or killing the patient. We are now in a position to assess the normative force of this distinction.

In neither of these cases are the harmful effects of the death directly intended. Hence they are merely caused or allowed in each case. Thus there is no difference between active and passive euthanasia on this score. (Incidentally, this helps to explain why Rachels's examples of Smith and Jones and their wealthy cousins [i.e., cases C and D above] are not sound analogies to active and passive euthanasia, respectively.)

The beneficial effects of death have a different status in each case, and this difference does seem to be morally significant. In both cases, the reason for bringing about the death of the patients is to spare them from pain, suffering, etc. However, in case G, this is carried out through a negative cause (i.e., refraining from resuscitating); whereas in case H positive or active steps (i.e., injecting curare) are taken to achieve this goal. Thus, in case G the benefit is *virtually bestowed, willfully caused;* whereas in case H the benefit is *actively bestowed.*

Now according to the normative principles that we worked out above and in Appendix II, actively bestowing a benefit is more meritorious than virtually bestowing an equivalent benefit. Our conclusion, then, is directly contrary to the claim of the critics of active euthanasia. Not only is there no reason to believe that active euthanasia is irredeemably wrong while passive euthanasia is justified, but active euthanasia is actually *more* meritorious than passive, everything else being equal.

This conclusion must be qualified on the basis of principles about rights. The discussion above concerns cases of voluntary euthanasia, in which the patients waive their right to life, and hence this right would not affect our reasoning. However, if the patient requests *not* to die, then active euthanasia would violate her right to life *plus* her right to have reasonable requests granted, any rights that arise from promises made to her, etc., whereas passive euthanasia would violate only the latter cluster of rights but not the right to life. Thus there is a more serious wrong involved in active euthanasia *in the involuntary situation.* This is the grain of truth in the criticisms of active euthanasia. But it is a mistake to generalize from this situation to the context of voluntary euthanasia. There the tables are completely turned.

GENERAL CONCLUSION

We have argued in this chapter that euthanasia is morally justified in a wide range of circumstances. The justification is clearest and

strongest in the circumstances described in Chapter Two, withholding extraordinary means, pp. 17–21. As each of these features is
weakened, the force of the justification for euthanasia is also less-
ened, until we reach a point along each continuum beyond which it
would no longer be morally justified to bring about an end to the
patient's life. We have not attempted to define these limits in any
concrete way. We do not believe that this is possible in any general
discussion. The judgment as to whether euthanasia is justified in a
given case must be based upon the specific facts of the situation.[29]
What we have attempted to do in this chapter is to indicate the kinds
of elements that are important for making such a determination in
the specific case. It is left to those who face these decisions in the concrete situation to work through this reasoning and arrive at a specific
judgment for the case at hand.

We turn now to other, more external, factors governing our concerns about euthanasia with an examination of the family as the
immediate next step. These considerations will mollify our conclusion that voluntary active euthanasia can sometimes be a benefit and
therefore may represent a positive duty.

NOTES

1. This has been a factor in court cases; see especially the O'Connor
case in New York State (Case 22, p. 234) and the Cruzan case in Missouri
(Case 21, p. 233), which the U.S. Supreme Court has agreed to review in its
1989–1990 term.

2. The court in *O'Connor* seems to concur with this assessment. See
Case 22, p. 234 and our discussion of it in Chapter Three.

3. H. T. Engelhardt, Jr., *The Foundations of Bioethics* (New York: Oxford
University Press, 1987).

4. The final scenes of the film *Whose Life Is It Anyway?* include such a
promise by Dr. Emerson.

5. Often such dialogue is missing in the clinical setting. Many problems
could be avoided if attention were paid to qualifications of general promises
made, explicit or implied.

6. For a qualification on this conclusion, see the case of Bert and Ernie
below, pp. 289ff.

7. Glenn C. Graber and David C. Thomasma, *Theory and Practice in
Medical Ethics* (New York: Continuum, 1989).

8. Pope Pius XII, "The Prolongation of Life," *The Pope Speaks* 4, no. 4
(1958), 393–398.

9. Gerald Kelly, "Notes: The Duty to Preserve Life," *Theological Studies*
12 (1951), 550–556 .

10. For a view different from ours see Germain G. Grisez and Joseph Boyle, *Life and Death with Liberty and Justice: A Contribuion to the Euthanasia Debate* (Notre Dame, Ind.: University of Notre Dame Press, 1979).

11. See Glenn C. Graber and David C. Thomasma, *Theory and Practice in Medical Ethics* (New York: Continuum, 1989); David C. Thomasma, "The Context as Moral Rule in Medical Ethics," *Journal of Bioethics* 5 (Spring/Summer 1984), 63–79.

12. Case 33, p. 248, also illustrates this point. Here the choice is whether to allow the patient to die from his bleed now, or six days later from his cancer.

13. See, for example, the discussion by Ramsey cited below and the authors discussed in Robert M. Veatch, *Death, Dying, and the Biological Revolution* (New Haven: Yale University Press, 1976), pp. 108–109.

14. Some moral theologians are willing to accept this conclusion. See, for example, Joseph V. Sullivan, *Catholic Teaching on the Morality of Euthanasia* (Washington, D.C.: Catholic University of America Press, 1949), p. 72. Gerald Kelly also accepts it, but describes it more accurately as a "useless ordinary means" rather than an extraordinary means. See his "The Duty of Using Artificial Means, *Theological Studies,* 11 (1950), 219. Both Sullivan and Kelly are quoted in Veatch, *Death, Dying, and the Biological Revolution,* p. 108. For recent discussion of this issue, see Joanne Lynn, ed., *By No Extraordinary Means: The Choice to Forego Life-Sustaining Food and Water* (Bloomington, Ind.: Indiana University Press, 1986), and Joanne Lynn and James F. Childress, "Must Patients Always Be Given Food and Water?" *Hastings Center Report* 13, no. 5 (October 1983), 17–21; Kenneth C. Micetich, Patricia H. Steinecker, David C. Thomasma, "Are Intravenous Fluids Morally Required for a Dying Patient?" *Archives of Internal Medicine* 143 (May 1983), 975–978; J. Paris and Richard McCormick, "The Catholic Tradition on the Use of Nutrition and Fluids," *America* 156, no. 17 (May 5, 1987), 356–361; John J. Paris and F.E. Reardon, "Court Responses to Withholding or Withdrawing Artificial Nutrition and Fluids," *Journal of the American Medical Association* 253 (April 19, 1985), 2243–2245; David C. Thomasma, Kenneth Micetich, and Patricia H. Steinecker, "Continuance of Nutritional Therapy in the Dying Patient," *Critical Care Clinics* 2, no. 1 (January 1986), 61–70; Rebecca Dresser and E. B. Boisaubian, "Ethics, Law and Nutritional Support," *Archives of Internal Medicine* 145 (January 1985), 122–124.

15. See, for example, the following suggestion in a recent issue of a well-known nursing journal:

> Here's a suggestion for EDs [Emergency Departments]: Instead of automatically placing an elderly patient on a ventilator, insert an endotracheal tube and manually bag him until a family member can be located to communicate his wishes. (Of course, that means we must tell our kin what we want before a crisis occurs.)
> I realize that my idea creates a staffing problem. A nurse or respiratory therapist must be present to squeeze the bag 16 times per minute. But it eliminates a problem that's far more troubling: when to unplug the ventilator.

Because if the staff takes my suggestion, the machine is never plugged in. (Joy Ufema, "Insights on Death and Dying," *Nursing 89*, 19, no. 2 [February 1989]: 79.)

16. *The Hastings Center Guidelines* appears to acknowledge this point indirectly in their proposal for "time-limited trials" of life-sustaining procedures such as respirators and tube feedings. Cf. *Guidelines on the Termination of Life-Sustaining Treatment and the Care of the Dying* (Briarcliff Manor, N.Y.: The Hastings Center, 1987), p. 26.

17. Susan Braithwaite and David C. Thomasma, "New Guidelines on Foregoing Life-Sustaining Treatment in Incompetent Patients: An Anti-Cruelty Policy, " *Annals of Internal Medicine* 104 (1986), 711–715.

18. This would be an application of *In re Conroy* objective test.

19. See, for example, President's Commission for the Study of Ethical Problems in Medicine and Biomedical and Behavioral Research, *Deciding to Forego Life-Sustaining Treatment: Ethical, Medical, and Legal Issues in Treatment Decisions* (Washington, D.C.: U.S. Government Printing Office, 1983), pp. 73–77.

20. Howard Brody, *Ethical Decisions in Medicine* (Boston: Little, Brown and Company, 1976), p. 72 (frame 243); 2nd ed. (1981), p. 234 (frame 796). Our list on p. 58 above is adapted from the list Brody gives.

21. See, for example, James Rachels, "Active and Passive Euthanasia," *New England Journal of Medicine* 292 (January 9, 1975), 75–80; reprinted in Robert Hunt and John Arras, eds., *Ethical Issues in Modern Medicine* (Palo Alto, Calif.: Mayfield Publishing Co., 1977), pp. 196–202.

22. See "When Death Is Not Imminent," above, pp. 32–37, especially p. 34; see also Appendix II.

23. Paul Ramsey, *The Patient as Person* (New Haven: Yale University Press, 1970), p. 151.

24. This situation is parallel conceptually (although not morally, due to differences in motive) to the case in Appendix II, p. 284, in which the neighbor carelessly omitted putting up warning signals to indicate the excavation, thereby contributing to your injury or falling into the hole.

25. James Rachels, "Active and Passive Euthanasia," in Hunt and Arras, eds., *Ethical Issues in Modern Medicine*, p. 199.

26. Ibid.

27. The right to rescue is especially strong in this situation where (a) the rescue would not be burdensome to the agent and (b) the agent has assumed responsibility for the safe-keeping of the victim.

28. Philippa Foot, "The Problem of Abortion and the Doctrine of the Double Effect," pp. 270–271, in Samuel Gorovitz, Andrew L. Jameton, Ruth Macklin, et al., eds., *Moral Problems in Medicine* (Englewood Cliffs, N.J.: Prentice Hall, Inc., 1976), pp. 270–271.

29. Graber and Thomasma, *Theory and Practice in Medical Ethics*.

Chapter Four

THE FAMILY'S PERSPECTIVE

A claim that voluntary active euthanasia might, indeed, be both a benefit to a patient and a positive moral duty to provide in certain limited circumstances must be balanced with other important considerations. Most often a purely philosophical or theological discussion of active euthanasia fails to take into account the sophisticated clinical distinctions and public policy concerns that surround the care of the dying. As a first step in addressing these kinds of concerns, we examine the role of the family, in particular its circumscription of the autonomy of its members.

As a loved one deteriorates with a terminal disease, increasing pressure falls on the family. Family members alternate between fear that their loved one will die, guilt-ridden wishes that the end will come soon, and hope that continued support can be beneficial.

Because our society does not properly support families who care for their loved ones in extreme circumstances, tragedies occur almost daily. Some of these were noted in Chapter One: young men enter a nursing home and kill their uncle with a German Luger; a mother poisons her severely ill child; an elderly mother is driven to try to kill her retarded and dependent son when she fears she can no longer care for him.

An elderly lady feels compelled to stab her dying husband over fifty times and kill him because he is suffering so much from terminal cancer. She then turns the knife on herself, but fails to kill herself. She is hospitalized, but the prosecuting attorney discounts the role of compassion. "Promptings of euthanasia are no excuse," he declares, "for murder."[1] A distraught father, Rudy Linares, pulls a gun on health professionals and detaches his fifteen-month-old near brain-dead son from a respirator to allow him to die.

Families undergo pain and suffering paralleling the pain and suffering of dying patients.

84

This chapter will examine the role of the family in making decisions about dying patients, hospice as a support for the family and a kind of community, and the reasons, if any, why a person could be kept alive or permitted to die for the sake of the family. In addition, we will examine requests of families to remove patients from life-support systems, as well as requests from families for inappropriate care.

An argument is constructed for a broadly-based treatment decision status policy for hospitals, based on the value system of patient and family. In this argument we will examine the strengths and weaknesses of living wills and advance directives, as well as the durable power of attorney.

We begin with a historical sketch of dying to show how it has only been in the modern era that persons have lost control over their own dying process.

HISTORICAL SKETCH OF DYING

Dying is at once a personal and social ritual.

In ancient, medieval, and even modern times, most persons were able to "sense" that they were dying. At that time, they would assemble their families and friends for some last words. During this assembly, they distributed their goods (later they were able to make out a will ahead of time for this purpose). After talking and praying, the dying person assumed a ritual posture to await death. Sometimes this was a seated posture (as among American Indians); sometimes it was a posture of folding one's arms across one's chest (as seen on sarcophagi of knights, kings, and queens).

The social ritual of dying paralleled the personal ritual. The family and friends assembled. They kept vigil around the dying person to assure him or her that the community support they had enjoyed through life was maintained. That same community recorded the last thoughts, the wisdom of the dying person. Psalms and prayers were said. The burial ritual simply extended this vigil until the body was in the grave.

Dramatic changes in health care have also changed this personal and social ritual. There has been an enormous increase in the technologization of care. Where once a cold compress might have been applied and one's hands held, now all sorts of interventions are possible, from intravenous fluids and nutrition, nasogastric feeding tubes, tubes implanted directly in a vessel or the stomach for feeding, bypassing cancerous obstructions, blood products and agents to prevent clotting or bleeding, and cardiopulmonary resuscitation to experimental treatments such as advanced chemotherapeutic agents, radiologic implants, artificial hearts, and transplants of other organs.

With the increase in technology came a corresponding increase in the institutionalization of care. Whereas formerly patients died at home in the midst of family, relatives, and friends, now they die in hospitals. Almost 80 percent of those who die each year die in institutions. Many of the personal freedoms enjoyed by dying persons have been lost as a result. Hospitals are excellent places to go if one wants to be cured of a disease, but they are terrifying places in which to die.

Also with the increase in technology and institutionalization came a corresponding increase in the institutionalization of care. No one person attends to the dying patient. Often different services are stacked up like planes at O'Hare field, waiting to attend the dying person.

In our hospitals it is actually difficult to die. There is little possibility to maintain the personal and familial ritual of dying.

In a technology-intensive hospital, it is difficult to sense that one is dying. The patient and the family often have no clues about what will be the final event. The dying process is disrupted in favor of doing all one can to preserve life. Hence it is hard to assemble family and friends for a last conversation. How many persons have gone to and fro from the deathbeds of their relatives, wondering if each trip would be the last? Even if one knows that death is approaching, there is a diminished chance that last words could be spoken. This is true because the prolongation of the dying process, if it is successful and provides a few more good days, weeks, or months, usually terminates in a process of severe pain during which the patient is heavily drugged.

People die in pieces. First their kidneys might go, then their liver, then their heart, their lungs, and finally their brain. During this process, they have invited into their bodies fluids, nutrition, antibiotics, surgeries of various sorts, respirators, nasogastric feeding tubes, and all sorts of other interventions. There is no one to preside over the moment of death, since the dying is spread out over so many moments. The physician's contact with patient and family is episodic (and often diminishes as death approaches). Nurses are more regularly present, but today they have many duties that appear to be more pressing than providing solace to the family. The family itself is diminished as a result.

THE FAMILY AND PATIENT DECISION-MAKING

Personal control of the dying process can be regained by appealing to a number of medical ethics principles, as we showed in Chapters Two and Three above. There the case for euthanasia was grounded in a personal right of the individual patient — a request to have his/her life ended, stemming from a personal judgment that s/he would be better off dead. We argued that this request should be interpreted as a waiver of the right to life and gives rise to an obligation on the part of others to carry out the patient's wishes.

The law has also recognized something like this right — especially in its negative aspect: the right to refuse treatment. A summary of prominent recent court cases is collected in Appendix III, and several of them are among the cases sketched in Appendix I. The most firmly established principle that emerges from these cases is the right of the competent adult patient to refuse treatment, even if foregoing this treatment will lead to death. This right is regarded as a personal right of the patient himself or herself, and the family supposedly has no say in the matter.

Of course, the pure case does not often arise in uncontroversial form. Although refusal of treatment is not, in and of itself, evidence of diminished competence, the situations in which refusals are proffered virtually always contain circumstances that raise questions about the patient's competence. For example, the patient may be in extreme pain and/or heavily sedated. News of a terminal prognosis unavoidably causes emotional reaction. The disease process itself may affect the level of reasoning.

Furthermore, patients rarely reach these decisions in isolation. The family typically figures into the decision-making process in some way or other. A variety of roles are possible here, including the following:

The family may *oppose* the patient's decision. In the case of Donald C. (Case 19, p. 229), the young man with severe burns whose prognosis was severe, permanent disability, Donald's mother strongly opposed his wish to forego treatment. She had lost her husband in the accident in which Donald was injured, and she could not bear to lose her only son as well. Furthermore, she was a very religious woman of a born-again persuasion, and she was concerned about the state of her son's soul. The thought that he would die before a personal conversion experience in the faith he had pretty much abandoned as an adult was abhorrent to her.

In Case 7 (p. 216), the wife of a depressed cancer patient dissents from his judgment that a recurrence of lymphosarcoma accompanied by persistent nausea and vomiting made "life not worth living." She pleaded with him to begin another round of chemotherapy in an attempt to establish another remission. Once the nausea and vomiting were brought under control by rehydration measures, he agreed to begin chemotherapy.

The contrast between these examples illustrates the dimensions of the problem. On the one hand, in Case 19, Donald C.'s Burns, we have a mother seeking to impose on an adult son values that she did not succeed in instilling in her son as she reared him. If his accident had not rendered him dependent, he would be able to assert his independence and live (or die) by his own values. On the other hand, in Case 7, the man suffering from lymphosarcoma and depression, we have a spouse who is best seen as *reminding* the patient of *shared* values that his present distress and discomfort have led him to lose sight of. In the latter case, it seems plausible to overrule the patient's current decision in favor of his wife's judgment about his more authentic wishes, even though the patient would not qualify as incompetent and even though the choice is fraught with uncertainty. In the former situation, it is implausible to substitute his mother's decision for the patient's, even though his state of depression appears far deeper than that of the patient in Case 7. The key difference here is that the mother in Case 19 does not make the decision on the basis of values that her son shares.

In Case 29 (p. 241), matters are less clear-cut. The patient, a sixty-three-year-old dentist in the terminal stages of throat cancer, gives the caregivers the fairly vague request that "nothing extraordinary be done." He is apparently more emphatic and perhaps more specific in messages he conveys to his. wife — but it is significant that he does not convey these messages directly to caregivers.

His wife asks the managing physician to initiate a gastrostomy to provide nutrition and hydration to the patient. The nursing staff is distressed, since they believe this is contrary to the wishes of the patient, judging from the messages they have overheard him conveying to his wife.

The first step toward resolving this situation is to ask the wife the basis of her decision — in particular, she should be asked to provide evidence that this is what her husband wishes to have done.[2] This question can initiate a discussion aimed at distinguishing her own needs and wishes from those of her husband. Such a discussion (ideally including the husband, to the extent he is able to participate) can help her to clarify her own understanding, as well as that of the caregivers.

The family may *defer to* the patient's decision even though they do not agree with it. In the case of "R. B.'s Leg Condition" (Case 30, p. 243), a fifteen-year-old boy who was active in sports refused amputation recommended as treatment for osteosarcoma. His parents were themselves undecided about this recommendation, but their son persuaded them initially to support his refusal despite their misgivings. Following further discussion, he and they relented and permitted the amputation; but, after several months of chemotherapy, the boy decided that the side effects were intolerable. He persuaded his parents to support this decision as well — the mother actively, the father passively by withdrawing from the situation.

Both these reactions are fairly common, especially when family members find themselves uncertain about the treatment recommendation. Reasoning that the patient should have the primary voice in the decision since he is the one directly affected, they will stop short of worrying through all their own misgivings and defer to the patient's wishes. The passive style of deference to the patient is characteristic of less verbal individuals — especially males of the "strong and silent" type, like R. B.'s father.

The chief difficulty with this approach is that the misgivings that are suppressed at this point may emerge to cause heightened guilt if the refusal of treatment has a fatal result. Painful as it would be to challenge the patient's judgment at this stage, the dialogue that would ensue from this response would bring matters to a more clearcut resolution than a noninformed deferral to the patient's wishes. The father in Case 30 is likely to experience an especially tragic bout of grief at his son's death — and it will be even more difficult for him to deal with it if he remains withdrawn and unable and/or unwilling to verbalize his feelings.

In ethical terms, we are inclined to argue that one *owes* it to family members to go beyond this position of deferring to the patient's wishes and prompt an open discussion of differences of judgment. The family ought to be the fundamental unit of values analysis.

The family may *concur* with the patient's decision. Edward Faulkner, the ninety-year-old patient in Case 23 (p. 235) and his wife appear to be in complete agreement in desiring that "everything possible" be done to sustain his life. Faulkner judged that his quality of life was satisfactory and desired to continue to live, even with significant impairments and handicaps. His wife agreed with these judgments wholeheartedly. The tragedy here is that the physician in the case did not concur with the Faulkners' assessment and that they did not learn of this difference of viewpoint until the physician had acted upon his judgment by foregoing resuscitation when Faulkner had a cardiac arrest.

The family may *assist* the patient in reaching a decision. We would maintain that the ideal role of the family is to participate with the patient (and, ideally, with health care professionals as well) in a process of joint decision-making. A family should be a values unit — not in the sense of a monolithic structure in which, e.g., the father dictates the value stance of all family members, but in the sense of the special place where exploratory discussions of value issues are conducted and conclusions about fundamental values and aspects of each individual's life-plans are developed. And there should be inter-linkages between the life-plans of family members; each should take into account the impact of his or her choices on each of the other members of the family and the future of this family unit. One of us (G. G.) has spoken elsewhere of a notion of "family autonomy."[3] In the ideal situation, it should be possible to speak of a common set of family goals (even if each individual member of the family has, at the same time, personal goals) and a common set of values (even if each member also has his/her own personal values) that are central to deliberation about momentous decisions that have an impact on the family as a whole. These values should be explored to such an extent by the family that they can support an assurance when patient values have not been expressed.

In our analysis of specimen cases of euthanasia in Chapters Two and Three, the concurrence of the family was one feature of the paradigm cases (see item 7 in Tables 1–5). Family concurrence strengthens our confidence in the soundness of the patient's judgment that he or she would be better off dead because we acknowledge the role of the family as the fundamental unit of value teaching, analysis, and application.

The family may *figure in* the patient's decision. Unfortunately, this ideal of joint decision-making is almost never fully realized and seldom even approached. More often, we have the patient making decisions on the basis of his or her individual goals and values — and, perhaps, his or her judgment as to what is in the best interests of other members of the family. For example, in Case 31 (p. 244), a man who has been diagnosed with carcinoma of the tongue does not even want his family to know of the diagnosis, much less to take part in his decision to forego treatment for the disease. Instead, he apparently attempts suicide — first by automobile and then by means of refusal of trauma care — in order to avoid having himself and his family face the disfigurement, suffering, and expense of attempting treatment. This approach does a grave disservice to his family — as well as putting his physician in an extremely awkward position. If the physician honors his refusal of treatment and his insistence that the family not be told the reasons behind it, the physician could be left to face an angry family who would be understandably inclined to sue him for malpractice for the death of the patient.

Surely there is an obligation, in this situation, to delay a suicide decision until one's family has been told the diagnosis and has had an opportunity to discuss its implications for the quality of life of the patient and the rest of the family. In a sense we argue here for a duty of a dying patient to discuss with family or friends his or her disease and the possible interventions desired.

If the family is so dysfunctional that they would be unable or unwilling to offer the patient support, comfort, and advice, this is a tragic commentary on the functioning of the family unit, as well as on the support systems of the wider society. But it does not, in itself, mitigate the duty to discuss. The duty turns to others in the patient's circle. If the patient is unable or unwilling to accept the support, comfort, and advice of the family, this is a tragic commentary on his mental health, as well as again on the support systems of the wider society. But again, this does not detract from the patient's duty to make his or her wishes known.

It is difficult to imagine conditions that would override this duty to share information and decision-making with one's family. A judgment (as the patient in Case 31 apparently made) that the family would be better off not knowing of his condition is not only paternalistic in intent, but misguidedly so. All evidence points to an increased burden of guilt and hurt experienced by the family of a suicide. A judgment that he can handle this situation better on his own rather than having to deal with the family's reaction is also misguided; the family may be able to offer support that would make his future course easier to bear.[4] A new closeness may be established among the family that has its beautiful side, even though the circumstances that prompted it are tragic.

Health professionals have a duty to join with religious institutions and other structures of society to bolster and support the family in this important role. Religious institutions and service clubs can assist by helping their members make their wishes known through instruments available in society, instruments like advance directives and living wills.

The family figures as a basis of the decision in a significantly different way in Case 32 (p. 245) and Case 14 (p. 223). In the former, Sharon Rose, a fourteen-year-old girl with an apparent recurrence of malignant lymphoma, chooses to honor the religious beliefs of her stepfather by refusing blood transfusion. She does not show much understanding or appreciation of the religious tenets in themselves, so one is left to conclude that her motives are (a) gratitude toward the stepfather for his kindness toward her and her mother, (b) a desire to avoid disrupting her mother's relationship with him so she will be well taken care of following Sharon's death, and (c) a desire to avoid disrupting her own relationship with him or her mother so she can receive support and comfort from both as she dies. These motivations are discerned by the social worker who analyzes the situation. It is unlikely that Sharon has articulated them in her own mind, much less discussed them with her family. In Case 14, Walter Arnold appears to be holding on to a pain-racked life in hopes of rewarding his younger son through an insurance payment for his faithful service to himself and his wife. He, too, has not discussed this motive with his family.

Difficult as it may be to do so, it would benefit both of these situations enormously if such a discussion could take place. Surely Sharon Rose's stepfather would be prompted to seriously rethink his theological position, at the very least, if Sharon made her true motives known to him. We would hope he would assure her that he could still accept her and her mother even if she made a decision to accept a blood transfusion. Similarly, the family of Walter Arnold should be able to come to some reconciliation if the whole picture were placed before them and they had opportunity to talk it through.

It would be an overreaction to say that failure to confer with family totally invalidates a refusal-of-treatment decision by the patient, but we would insist that it casts significant doubt on its validity. Family debate is the crucible in which value decisions are refined and clarified.

The family may agree with the patient's decision in principle, but be unwilling or unable to carry it out. Both Case 33 (p. 248) and Case 18 (p. 228) exemplify this situation. In Case 33 (M. H.'s GI Bleed), the family of a middle-aged man with metastatic carcinoma of the colon concurs with the patient's decision to die at home, but they become frightened when he begins to bleed "from both ends" and therefore they call emergency medical services. In Case 18 (Mr. Downmore's Intubation), the brother of a fifty-four-year-old male with metastatic cancer of the rectum who is receiving terminal care at his brother's home becomes distressed by the patient's obvious pain and his seizure activity and calls emergency medical services to take him to the hospital.

In both of these cases, better advance information about what to expect, as well as better support services through a hospice program, might have made it possible for the family to carry through the patient's wishes. We will discuss these matters later (see p. 113).

The background issue here has to do with intrafamilial and intrapersonal conflicts of values. As we saw in our detailed analysis of cases in Chapters Two and Three, these decisions are complex and riddled with conflicting values and principles. A decision is made by working through these complexities and, finally, sorting out priorities among the values and principles involved — as we did in our analyses in Chapters Two and Three. However, it should not be surprising to find that misgivings may remain, and especially that they may resurface at times of stress when factors that counter the final decision are prominent. Thus, the families of both M. H. and Downmore may have come to the conclusion that the patient would, all things considered, be better off dead and thus should be allowed to die; but when they are faced with obvious signs of discomfort or other unpleasant aspects of the dying process, they are reminded forcefully that this decision also causes the patient some harm.

There is no way to obviate the anguish of these situations. The only way to meliorate it is to remind oneself of the course of argument that led to the decision initially — that, despite the contrary considerations, the option embarked on was the correct one. And, we would contend, the best way to keep the full dimension of the argument firmly in mind is (a) to have reached it through a thorough discussion involving the family as a whole, in which misgivings had an opportunity to be completely aired and debated, and then (b) to remind oneself of the reasons behind the decision by recapitulating it regularly during the course of carrying it out.

The family may *make* the decision on behalf of the patient. In some family situations, one or more other members of the family may make the decision on behalf of the patient even if the patient is (at least marginally) competent. For example, in Case 34, although it is true that the patient, Pamela Hamilton, was only twelve years old when Ewing's sarcoma was diagnosed, it might have been possible — with the proper consoling support — to allow her to participate in decisions about her own treatment. However, the religious sect in which her father was a minister was strongly paternally dominated; and hence it was extremely unlikely that any form of "democratic" family decision-making would be fostered.

In other cases, the patient may encourage others in the family to dominate the decision-making process — perhaps as a support to personal denial, perhaps as a family dynamic that has become customary. If we regard individual autonomy as an optional value, this family style may not present a problem. However, if we regard personal, rational autonomy as not merely a value but a duty, then it may be necessary to encourage families to bring the patient more actively into the decision-making process whenever possible. Some children's cancer treatment centers, for example, make it a point, even in the case of young children, to provide information directly to the patient, offer the patient significant choices about treatment within the facility, and encourage the parents to involve the child in the fundamental treatment decisions. One question that arises about Case 35 (p. 252) is why the thirteen-year-old patient with a congenital kidney blockage had not been brought into the decision-making. Surely by age thirteen he was capable of understanding what is at stake and taking some part in discussions about his care. Sometimes older patients have been treated throughout their lives in a paternalistic way, such that to engage them in decision-making about their own care while dying becomes very difficult. In the case of "Momma" (Case 36, p. 254), the family's protection of their Italian mother from any bad news made the job of a surgeon extremely difficult. Is it his task to try to alter habits of many years standing in favor of engaging her in her care?

The family may *disagree among themselves* about the decision. The ideal of value unity is not, of course, always reached in practice. There may be fundamental disagreements among family members about the elements of a decision. Sometimes, as in the case of Walter Arnold's family (Case 14), this may stem from lack of information on the part of some or all the family. In other cases, it may stem from disagreements about the interpretation of values and principles in a given situation (e.g., what counts as an "extraordinary" measure, what aspects of treatment are "indignities," what should count as an "undue burden"?). In still other cases, a fundamental disagreement about values may lie at the heart of the dispute. This sort of situation is more likely to arise when the family has not maintained close contact for a period of time. It seems that it is nearly always the sister or uncle who comes to the terminal bedside from hundreds or thousands of miles away who views the situation differently from the family members who have remained in close contact with the patient and each other over the years. This consideration will play a role in one suggestion for enabling legislation to be found in the final chapter.

These disagreements, too, can be best handled by extended, open family discussion. Tragically, often the most important participant (the patient) is unable to participate by the time the whole family has gathered.[5] This fact underscores the importance of beginning these discussions long before the onset of illness, as we shall recommend in our discussion of advance directives below (pp. 108–109).

The family may *remain indifferent* to the patient's decision. In many ways, this is the least desirable of all the stances detailed here. Even if there is sharp disagreement within the family, there is a basis for resolving the conflicts as long as communication remains open. In the face of indifference, the patient is deprived, not only of the compassion and support a family ought to provide at time of crisis, but also of the challenge to articulate and defend fundamental values that a family discussion could prompt. Corresponding to the dying patient's duty to discuss his or her disease with the family and care-givers, there is a duty of the family to support and encourage this discussion among its members.

As disruptive as family disputes at this time may be within the institutional setting, it is almost always worse for the patient if peace and quiet takes the form of isolation and abandonment. Professional caregivers can perform some extremely valuable service to meliorate the patient's feelings of isolation. But, even at their most compassionate, professionals can never completely fill the void left by indifferent family members. We cannot expect strangers to supplant the role of the family, even if they are as dedicated to the dying patient as are most nurses, doctors, social workers, and others.

ETHICAL ISSUES WITHIN THE FAMILY

Thorny ethical issues arise as the family deals with terminal illness of one of its members. Parents of a homosexual son may have reacted in the past with denial or rejection of his lifestyle; how do they respond when he informs them that he has AIDS and wants to come home to die? Suppose, as his disease progresses, he indicates a desire for a visit from his lover? These situations test the value commitments of all the individuals involved.

Suppose the family of the man with carcinoma of the tongue (Case 31) is informed of his condition. How should they respond to his initial suicide attempt? It would hardly be constructive to proclaim their feelings of rejection due to the fact that he had not planned to make them aware of his diagnosis; but it would hardly be honest to ignore these feelings. What should be their response if he continues to insist that he will refuse treatment for the carcinoma? They are bound to feel, to some extent, that his decision reflects the judgment that continued association with them will not be worth the cost in pain, disfigurement, etc. of treatment. Thus they will go through some of the same gamut of emotions as a family who has been abandoned by one of its members. On the other hand, their compassion for this loved one will disincline them to urge him to a course of action that will involve pain and suffering. Added to this will be the inevitably guilty worry that they may be counseling him to the course of action that serves *their* interests, and perhaps not *his own.*

Families are the fundamental units of support in tragic times. As Robert Frost put it: "Home is the place where, when you *have* to go there, they *have* to take you in."[6] But nowadays the resources of the extended family are not readily available. This is an irony. At the time the technological environment created by massive advances in medicine cries out for the family's support as a corrective, the family itself no longer can provide that support because it has weakened in our society.

Instead of a large family circle who could each contribute to caring for a seriously ill loved one, we have families scattered over large geographical distances, so the question becomes: "Who will tend Mom?" where this will be an exclusive assignment. Furthermore, there is unlikely to be one family member (typically, in the past, the youngest daughter — though sometimes the youngest son, as in Case 14) willing to devote a portion of his or her life to caring for a debilitated loved one. Everybody has career plans, and all are eager to get on with them as expeditiously as possible (often today not even pausing to "start a family" of their own).

This raises large questions about the obligations of family members toward seriously ill members. Questions can be raised at both extremes: some ill members may demand too much, expecting others to shelve their own life-plans to provide intensive and lengthy personal care; other ill members may not demand enough, forbearing from requesting even minimal support that would comfort them in their anguish.

It is the responsibility of the family as a unit of support to steer between these extremes. It only compounds the tragedy of the terminal illness of one loved one if the life of one or more others is inalterably wrecked in the process of caring for them as they weaken and die. However, it is also a tragedy if a loved one dies longing for comfort that we could have provided without undue burden if we had taken the trouble to ascertain their needs and work to meet them.

The distribution of benefits and burdens within the family might not satisfy objective standards of fairness; but, if not, any departure from impersonal principles of justice ought to be negotiated openly and freely within the family on the basis of both mutual respect and mutual affection/love/compassion.

THE FAMILY AS SURROGATE DECISION-MAKERS

In Chapters Two and Three, we argued that the patient's own judgment is central to euthanasia decisions. The paradigm cases of justifiable euthanasia are those in which the patient explicitly requests to have life ended (cf. item 5 of Tables 1–5 in Chapter Two and Table 8 in Chapter Three), a situation that we called "voluntary" euthanasia (see Table 6, p. 50). Furthermore, we emphasized that the quality of life judgment (item 6 in Tables 1–5, 8) must be made from the patient's own point of view.

In the previous section of this chapter, we argued for the importance of family debate in forming and clarifying the decision for a competent patient.

When the patient is incompetent, their request and quality-of-life assessment are not directly available; and thus the relative importance of family judgment increases. The formerly competent patient may have provided an explicit advance directive (see p. 108 below), and/or there may be a basis for presuming their wishes — but even these may require interpretation and refinement in the crucible of family discussion (just as they would have, with the patient participating, if they were competent). Thus, for families that have been functioning actively as a values unit, there is every justification for relying on the family to make decisions on behalf of the patient. Not only does this provide more reliable information about what the patient would have wanted than caregivers are likely to have gained from their shorter-term and limited association with the patient, but it also brings in key elements that would have influenced the patient's decision. In part, this constitutes the patient's value history.

To the degree that there is *either* value disunity *or* a lack of mutual affection and concern within the family, however, the reliance on family decisions becomes less justifiable. Hence health care professionals have a responsibility to monitor the functioning of the family and to challenge decisions that go against the patient's wishes (if these can be ascertained with any degree of reliability) or their best interests.[7] It must be stressed that the standard by which family decisions are to be evaluated is *not* the patient's best interests as the caregivers view them from their own value perspective, nor even the perspective of the patient alone, but *the value perspective of the family unit which includes the patient.*

However, the value of family autonomy and privacy must not be dismissed lightly. There should be a strong presumption that the family represents the wishes of the patient. This presumption is rebuttable, but only by significant contrary evidence. Thus, for example, in Case 29 ("The Wife Has Her Own Ideas," p. 241), it is quite possible that the patient will be reluctant to take part in a discussion with caregivers. If so, we may have to rely on the wife to make decisions although the suspicion remains that her decisions are not coincident with her husband's wishes. We can *invite* him to express his wishes directly to caregivers. We can do much to facilitate such a discussion. But if, in spite of these measures, he prefers to communicate only with his wife about these matters and to leave it to her to make the decisions, we must, ultimately, honor this wish of his.

For the patient who has never been competent (e.g., newborns, the severely mentally retarded,[8] victims of severe childhood mental illness), the family is still the fundamental unit of value analysis and thus the primary decision-maker. This is so for several reasons. First, it can be presumed that the value stance of the family would have been instilled — at least to large measure — in the individual if he or she had been able to participate competently in family life. Second, the affection and compassion within the family normally makes the members unusually sensitive to the best interests of the patient. Third, the family will be responsible for continued care of the patient and thus they are the ones most directly affected by the consequences of these decisions.

It is thus extremely regrettable that the succession of "Baby Doe rules," which were issued by the Reagan Administration from 1982 to 1985,[9] provided little or no role for the parents in the decision-making process. The final version of these rules, which applies standards of child neglect and abuse in this situation, appears to us to appropriately embody the presumption that decisions are adequate unless there is strong evidence to the contrary. Unfortunately, this version of these rules still focuses almost exclusively on the physician's professional judgment and thus does not give adequate recognition of family autonomy.

Perhaps it might be argued that family autonomy is honored precisely by its *omission*. The fact that family decisions are not mentioned might be interpreted to suggest that they are none of the regulators' business, but rather a private matter between the family and the physician. However, we would contend that family autonomy requires a more active affirmation than this. To set guidelines (and penalties) for physician decision-making without prompting the physician to consult with the family is to invite the physician to make decisions unilaterally — an unfortunate reversal of hard-won trends of the past decade.

Thus, it invites responses like that in Case 38 ("Jenny's Heart Condition," p. 256), where the parents are not even told all the available options. One can sympathize with the benevolent motives of the physicians in approaching the situation in this way. They regard themselves as advocates of the patient and also they are trying to spare the parents the anguish of making a difficult decision. However, this is what families are *for*; and, if the temporizing surgery is a genuine option, they really ought to be apprised of it and take part in the discussions about whether to go for it. If the reasons *not* to attempt this procedure are genuinely convincing, they ought to be persuasive to the parents as well as to the health care team. Bringing the parents into the discussion will have the advantage of prompting the caregivers to articulate and defend their judgment in explaining it to the parents.

This stance also leads to tragedies like the case of Daniel McKay (Case 39, p. 256) and the recent case we call "I've Got a Gun!" (Case 40, p. 258). In both of these situations, the hospital personnel had arrogated the decision about treatment entirely to themselves with insufficient attention either to the wishes of the parents or to their anguish. In both cases, the infant's father finally felt driven to take matters into his own hands in a desperate way — by a brutal, active killing in Case 39, in an armed stand-off in Case 40. Perhaps the dramatic and frightening outcome could have been averted in both these cases if caregivers had brought the family more actively into the decision-making process from the start.

More difficult is the situation in Case 41 ("Baby Boy Miller,"

p. 259). The ambiguities in the diagnosis render any decision problematic, and the absence of input from the infant's mother and the
accompanying emotional state of the father (especially in Scene 3)
also raise questions about the soundness of his decision. And, yet,
his wishes cannot merely be dismissed. They should clearly have a
major role in the decision to be made.

These decisions made by family may take into account interests of
the family as a whole (just as they would have if the patient were an
active participant in the family discussion). For example, in Case 42
("Grandma or the House," p. 262), the family of an elderly woman
cites as one consideration against continued treatment the prospect
of losing the family home because of the expense of treatment.

FAMILY PATHOLOGIES

When the family requests inappropriate treatment. We would maintain that the thinking in Case 42 immediately above is *not* necessarily
inappropriate. There is a tradition of argument in moral theology going back several centuries that acknowledges that a medical treatment
may be classified as extraordinary or gravely burdensome on account
of the expense involved. Along with its other functions, the family
is an economic unit; and decisions must be made about allocating
financial resources in accordance with family values. The caregivers
in this case were extremely uncomfortable with this element of the
family's reasoning — to the point that, although they had been sympathetic to the family's request to discontinue treatment up to this
point, their sympathies changed when they discovered that money
issues were influencing the family's thinking. We would contend that
this reaction by the caregivers was misguided. If factors independent
of the monetary considerations were strong enough by themselves to
justify limiting treatment, this support should not be diminished by
the introduction of financial issues, even if (as we would dispute) it is
not strengthened by this factor. The reaction by the caregivers may
be, in part, a matter of coming to question the *motives* of the family.
The concern is that the other arguments by the family were rational-
izations masking a selfish and uncaring attitude. However, we would
contend (a) that this financial judgment itself is not selfish, but rather
appears to be an application of values shared by the family (including
the patient herself) and (b) that their concern might prompt the caregivers to review their own reaction to the family's earlier arguments;
but it is not, in itself, sufficient reason to reject these arguments. If,
on re-examination, they find the *arguments* sound, they might still be

decisive in the decision-making of the caregivers, even if they were not operatively decisive for the family.

Case 43 (p. 264) raises similar issues, here complicated both by evidence of dysfunction within the family and by difficulties in communicating with them. The patient, whom we call Bobby Nourse, had abandoned his family years before and has had virtually no contact with them since. Yet his son and daughter, now adults, are the only family available with whom to confer about treatment decisions. Reaching the daughter is difficult enough, but the caregivers have never been able to talk with the son directly. And it is he (according to the daughter's reports) who has objections to limiting treatment. His reported reasoning was based on religious values, but the caregivers could not avoid considering the possibility that part of the motivation here might be vengeful. The fact that the daughter rarely visited her father in either the nursing home or the hospital and the son never visited raised questions about the depth of their compassion for him — questions that were only compounded by the analysis of the daughter's affect when she discussed her father's situation with caregivers.

We would argue that the caregivers have an obligation to their patient in this situation to make direct contact with the son. For one thing, they need to explore with him the nature of the religious values he is applying to the situation. It might be possible to convince him *within the context of his own tradition of reasoning* that the limits of an obligation to treat have been reached. It might be helpful, in this regard, to ask the hospital chaplain to contact the son's minister, in order both to explain Nourse's medical condition and to explore the theological reasoning involved — and, perhaps, even to challenge it. To attempt this is well worth the effort — both because it might inspire family support that would benefit the patient and as a defensive measure against possible legal action by the family.

Further, it needs to be determined what reason (if any) there is to believe that these values are shared by the father — for, ultimately, it is *the patient's* values that are decisive in a dysfunctional family. If we were to learn from the son that his religious tradition is that in which he was brought up by his father, the next question would be whether there was reason to believe that the father still pays allegiance to this viewpoint at present. If we were to learn of a fairly recent expression of allegiance by the father (e.g., an approving comment about the son's religious devotion, or perhaps merely a small recent donation to the church), then the son's wishes should be weighed heavily. If, on the other hand, we were to learn that the father had explicitly repudiated religion or that the son had turned to this tradition entirely on his own, then the son's viewpoint ought to carry little weight in the final decision.

Case 13 (p. 222), which we call "The Transfused Cat," raises somewhat different issues. The evidence is strong that the patient's daughter is approaching the situation with pretty much the same values the patient herself would have employed. The questions are (a) whether the patient's own expression of these wishes would have been honored if she had made them known herself (say, through a living will, a prior detailed conversation with the physicians, or other clear advance directive), and (b) whether it makes any difference that the daughter is here representing her wishes as her surrogate. On the latter point, the President's Commission insists that it *does* make a difference:

> there are certain decisions that a patient might be permitted to make because of the strong protection afforded self-determination but that are outside the discretion of a substitute decision-maker. The line is drawn at actions whose potential adverse effects on well-being, as that concept is commonly understood, are so great that they can be permitted only when sufficiently directly chosen by a competent patient.[10]

The Hastings Center Guidelines express a similar reserve, but only about surrogates who are neither family nor close friends:

> Some maintain that [an appointed] surrogate, who is not a family member or concerned friend of the patient, but may instead be a stranger, should have more limited discretion than a family or friend surrogate and perhaps should be subject to closer review. No wide agreement exists on this however, or on the standards and mechanisms that would be used to further confine the discretion of a "stranger surrogate." We recommend that surrogates appointed for patients who lack them at least be held to the standards applied to family or friend surrogates.... [11]

We would contend that caregivers have some obligation in *every* case to determine that the surrogate is applying values that would be shared by the patient. Structural factors are one important piece of evidence here — i.e., the adult child who lives nearby and has communicated with the parent regularly through the years is more likely to be in touch with the parent's values than the child who lives thousands of miles away and has communicated or visited infrequently. However, this is prima facie evidence only. It may be rebutted by contrary evidence that the distant child was actually closer to the parent than the nearby one.* Further, even in the absence of contrary

---

*Once again this situation confirms our conviction that general policies lack sufficient specificity to assist in decision-making in concrete cases.

considerations, such external, relational signs of shared values ought
to be supplemented by direct evidence of the patient's thinking. The
family ought to be able to cite specific things the patient has said or
done that express these values. One of the strengths of the *Conroy*
opinion is its insistence on this sort of evidence in connection with
what it calls the "subjective" test.[12]

There are two chief difficulties with the requirement that caregivers explore this sort of evidence: (a) it is time-consuming, and
perhaps not reimbursable, and (b) it might be seen as an invasion of
the privacy of the family. However, we would argue that these need
not be insurmountable obstacles. The importance of this in order to
serve the welfare of the patient makes it worth some time and effort;
the process of trying to obtain it may lead the caregivers to develop
a degree of intimacy with the family that will be comforting to them
and will make the decision-making process easier on all concerned.
Caregivers should, of course, respect limits to intimacy that the family indicates; and family members must similarly respect the other
demands on caregivers' time.

The family has needs, too; and there might be times when it is
appropriate for caregivers to take a step to serve these needs even
when they are not coincident with needs or known values of the
patient. One such situation is illustrated in Case 44 ("When Did
Billy Die?" p. 265). The American College of Physicians *Ethics Manual* acknowledges the appropriateness of the physicians' decision in
Case 44: "There may be circumstances in which the physician may
elect to support the body when clinical death of the brain has occurred...."[13] Of course, it is possible to carry this too far. Case 45
("Grandpa's Grandpa," p. 267) is a *reductio ad absurdam* of giving
primacy to family convenience, as well as of the unchecked use of
technological prowess.

Striking the proper balance in deferring to family needs and values
requires discerning judgment. The case of Walter Arnold (Case 14)
and the case of the jeopardized family home (Case 42) both show
that no one *type* of factor can be ruled out of consideration altogether. If we can assume that the patient himself or herself cared
about the welfare of his or her family (and this is, of course, a rebuttable presumption), there is warrant for giving considerable weight to
the needs and values of the family.

These needs must, at the same time, be addressed in other ways.
If denial on the part of the family is prompting caregivers to sustain
a patient who is brain-dead (as in Case 44), it is not enough to "wait
it out." Active measures, employing both professionals within the

institution and the family's community support system, must be initiated to resolve this denial as rapidly as possible and with minimal trauma to all parties.

Treatment requests may be inappropriate on either or both of two grounds: (a) when it is contrary to the wishes of the patient and/or (b) when it is medically contraindicated. The latter of these will be dealt with in Chapter Five. We explore the former here.

If caregivers are concerned that the family's choices are contrary to the wishes of the patient, considerable diplomatic and negotiating skills are called for. Removing decision-making from the family through a heavy-handed mechanism such as court action to appoint a guardian should be a last resort.[14] Much to be preferred is handling the matter through informal negotiations. The first step here would be to be sure that the family fully understands the patient's medical condition. Then they should be (gently) queried about the basis of both their understanding of the patient's values and their application of these to the case at hand. An open discussion of differences between family and caregivers in perceptions about these matters may prove illuminating to both parties. A mechanism like the Hospital Ethics Committee can be helpful in facilitating this sort of discussion. If agreement is not reached through this sort of "fact-finding" discussion, it may be necessary to take a "contracting" stance, where caregivers indicate the limits to how far they would be comfortable going in accommodating the family's choices. With the right attitude and accompanying emotional support to families, it should be possible to come to a resolution in all but a very few cases of this sort.

Some families may be paralyzed with indecision — finding it impossible to make an explicit life-or-death decision about a family member. In this situation, caregivers may choose to approach the choices somewhat obliquely with communications like: "Perhaps we should say that our goal will be to see that he does not suffer unduly" or "Unless you indicate a contrary wish, I do not plan to initiate aggressive life-sustaining measures." A balance must be struck between the requirements of informed consent, on the one hand, and, on the other, avoidance of cruelty to the family by forcing them to face unwillingly a decision they will find it difficult to live with after the patient's death.

Here again, if personal autonomy is seen as a duty and/or a significant value, we may be doing the family a disservice by "protecting" them from such decisions. On the other hand, health professionals cannot be expected to rectify overnight patterns of nonautonomous decision-making that may be deeply ingrained. Furthermore, a life-

or-death crisis is hardly the ideal time to expect family members who have heretofore avoided taking personal responsibility for choices to begin to exercise personal autonomy. (This does sometimes happen, but we should not *count* on it.) Prompting personal autonomy may, of necessity, have to be made a long-term goal — perhaps integrated into grief counseling — rather than insisted upon at the moment of crisis-laden choice.

Who constitutes the family? Case 46 raises this question with a vengeance. Mr. Burntree's "lady friend" appears to be in a better position to judge his present wishes than his daughters are. She demonstrates her concern for him by her presence and attentiveness while he is hospitalized — whereas the daughters merely telephone. She should, of course, be observed (as should family members) for signs of self-serving reasoning; and she should be queried about direct evidence of his wishes. But, in the absence of contrary evidence, she should be considered more suitable to take the family role in decision-making than the daughters.

The concept of "family" is, above all, a *functional* notion. Especially in this day of the dissolution of the traditional family unit through divorce, estrangement, divergent lifestyles, and geographical separation, caregivers must seek to ascertain who in the situation is functioning as the patient's unit of support and values analysis. A close-knit circle of friends who have lived together for many years in a retirement community ought to be considered, at the very least, as *part* of the family — and perhaps as a more important part than relatives by blood or marriage.

One mechanism the patient can employ to make these relationships clear is by executing a durable power of attorney for medical care decisions, which names one or more persons to act as surrogates when they become incompetent to make health decisions. Less formally, one might include in one's living will some specification like the following: "It is my wish that the following persons be included with my family in discussions about decisions to be made about my care...."

The case of Kenneth Wright (Case 47, p. 271) involves the functional notion of family. Wright was a young man who could not bear to continue to live as a paraplegic. He persuaded two friends to supply him with a shotgun and to take him out into the woods where he could kill himself. Although manslaughter charges seem too harsh for them, we would be critical of these friends for the way they carried out their extended family role. We would interpret this situation (admittedly on skimpy evidence) as one of deferring to the patient's wishes with which they do not necessarily agree, and we would contend (as we argued in discussing this category of cases on p. 89 above) that these friends should have registered their disagreement with his judgment and should have prompted him to reexamine it in the light of all possible prospects for a positive quality of life for himself. They should probably have enlisted other friends and Wright's "real" family in these discussions. (We would urge, as well, that he be put into contact with some people as much like himself as possible who had managed to find a satisfactory quality of life in a wheelchair.)

The case we call "Please, Please Kill Me!" (Case 48, p. 271) illustrates how complex and thorny family dynamics can become in these tragic situations. Jamie Lou Martin was paralyzed "from the lips down" in an automobile accident. Her own family was unresponsive to her repeated requests to die, but a friendly neighbor (who was neglecting his own wife and children in attending Jamie by the hour) did kill her at her request. Now the family remains bitterly divided in their attitude toward him. Extremely dysfunctional family dynamics are moving toward resolution very slowly, if at all.

Jamie's own wishes were crystal-clear: she persistently and emphatically made it known that she judged that she would be better off dead. She attempted to achieve this goal by passive euthanasia measures, but legal ambiguities and strong family wishes to maintain her life made this impossible. Thus she was driven to the desperate act of goading a vulnerable, love-struck neighbor into employing direct, active mercy-killing.

The reasonable person approach. In situations in which neither information about the patient's wishes nor family or friends to act as surrogates are available, decisions may have to be made through a "reasonable person" approach — i.e., what the average thoughtful person is likely to desire. In this connection, one thing that is needed is more data about what people normally desire. The best data is that gained explicitly from the patient or from a legal guardian who has been appointed with a durable power of attorney for health care. But we should not ignore the kind of grassroots data that is already available regarding intensive measures to preserve life.

In 1976, an NBC-TV opinion poll indicated that 72 percent of the American public did not believe that doctors should use mechanical means to prolong a person's life when there is no chance of recovery.[15] There is still plenty of room for interpretation in this statement, but the view seems to have held rather steady for more than a decade.

The issue of the right to die is the most important of a number of patient-rights issues. In a two-year project a coalition of health organizations in Colorado sent out a thirty-one-question survey on critical care issues. More than 30,000 questionnaires were distributed and more than 10,000 responses gained. Despite the wide range of respondents, tremendous consensus emerged on many issues. All the consensus issues had to do with the right of individuals to control their own decisions about health care.

Eighty-three percent agreed that physicians have an obligation to follow one's wishes, even if the physician did not agree with them. 82.2 percent agreed that they would *not* want their family to have the right to change their directives about organ donation, withholding food and fluids, and other matters. 85 percent did not want to be artificially maintained during a dying process. They disagreed with the following statement: "If I become permanently unconscious and couldn't eat normally, I would want my life maintained with artificial feedings." 62.8 percent did not want to be kept on a respirator if there was no hope of living off one, and if they remained mentally alert. 71.8 percent supported a statement that said that as a family member, I would support a loved one's decision not to be maintained with food and fluids. Individuals wrote in the margins. One statement seemed to summarize the perceptions of most of the respondents: "I believe it is imperative that we the patients, and their families, have a choice in the kind of medical treatment we receive."[16]

As can be seen in the data that have been assembled, decisions individuals make have an impact on the family. Further, the family itself either is expected to support the individual's decision, or it is expected to have a role in implementing those decisions. When a patient has not given directives, families expect to be able to make them for the patient, presumably based on their knowledge of the patient's value system. Over 2,100 Orange County men and women attending meetings sponsored by California Health Decisions, a group like the Colorado group already cited, filled out treatment decision questionnaires. Over 71 percent agreed and 14 percent were not sure that "if a close relative is in a coma and not expected to recover, I should have the right to direct the doctors to withhold artificial feeding."[17]

Despite a general feeling by most persons, and even by specialists in medical ethics, that there is no valid reason for continuing the technology of medically-delivered fluids and nutrition when "there is no hope of an improvement in the patient's prognosis," there is still no real clear consensus in society about withholding or withdrawing this technology in practice.[18] This is particularly true for patients in various end stages of dementia in nursing homes. Even though patients may not be seen as "dying," their loved ones, usually sons and daughters they no longer recognize, wonder whether not feeding them simply starves them to death, or whether their parents or aunts and uncles "die of the underlying disease"?

Specific decisions in these circumstances should probably be put into the hands of a surrogate, even if we must solicit a person who is a stranger to the patient to act in this role. Although the logistics of enlisting private citizens to act as surrogates for strangers may be difficult, such a program is worthwhile for at least two reasons: (1) it adds the voice of a health care "consumer" to treatment discussions, which is a point of view that it is beneficial to all parties to have represented; and (2) it prompts the laypersons who act as surrogates to think about these decisions — both in the case of the patient for whom they serves as proxy and in their own cases — and provides them with some insight into the exigencies under which such decisions must be made.

A widespread program of volunteer surrogates might prompt most of those who serve to go back to their own families and discuss their wishes about limits to treatment in terminal care. In time, this might, in turn, reduce the number of cases in which caregivers are left without guidance from the patients themselves through a living will or other advance directive.

ADVANCE DIRECTIVES

The rationale of advance directives has often been misperceived — not least in the legislative language of statutes that support them. The Tennessee statute is typical in this regard. In the preamble to the statute, the legislative intent is stated as follows:

> The general assembly declares it to be the law of the state of Tennessee that every person has the fundamental and inherent right to die naturally with as much dignity as circumstances permit and to accept, refuse, withdraw from, or otherwise control decisions relating to the rendering of his or her own medical care, specifically including palliative care and the use of extraordinary procedures and treatment.[19]

The concept of "natural death" (repeated, in Tennessee as in many other states, in the title of the statute: "The Tennessee Right to Natural Death Act") is a red herring. Nobody wants to be cut off from pain control measures and other aspects of comfort care and the emotional support health professionals are trained to provide as they die.[20]

The notion of "death with dignity" is somewhat more meaningful; but, as we pointed out in Chapter Two, it is vague in the extreme. The notion of "extraordinary" procedures is also quite vague.

The important element of this statement is the concept of *control*. An advance directive is a mechanism by which patients can maintain control of decisions about their treatment even after they are no longer able to exercise active participation in decision-making. The point is that a patient's right to refuse treatment is not lost when the patient becomes incompetent.

Living wills. Surrogate decision-makers are expected to try to ascertain what the patient's wishes would have been even if the patient has left no direct indication about them. Clearly, if the patient has made his or her wishes known — even in informal ways — these have some claim to be honored. A formal expression of wishes to limit treatment indicated in a formal living will document carries considerable weight both ethically and legally in the absence of enforcing legislation, since it represents an emphatic indication of the patient's wishes. When backed by legislation that provides mechanisms for execution and enforcement, a living will directive is weightier still — sometimes involving penalties for failure to carry it out.

It is important to see these variations as stages along a single continuum rather than as distinct situations. It would be a serious mistake to think that one need not conduct extensive informal discussions with one's family, for example, because one had executed a living will directive in a state that gave this legal force. We would contend that, even in these states, the living will should be viewed as one step in a fuller process. No written document can anticipate the full range of situations that might arise and the full set of values that might be brought into play in decision-making in terminal care situations. Terms like "heroic" or "extraordinary" measures or "death with dignity" leave wide scope for interpretation in application to the specific situation. Execution of a written living will directive should be both preceded and followed by extensive discussions with family, friends, and caregivers. Prior discussions can bring to light what the issues are — i.e., what kinds of situations are likely to arise in terminal care, what technologies might be considered and their emotional impact and value implications.

Caregivers will have a chance to communicate their personal attitude toward limiting treatment and what, if any, boundaries they would be unable in conscience to cross. Family and friends will have the opportunity to challenge the patient's value claims and to indicate their own judgments about the key values in this situation. After the document is executed, discussions should continue, now focused on applying the general guidelines enunciated in the living will document to the situation at hand. Once a patient is diagnosed with a terminal illness, and as the illness progresses, specifics about the course of the illness and treatment choices to be faced can be communicated and discussed in detail.

If a procedure like this has been followed in advance, involving key caregivers and the whole of the patient's circle of family and close friends, there should be little uncertainty or disagreement when the time comes to limit treatment. The patient's wishes, clarified and tested in the crucible of extensive discussion with family and caregivers, should be clear and acceptable to all parties. Thus, the living will becomes an occasion for increased communication and trust among caregivers, the patient, and family in light of the two principal duties we have articulated: the duty of the patient to communicate his or her desires about the terminal illness and its treatment, and the duty of the family (and caregivers) to support the patient and this painful process. The living will is a helpful instrument if it mirrors such discussion.

These general principles are not always operative in the dramatic cases that reach the court system in some states. For example, in what was characterized as a setback for the right-to-die movement, the Supreme Court of the State of Missouri forbade the withdrawal of artificial nutrition and hydration through a gastrostomy in the case of Nancy Cruzan, who lay in a permanent vegetative state for five years as a result of an automobile accident (see Case 21, p. 233). If the feeding continues, she might be expected to live another thirty years in this condition. In spite of evidence of a "somewhat serious conversation" in which Nancy had indicated that if sick or injured she would not want to have her life continued unless she could live "halfway normally," the Missouri Supreme Court held (in a hotly debated 4–3 ruling) that the constitutional right to privacy is not expansive enough to apply to lifesaving treatment.

In this ruling, the court brushed aside the nearly one hundred court cases in twenty states, and the living will statutes in thirty-eight states, including Missouri itself. The overwhelming majority of these court cases were decided in favor of the right to die.[21] These cases also affirmed the role of families or other decision-makers, who are able to say in the absence of written preferences from patients, that the patient would not have wanted the treatments in question.[22] The statutes are based on the right of individuals to determine their own treatment, especially when they are dying. The Cruzan court viewed these as simply based on a desire to interpret the law in favor of one's right to die. Clearly, only the United States Supreme Court, which has agreed to hear this case in its 1989–1990 term, will be able to make the final interpretation of the constitutional right to privacy (assuming they address this issue in their opinion).

The Cruzan decision demonstrates that one can interpret the law in many ways.[23] This is certainly not the way we would want it interpreted, especially in view of our consideration of the obligation to provide a benefit to patients who express their wishes about their death ahead of time. At risk, too, and not very well examined in this and related court decisions, is the right of the family to advocate and interpret the preferences of their loved ones who become incompetent.

One problem in the Missouri case was with the specificity of wishes. In this regard, the court built upon an earlier and less restrictive judgment handed down in New York regarding Mary O'Connor (see Case 22, p. 234). The decision in New York is considered less restrictive because it did not deny the right of patients to express advance directives, nor deny that the family had a role in attesting to and interpreting those directives. The doubt they raised was whether O'Connor made any specific reference to fluids and nutrition in stating her wishes to her two daughters, both of whom were practical nurses. The daughters and friends were able to testify to her constant and explicit desire never to "be a burden to anyone," "not to lose my dignity"; that it was "monstrous" to keep someone alive using machinery when they are "not going to get any better." She held that people who were suffering very badly should be allowed to die. Several times she told Helen, one of her daughters, that if she became ill and could not take care of herself, she would not want her life to be sustained artificially.[24]

A trial court approved removal of fluids and nutrition after her progressive deterioration following a series of strokes. She was in a geriatric institute at the time. The appellate court affirmed that ruling, but when the institute went to the New York Court of Appeals, it issued a surprise ruling. After affirming the ideal situation of having advance directives from the patient herself, or a living will (which is not yet legally enforced in New York), and acknowledging that repeated oral expressions are important, the rulings of the lower courts were overturned because the patient's statements, as expressed by family and friends, were "not clear" about application for withdrawing fluids and nutrition.[25]

The Society for the Right to Die commented on this case with respect to the role of the family, as follows:

> ...the underlying assumption is that to permit ending treatment without clear and convincing evidence would lead to abuse of the vulnerable elderly. Other courts and authorities...have strongly held that decision-making when the patient is incompetent is best discharged by family members who know and care for the patient, rather than health care providers or courts, to whom she may be a stranger.[26]

The Court's position is that there is nothing more than conjecture about whether O'Connor would have wanted the fluids and nutrition withdrawn. One suspects, however, that a more conservative concern about many vulnerable individuals has now surfaced. This concern has as a deep background, the Nazi experience, which we will examine in Chapter Six. Yet the question remains, how specific can or must individuals be about the future contingent possibilities of their health? It seems sufficient to us to take the "family principle" seriously, that lacking any other data, families are the best interpreters of their loved one's wishes, unless, of course, the family itself is judged incompetent to speak for their loved one for one reason or another.[27]

Durable power of attorney. Another form of advance directive is to designate one or more specific persons to make decisions on one's behalf. The chief advantage to this approach over a living will document is that it can be more responsive to the particularities of the situation. The living will is, of necessity, phrased in generalities; and thus it is left primarily to the physician to interpret the application of these general instructions to the case at hand. As the *O'Connor* case demonstrates, this can pose quite a problem in an unusual situation, or in the case of a conservative court.

Through a durable power of attorney for medical decisions, the patient transfers decision-making authority to one or more specific named individuals. There are no restrictions on who may serve in this capacity: family members may be designated, but the designee may be a close friend (or minister or attorney) instead of, or in addition to, family.

It should be recognized that this is a considerable burden of responsibility to place on an individual. That individual may, quite literally, be making life-or-death decisions. Even though the law does not require it, ethical principles would clearly mandate obtaining prior agreement from the individual(s) chosen to serve in this capacity. Further, fairly extensive discussions with the person(s) are called for in order to help them understand fully one's wishes and the values upon which they are based, as we have already indicated.

Although advance directives are usually discussed in the context of refusing certain treatments, it should be pointed out that any of these same mechanisms could be used to convey the wish to sustain life as long as possible by means of every procedure available. These mechanisms are not "pro-death" or "anti-life" instruments; what they are about is control. To put the same point in a slightly different way, it might help to remember that our argument for allowing certain forms of euthanasia in Chapter Two (see p. 51) was based on the right to life and the possibility of waiving this right. But it is also possible, of course, to refrain from waiving the right and instead to claim it.

The limits to what can be mandated by means of an advance directive are set by the same principles discussed in Chapters Two and Three. It is not fair to ask others to assist us in ways that would violate their own conscience, or that would violate their own moral rights, or that would impose a grave burden upon them, or that would expose them to legal jeopardy. Extensive family discussion of one's wishes is the crucible in which these, as other matters, should be arbitrated. (We will discuss another limitation — medically contraindicated treatment — in Chapter Five.)

HOSPICE

The philosophy of hospice was encapsulated in a nutshell by a hospice nurse who said to one of the present authors: "Surveys show that more than 80 percent of terminally ill persons prefer to die at home, whereas more than 80 percent of their families prefer *not* to have them die there. The goal of hospice is to overcome this discrepancy."

Hospice attempts this by providing medical and other forms of support to ill persons and their families and by developing goals that amount to a form of voluntary, passive euthanasia. Some hospices offer residential facilities; some operate entirely by providing support services to patients at home; some combine these two approaches; still others may continue to serve patients who have been hospitalized. What all these units have in common is a set of guiding principles or goals, which we might summarize as follows:

1. Efforts to prolong life are no longer appropriate.

2. The goal of care ought to become, instead, to provide the ill person with the means to be as comfortable as possible and to maintain his or her dignity to the extent possible.

3. Thus, the acute-care hospital no longer seems an appropriate setting for care. Its resuscitation equipment, rescue teams, and high technology treatment facilities ought not to be employed.

4. The most clear-cut way to avoid use of these modalities is to move the person to a facility where it is clear to all involved that they are not available — ideally, to the person's home, where personal dignity can be maximized by the family and where the setting contributes to personal comfort.

5. Medical technology should be focused on pain control and other aspects of comfort care.

The involvement of family is clearly of central importance to these goals. If the ill person is to be maintained at home, the burden of day-to-day (and, indeed, minute-to-minute) care almost always falls on the family.[28] The role of hospice here is (a) to train the family to carry out their care functions, (b) to supplement their care by delivering treatments that require technical skills beyond the capability of family, (c) to function as liaison between the family and the physician, and (d) to provide emotional support to the family in coping with the inevitable stresses of their role.

One real problem with carrying through the decision not to employ life-prolonging measures is their widespread availability. Even if the ill person is at home, a call for an ambulance at a period of crisis (cf. Case 33, p. 248, and Case 18, p. 228) may bring a rescue squad armed with sophisticated resuscitation equipment and techniques, and a mandate to use them. Avoiding this may require a DNLH attitude, a Decision Not to Leave Home. [29] When the dying family member suffers a sudden attack, it takes courage not to call the Emergency Medical Service (EMS). Some hospices makes signs for the refrigerator saying, "Do Not Call EMS."

This is another way of honoring the fact that families should not and cannot require that patients stay alive. Yet they try to. "Please don't die on me, Harry"! they may shout. Harry tries to hang on, so that he does not disappoint his wife. For this reason, Eric Cassell developed a permission model for dying patients and their families. According to this model, near the end of a patient's life, Dr. Cassell would assemble all the family members and the patient, and they would formally give the patient their permission to die. This insured that the patient would not "hang on" unnecessarily, and by doing so, prolong his or her own pain and anguish.[30]

CONCLUSION

Generally speaking, the family is in the best position to help make critical decisions about incompetent patients. They best know the values of the patient, and whether the patient made any formal or informal requests about treatment. If the family cannot relate what the patient wanted, they may be able to relate what the patient *may* have wanted on the basis of the patient's value history. Barring that, as Shannon and Walter argue, "the family is still the appropriate decision-maker. The family has a socially recognized relation to the patient and can be presumed to have the best interests of the patient in mind."[31] We have called this the "family principle" and we have explored in this chapter how it might be used in clinical cases.

As Fenella Rouse emphasizes, "The legal history of withholding and withdrawing treatment has been very much concerned with the extraordinary cases and, I think, has provided very little guidance for us in the everyday care of dying people."[32] A broadly based Treatment Decision Status (TDS) policy in hospitals and other institutions is one useful way to implement the involvement of patient and family in decision-making in routine care.[33] In a Treatment Decision Status policy, all entering cancer patients (and other critically ill patients) — together with their families — would, as soon as possible, have a thorough discussion of all interventions that are likely, with an attempt to elicit their choices about all of these, from ordinary nursing service like suctioning the respirator to radical and expensive interventions, as soon as possible. If patients have executed a living will and/or durable power of attorney, these should be examined and discussed in the detail we have proposed. For those patients who have left few or no instructions about what they would like to have done during their dying process, physicians and families must speculate what they would have wanted based on family values.

Families are often exposed and vulnerable during the deaths of loved ones. Society should be supportive. Specific measures for family support should be instituted in acute and long-term care settings. Furthermore, families need the assurance that only legislated rights can bring. First of all, they need assurance that they will not remain powerless and emotionally raw while a loved one suffers a painful death. Second, the proper role of families in making health decisions for a loved one needs to be spelled out in the law. We suggest an example at the end of Chapter Seven.

NOTES

1. "Bond for Leona Andresen Reduced," *Chicago Tribune*, February 2, 1989, sec. 2C, 4.

2. This is recommended in the *Conroy* opinion at 1229.

3. John A. Eaddy and Glenn C. Graber, "Confidentiality and the Family Physician," *American Family Physician* (January 1982), 141–145. We might add that critical comments on the notion of "family autonomy" are found in B. Hoffmaster and R. Christy, *Ethical Issues in Family Medicine* (New York: Oxford University Press, 1988).

4. For a contrasting view, see Jacob Oser, "Oral Cancer: Coping with the Changes," *Kangogaku Zasshi* (Japanese Journal of Nursing) 44, no. 10 (Oct. 1980), 1060–1062.

5. See Howard Brody, Guest Editor, *Theoretical Medicine* 8, no. 3 (October 1987), entire issue devoted to the role of the family in medical decisions.

6. Robert Frost, "Death of the Hired Man," *The Poems of Robert Frost* (New York: The Modern Library, 1946), p. 41.

7. E. D. Pellegrino and D. C. Thomasma, *For the Patient's Good: Towards a Restoration of Beneficence in Health Care* (New York: Oxford University Press, 1988).

8. See Case 37, p. 255.

9. See 47 *Federal Register* (June 16, 1982), p. 26027; 48 *Federal Register* (March 7, 1983), p. 9630; *American Academy of Pediatrics v. Heckler*, No. 83-0774 (April 14, 1983); 48 *Federal Register* 129 (July 5, 1983), pp. 30846–30852; 48 *Federal Register* 6 (January 12, 1984), pp. 1622–1654; 49 *Federal Register* 238 (December 10, 1984), pp. 48170–48173; 50 *Federal Register* 72 (April 15, 1985), pp. 14893–14901.

10. President's Commission for the Study of Ethical Problems in Medicine and Biomedical and Behavioral Research, *Deciding to Forego Life-Sustaining Treatment: Ethical, Medical, and Legal Issues in Treatment Decisions* (Washington, D.C.: U.S. Government Printing Office, 1983), p. 133.

11. *Guidelines on the Termination of Life-Sustaining Treatment and the Care of the Dying* (Briarcliff Manor, N.Y.: The Hastings Center, 1987), p. 26.

12. *In re Conroy*, 1229.

13. American College of Physicians, *Ethics Manual* (Philadelphia: American College of Physicians, 1984), p. 26.

14. It is widely held that in the Linares case ("I've Got a Gun" — Case 40, p. 258), poor legal advice caused a great deal of the problem. It was not necessary to "go to court" to make an ethical decision.

15. "Annual Conference Notes Progress Toward Goals," *Euthanasia News* 2, no. 1 (February 1976), 1.

16. Rebecca Mashaw, "Colorado Speaks Out on Health," *Frontlines* 5, no. 3 (December 1988), 8.

17. Alan Otten, "Local Groups Attempt to Shape Policy on Ethics and Economics of Health Issues," *Wall Street Journal*, May 25, 1988.

18. Thomas Shannon and James Walter, "The PVS Patient and the Forgoing/Withdrawing of Medical Nutrition and Hydration," *Theological Studies* 49 (1988), 623–647.

19. *Tennessee Code Annotated*, § 32-11-102.

20. H. T. Engelhardt, Jr., argues that autonomy includes "the right to be left alone." This "right" would clash with the common experience of the dying that they don't want to be left alone. See H. T. Engelhardt, Jr., "Advance Directives and the Right to Be Left Alone," in C. Hackler, R. Moseley, and D. E. Yawter, eds., *Advance Directives in Medicine* (New York: Praeger, 1989), pp. 141–154.

21. "Right-to-Die Backgrounder," Society for the Right to Die, January 1989. Available from the Society for the Right to Die, 250 W. 57th St., New York, NY 10107.

22. Ibid., p. 2.

23. "Right-to-Die Movement Takes Turn Toward Hard Times," *Medical Ethics Advisor* 5, no. 1 (January 1989), 1–16.

24. "O'Connor Case Highlights Problem of Incompetent Patient with No Living Will," *Medical Ethics Advisor* 5, no. 1 (January 1989), 13–16.

25. Ibid., 15.

26. As quoted in Ibid., 15–16.

27. See the chapter on family decision-making for incompetent patients in Edmund D. Pellegrino and David C. Thomasma, *For the Patient's Good: The Restoration of Beneficence in Health Care* (New York: Oxford University Press, 1988), pp. 162–171.

28. See "A Death in the Home," in Harold Bursztajn, M.D., Richard I. Feinbloom, M.D., Robert M. Hamm, Ph.D., and Archie Brodsky, *Medical Choices, Medical Chances: How Patients, Families, and Physicians Can Cope With Uncertainty* (New York: Delacorte Press/Seymour Lawrence, 1981), pp. 319–348.

29. Gene H. Stollerman, "Decisions to Leave Home," *Journal of the American Geriatrics Society* 36 (1988), 375–376.

30. Eric Cassel, "Permission to Die," *Bioscience* 23 (August 1973), 475–477; reprinted in John A. Behnke and Sissela Bok, eds. *The Dilemmas of Euthanasia* (New York: Doubleday, 1975), 121–131.

31. Shannon and Walter, "The PVS Patient," 646.

32. Carla Carwile, "Reclaiming Rightful Power," *Frontlines* 5, no. 3 (December 1988), 1.

33. David C. Thomasma, "Ethical and Legal Issues in the Care of the Elderly Cancer Patient," *Clinics in Geriatric Medicine* 3 (August 1987), 541–547.

Chapter Five

EUTHANASIA AND THE MEDICAL COMMUNITY

The traditional resistance of the medical community to voluntary, active euthanasia will be subject to critique in this chapter. The vitalist principle, that all life is sacred and must be protected at all costs, is rejected. Yet the dedication of physicians to the patient's best interests requires some significant commitments to the value of human life. Earlier discussion from Chapters Two and Three about the right of patients to request assisted suicide or voluntary euthanasia and our duties or obligations (if any) to provide it will be re-examined here from the point of view of physicians and other health professionals. Does the right of the patient to request euthanasia (if ever there is one) obligate caregivers to provide it? Can others, the caregivers for example, be placed in the situation of having to provide a benefit to others that may violate, not only their consciences and their professional codes, but also their fundamental commitments to the value of human life?

GOAL OF MEDICINE

The goal of medical care should not be life-prolongation per se.[1] Dedication to prolonging life per se is a vitalist position that, as our discussion thus far has already indicated, must be eliminated in any discussion of euthanasia, active or passive. Euthanasia as an option in care for individuals rests on the presumption that death itself can sometimes be a benefit greater than life preservation.

Exploration of this claim requires some metaphysical thinking. Is life a good in itself? Or is it only an instrumental or conditional value, a means to provide the basis for other values? Or is it instead what James Walter, a theologian, calls a "created and limited metaphysical good" — that is, a moral instrument in the ability to pursue goals.[2] If so, it follows that medicine must serve the purposefulness of human life, not just physiological life itself. Health is a condition of possibility of the pursuit of other values that transcend physical life. As Walter argues:

> When medicine cannot any longer promote this goal for a patient at all, or when, by its interventions, medicine will place a patient in a condition that makes the pursuit of purposefulness too burdensome, then medicine has reached its limits *on the basis of its own principal reason for existence.*[3]

Hence the proper goal of medicine ought to be the assistance of individuals in pursuing their personal, family, and social goals by means of health. This was one of the major bases for rejection of the actions by the young ob-gyn resident in "It's Over, Debbie" (Case 1, p. 208). The twenty-year-old dying cancer patient was described by the resident who wrote the piece as saying, "Let's get this over with." Yet the resident also wrote that when he first entered the room and met the patient "the room seemed filled with the patient's desperate effort to survive." The young doctor, without knowing any of the patient's values, promptly injected her with 20 milligrams of morphine sulfate and watched, rather narcissistically, as the morphine took effect on her respirations. The patient died as a result of both his action and his apparent intent. Eugene Kennedy, normally a supporter of rather liberal causes, noted in an editorial published shortly thereafter:

> One would have to travel into the heart of darkness itself to find a physician whose experience matched even roughly that of the author of this piece. For where, even in the relativistic shambles of American culture, could you find another physician willing to end a patient's life with less information than the average hit man gets about the life and habits of an intended target?[4]

Emphasis on patient choice was central to our argument in Chapters Two and Three, but from the point of view of physicians and other health providers, supporting "choice" alone about euthanasia is insufficient. Any request for euthanasia must be set within the context of the doctor-patient relationship and the health care system. This context emphasizes the importance of acting for the patient's benefit.[5] We become concerned as a society, for example, when what we called "social euthanasia" takes place, when people cannot get access to health care, or when, as the data suggests, fiscal squeeze increases the death rate in hospitals from 6 to 10 percent.[6] Our revulsion to this situation stems, in large measure, from its failure to provide benefit to patients in need.

Other guidance is also required to cope with modern medical technology and the range of available interventions when we become seriously ill. A very sophisticated bond is created between the dying patient and the physician. This bond entails immensely complex medical and psychological interactions. Very few patients ask outright to die, even those who are very ill. (Hence the category of "voluntary" euthanasia (see item 5 in Tables 1–5, 8, in Chapters Two and Three) is a relatively unpopulated category.) Patients who are dying have a profound wish "to feel that they are still part of the world of the living, that they are listened to and appreciated for what they can offer."[7] Egilde Seravalli of the Beth Israel Medical Center in New York further notes in this regard:

> Whenever I have been with someone in the final stages of a fatal illness, I have found myself unable to communicate with the dying person as I did before. I have sensed a growing separation that led to uneasiness the moment I entered the room.[8]

One reason for this uneasiness in communication is that we often feel that the world of the dying should not be violated, that the dying person should initiate reaching out to us and not vice versa. This is a misguided notion of respect for autonomy, interpreted as the "right to be left alone."[9] The will to live typically continues almost to the moment of death. And the role of the physician in providing hope, not optimism necessarily,[10] but hope based on that will is a major reason why physicians should not perform active euthanasia as a general social policy.

This point needs elaboration before turning to the other sections of this chapter.

GUIDING PATIENTS THROUGH RISKY PROCEDURES

Medicine has made major technological advances. We usually think of such advances in terms of gleaming chrome whirrings, plastic tubing lacing a body, and bleeping graphs punctuating the silence in the background. But much of the machinery of modern medicine supports an even more impressive armamentarium of surgical, chemical, and biological interventions.

Among the surgical interventions for very ill patients are bypass surgery, transplants, shunts around cancerous tissue, laser brain tumor operations, making new stomachs out of intestines, realigning the spine, and placing feeding tubes directly into the stomach to support dying patients.

Among the chemical interventions are a wide variety of drugs to control both the electrical and plumbing malfunctions of the heart, chemotherapeutic agents that are essentially poisons to kill cells (unfortunately often good and bad alike), drugs that improve mental function, some that improve cardiac output, pills to control high blood pressure, insulin to control diabetes, and the chemicals used in kidney dialysis to replace the failed kidney function.

Among the biological interventions are proposed genetic manipulations like artificial proteins to bond with the HIV virus, artificially created antibiotics, and the newer forms of cancer therapy, especially Interleukin 2.

All of these technologies have their own side effects. For example, a patient with spreading intestinal cancer may be offered an experimental therapy that, coupled with radiation, will almost certainly shut down one kidney. Such a patient may protest that she does not want to live the rest of her life with just one kidney! Yet, she may have only months to live anyway. In addition, most people can live with only one kidney for the rest of a relatively normal life span.

Every time a new procedure or experimental therapy is announced, the range of choice available for patients expands. Thus, not only is the technological capacity of today's medicine increasing, so is the range and complexity of its ethics. In the past, the physician was expected to choose the best treatment for the patient and recommend it. Partly because of experimental therapies, this sort of traditional medical paternalism is fading. In its place, increasing emphasis is put on patient decision-making and autonomy. The physician "guides" the patient by holding out hope in these technical interventions.[11]

These two dramatic alterations in medicine — its technological capacity and ethical challenges — create special difficulties for patients faced with serious illness. Experimental therapy is, by definition, unproven. Not only that. The physician cannot recommend an experimental therapy over standard therapy on the basis that it will be better. It may turn out not to be. Rather the recommendation is generally based on a negative judgment — that previous therapy has not worked well. Further, the physician cannot tell patients what to do in this regard. They must grapple with their own values and courage. Aspects of this problem are examined under three subheadings: The psychology of choice, the bell-shaped curve, and quality of life judgments.

The psychology of choice. Choices are influenced by our values and our goals. Choosing among therapies starts as a no-win situation. Typically, patients face the following facts:

- They have a serious disease that will cause them to die.
- Standard therapies have not been successful in either stemming the disease or prolonging life.
- Experimental therapy is available.
- This therapy presents a greater risk than standard therapy.
- A choice between standard therapies and experimental therapies is possible.

But what is the choice? The choice is between probabilities. The probability is high that one will die soon. On the one hand, standard therapies offer little to increase the probability of survival. On the other hand, experimental therapies are untried and may or may not increase survival. In fact, they *may* lessen it. But there is some reason to believe (based on animal studies and/or rational analysis) that they may improve one's prospect.

Many patients reason that taking the best shot means increasing their risk at present by consenting to the study, on the chance that they may be able to live longer. Experimental therapy in some fields, such as cardiology, may not offer a greater chance at longevity, but rather a better quality of life during the time remaining. Therefore other patients may choose the risk of experimental therapy in favor of a greater quality of life. Still others decide that, in a no-win situation, they would rather not put themselves at greater risk. Rather than longevity, this group of patients seem to value present quality of life — to maintain the present course while they die. ("Better the devil you know.") Further still, others weigh heavily the value of helping medical research and future generations. These patients want to make the best out of a terrible situation. Nonetheless, this is usually a secondary consideration for most patients.

Of major importance in making choices is how they are framed. Here the patient's values run headlong into those of the physician. If the physician puts the possibilities for cure, remission, or improved function in the most positive light, then the patient will tend to choose in favor of the research protocol (some studies suggest 70 percent of persons will do this consistently). If exactly the same possibilities are cast in a negative light, about the same percentage of patients would choose not to participate.

Imagine being faced with a decision to accept an invitation to participate in a study to test the ability of a new drug to increase your heart's efficiency. You have a heart condition that does not let you get out of bed, because you become out of breath with the least exertion. If the physician encourages you to try this drug because you may regain more function, you would tend to accept it (even if the benefits are probably only an ability to shuffle toward the bathroom on your own, and then back into bed). By contrast, if your physician discourages you from entering the study on the grounds that the benefits are so miniscule compared to the risks, then you would tend not to accept the invitation.

The reasons for this phenomenon are not hard to find. Patients honor and respect their physicians. Their physicians' advice is very important. Many physicians "pre-judge" the clinical trial and would not offer it to their patients unless their expectation is that it will improve upon the standard of care.[12] The problem with experimental medicine is, of course, that the physicians' past experience and clinical hunches are not reliable guides in this context. The study is designed to compare therapies scientifically. A central feature of the study is that previous research using animals or laboratory results suggests one therapy may be better than another. But here is the rub. We do not know in advance that this is the case when used in human beings.

Past standard therapy for prostate cancer, for example, included castration (called orchiectomy) and radiotherapy (x-ray treatment to the prostate). A new study might compare this treatment with newer forms of chemotherapy on a randomized basis. No one knows for sure if the newer forms of treatment will be better than the old. The point of the research itself is precisely to answer this question. In addition, the patient consenting to the study will have a computer choose whether or not he is to be castrated (i.e., which arm of the study he is to be put on). Although the consent form might refer to this as a "simple medical procedure," most patients would view it otherwise. Recall, too, that the consent to be treated in the study is really a consent to participate in the comparison of therapies (which sometimes include a placebo). One does not know in advance (and often not during the trial itself) which treatment will be offered. One only knows that past therapies have been rather ineffective, i.e., one will die soon from the disease in any event. And yet the past therapy may be all one will receive.

This point is only slightly different when considering established medical procedures that carry substantial risk. In such cases, physicians can describe the risks and benefits but they cannot predict how a specific patient might react. If there is a 10 percent mortality rate for the procedure, that "percentage" only describes past experience with like patients. The population to which we might be compared in this risk might be favorable to us. We might be forty-five years old, and most of the others in the past were over sixty-five. Or it might be unfavorable. We might be forty-five and have significant heart disease and diabetes, while others in the risk population did not have these complications. The physician then must weigh all the variables and still make a suggestion about proceeding. His or her clinical hunches are only that. They cannot firmly predict how we will do after the procedure is finished.

These issues are illustrated in Case 38 ("Jenny's Heart Condition," p. 256). The most promising hope for survival that the surgeons have to offer is a temporizing operation that, at best, will keep Jenny alive for a year or two until she can be evaluated for a definitive corrective procedure. The immediate procedure has a high mortality rate, so it might kill her outright, and it will certainly produce severe debilitation. The alternative is a high probability that she will die within a few weeks or months of congestive heart failure — but without the expense and burden of the surgery. The fact that Jenny is confirmed by genotyping to have Down's syndrome affects the decision in at least two ways: (a) since Down's syndrome is frequently associated with multiple cardiac anomalies, it probably lessens the chance of success for the future corrective surgery; (b) rightly or wrongly, it will also undoubtedly influence everybody's thinking about the benefit-burden ratio of this expensive and otherwise burdensome procedure.

Further, experimental studies themselves often compare therapies by assigning one or the other intervention by lot to the patient. Case 49 ("Elizabeth Thomas's Leukemia," p. 272) illustrates such a protocol and some of the difficulties that it can raise. The Thomases have strong misgivings about radiotherapy, one of the treatments their child might be assigned in the randomization at one stage in the experimental procedure. Some of their misgivings are cleared up by extensive discussion that clarifies some misconceptions on their part. But even when they do agree to admit Elizabeth to the study, it is clear that they do so with considerable reluctance. They would clearly prefer to be given the nonradiation arm of the protocol directly, rather than take the chance of being assigned to the radiation arm. However, since all these treatments are experimental, they are available only under research protocols that incorporate randomization into their design.*

---

*Sometimes new unproven treatments can be used through an emergency procedure called compassionate use. Sometimes, also, one "arm" of the study represents a standard therapy that can be employed.

In many cases, neither the patient nor the physician knows which therapy is being given. This is called a "double-blind" study — both the patient and the physician are in the dark. It is the preferred method, according to the canons of scientific evidence, since it neutralizes bias and the placebo effect a physician might bring to the relationship with the patient — healing just by being expected to heal.[13] In some studies placebos may be given to measure this effect directly; although patients are generally informed that they *may* receive a placebo, neither they nor their physicians will know if they *have*. Thus, persons with proven hypertension might be asked to participate in a study to evaluate new medication to control this disease. First, they would be taken off their current medicine. Then they would be given the new "pill." Some persons would receive sugar pills (placebos) and their old medicine, now disguised to look like the new one. Others on the study would receive the new medicine. All pills would look alike.

Finally, many therapeutic studies use historical controls. This means that the current therapy is initially judged to have such promise compared to past (historical) therapy, that it will be studied against reports of progress in the past. It will not be compared to another treatment in the study itself. An example of this method was used in making a new drug, AZT, available to persons suffering from AIDS. The drug was initially being studied using an ineffective comparison (to eliminate bias), but it quickly became apparent that it did produce enough of a benefit (it does not cure the disease, but it does appear to slow its progression) that for reasons of compassion, it was made immediately available to all. Scientists have now discovered that the AIDS virus can become immune to AZT after awhile.[14]

Another example is Interleukin 2, mentioned earlier. A dramatic new method of attacking otherwise incurable cancer, IL-2 involves removing one's blood, tagging certain cells as killer cells, and then reintroducing the cells into the body. The risks include death itself, destruction of the kidneys, hepatitis (at some centers studying the therapy), and other major problems. Nonetheless, only patients who have cancers that are impervious to other forms of treatment are accepted for this study. Their progress is measured against historical experience with their disease using chemotherapy and radiation. In return for the increased risk, patients may possibly gain an average of four months of additional survival compared to past treatment.

A decision to accept risky treatment is *not* to be considered a choice of euthanasia. (It might be so regarded if the patient were motivated to agree to the treatment by the hope that the "worst case" outcome will come about, thus ending life relatively quickly; but this is rarely, if ever, the patient's reasoning for agreeing to participate in experimental treatment.) A choice *not* to try a risky experimental procedure can be regarded as a type of euthanasia. The patient indicates that he or she would prefer to allow the disease to progress toward its fatal outcome rather than undergo the risks, uncertainties, and hassles of the experimental procedure.

The bell-shaped curve. Given the risky business of advising patients in the presence of so much uncertainty, some physicians help patients decide by describing "the bell-shaped curve." This is a curve drawn on a graph of a population of patients' experience with survival from the disease in question. For example, a number only make it a few days or weeks. Gradually more patients live several months to one and one-half years. Then the number of patients who live longer falls off dramatically. Only one or two make it five years. This is the case with cancer of the pancreas, for example, no matter what doctors do to treat it. The shape of the graph showing the survival of a number of patients, the population curve, looks like a bell.

When a patient who is newly diagnosed to have pancreatic cancer asks how long she has to live, the physician can remain "value neutral" about the possibilities (and not unduly persuade the patient to accept or reject therapies) by saying that some persons die in a matter of weeks, more last from several months to a year, and a very small number survive beyond one year. The physician would point out that the patient may fall anywhere along that path.

Then possible treatments may be discussed, the results of which also represent bell-shaped curves. In the case of pancreatic cancer, interventions are rarely if ever successful. So the proper way of framing the discussion is to indicate to the patient that any experimental therapy carries its own risks of reduced survival and a high probability of only extremely modest gains. The gains might be represented as shifting the bell-shaped curve a few months forward toward longevity. That is to say, rather than inadvertently holding out firm hope that a patient will gain some survival by consenting to an experimental treatment plan, the physician would only promise a *possible* improvement within the bell-shaped curve. This is a sophisticated point. But it can be explained this way.

No one knows where the patient falls on the curve; no one knows whether that placement will be affected by a new experimental therapy. The patient may even die earlier than he or she would have had they not accepted the experimental therapy (as we noted in the discussion of "Jenny's Heart Condition," Case 38, p. 256) — i.e., although the curve as a whole might be shifted forward, one's position within it might change for the worse. Depending on the disease (fortunately not all are as intractable to treatment as pancreatic cancer), the percentage or probability of moving the curve forward is what should be discussed) instead of the (unanswerable) question of where one's own survival chances fall within the curves. Is the probability high or low that the experimental therapy will move the curve forward? How much of an advance can be realistically hoped for? This is another way of stating the overall risks of the procedure for all patients who have accepted it in the past.

This sort of reasoning can be highly frustrating to patient and physician alike. What we want to know, of course, is not how *most* people do, but how *we* will do. But this is knowledge that cannot be obtained by the methods of science. Through greater specificity in the comparison group (e.g., not all those with pancreatic cancer, but all those with our specific type and extent of cancer, in our age range, and with a medical history similar to ours), a more reliable probability figure can be derived. But the result of this will still be a bell-shaped curve — albeit one that is a subset of the global one — and nothing but clinical hunch can specify our placement on that curve. In making decisions about accepting treatment, therefore, we are forced to compare, not only trade-offs between values, but also probabilistic assessments of the value (and disvalue) outcomes.

Further, gathering the information to make these more specific assessments is itself a procedure with benefits and burdens of its own. In the case of Sharon Rose (Case 32, p. 245), the physicians debated whether to take the trouble to determine whether her lymphoma had returned. If their decision about whether to go along with the family's wish to forego blood transfusions would be unaffected by the outcome of these diagnostic tests, it does not seem to be worth the time and trouble to everyone concerned to obtain the more specific prognostic knowledge that would be obtained from them.

Quality of life. Most of the discussion about results in experimental medicine revolves around longevity. In a heart transplant program, the success rate is measured by the percentage of patients who have lived one year, five years, and more. The five-year survival rate is most often used as a benchmark for all experimental efforts, especially in cancer treatments. It is a convenient way to compare therapies. One asks: how many patients made it five years on this treatment?

Naturally, physicians, nurses, and other health professionals are concerned about the well-being and values of their patients. But these quality of life factors are less amenable to measurement than is longevity.[15] Yet quality of life is an important consideration for most patients. It is often left out of the discussion of chemotherapeutic trials. As noted earlier, however, it is a centerpiece of other research medicine, such as cardiology, when only an improved function rather than increased lifespan, can be offered.

Suppose one patient on a study lived five and one-half years, but during that time, entered the hospital a total of ten times, spending over half of his or her days during those years confined in a bed. During that time, the patient's family spent innumerable hours at the bedside in the hospital, and the economic burden on the family was dramatically increased. On the same study, another patient lived only two years and three months, but had to be hospitalized only twice. She died at home, and her family was not unduly stressed.

How can these two outcomes compare? In terms of longevity — the five-year survival rate — the second person fared much worse than the first. Yet in terms of family and economic values held by the patient, the second person might be considered to have had a more successful result from the therapy than the first. This cannot be measured scientifically. Nor can it be presented by discussion of probabilities of survival.

The use of survival probabilities is actually predicated on an assumed value that the patient, like all of us, wants to live as long as possible. But patients often possess a complex of values, only one of which is longevity. It is important to consider these other values in any dialogue with the physician about experimental therapy and risky medical procedures. The possibility of the treatment plan having a negative impact on other values besides longevity should be thoroughly discussed before proceeding. Thus, a patient with pancreatic cancer may quite realistically choose not to accept any further treatment and enter a hospice, so that he does not become a burden on his family or use expensive medical resources that might benefit others and/or so that he does not have to suffer the nausea, weakness, etc. that attend potent chemotherapies.[16] These considerations are his values, values other than longevity. Another patient with the same disease may choose an all-out assault on it, because she has just started a veterinary practice and wants to leave as much of a business as possible in place for the family after she dies.

Decisions about medical treatments are sometimes made in the midst of heart-rending uncertainty. The risks and benefits are not only difficult to predict with any degree of assurance, but they are most often measured in terms of longevity. Longevity may not always be the most important value when patients face almost certain death no matter what they choose to do. For example, in Case 16 (p. 226), Mr. Meissner decides that the effect of the chemotherapy in slowing the progression of his head and neck cancer is merely prolonging the agony. He requests active euthanasia, which his physician refuses to consider; but the physician does offer to discontinue chemotherapy, continue aggressive pain control measures, and to withhold antibiotics if infection develops.

Research medicine is an important part of modern health care. Patients should be encouraged to participate in this effort by minimizing their risks and by public support, so that the economic burdens can also be decreased. But in the end, a choice for a better or a longer life rests on the degree and nature of the risks the patient chooses. Patients weighing probabilities under the advice of their physicians need support and guidance about the impact of the various options on their most profound values.[17] More than their lives are at risk; and their lives may not be the most important values at risk.

DUTIES OF HEALTH CARE PROVIDERS TO THE DYING

The same sort of exquisitely individualized advice and direction discussed above for seriously ill patients who must face death as a possible outcome must also be part of the armamentarium of doctors who must help a patient die. As Wanzer et al. note:

> Nowhere is [continually adjusted care] more important than in the control of pain, fear and suffering. In the patient whose dying process is irreversible, the balance between minimizing pain and suffering and potentially hastening death should be struck clearly in favor of pain relief.[18]

The principle of "continually adjusted care," which is central to this article, is important. We will return later to the recommendation in this article regarding assisted suicide. For now, suffice it to say that assisted suicide is regarded as a supplement to the principle of continually adjusted care, and not an extension of it.

The problems encountered in caring for persons who are dying are excruciatingly difficult. Among them are issues of intervention, support, care, and compassion during a period of severe physical and emotional changes in the person (and family) being cared for. These latter changes include increasing weakness, resorting one's values, increased medicalization of one's life, and eventually, when dying, of saying good-bye and "letting go." Family support is also crucial, as we discussed in the previous chapter. At the same time, health care professionals must maintain and improve their own quality of care, both as persons and as professionals. The most important feature of this care (as we pointed out in the previous chapter) is their own counseling of the dying patient: "Physicians have an obligation," say Wanzer and his co-authors, "to consider timely discussions with patients about life-sustaining treatment and terminal care. Only a minority of physicians now do so consistently."[19]

Sorting through clinical ethical issues as they arise in a particular case can therefore be challenging, to say the least. This section focuses on the range of professional duties toward the dying patient. These are presented as an expansion of the principle of continually adjusted care.

Professional duties of health providers are discussed under problematic headings, rather than defining them in terms of standard obligations. In this way, the challenges of practice can be explored in a way that leads to new proposals for the ethics of caring for the dying. These proposals are offered at the end of a brief exposition of each problem area.

The technological imperative. Technology enters clinical dilemmas by its inducements to respect means over ends, and current interventions over a more complete assessment of the good of the patient to be served. This technologic imperative fosters a bias toward intervention that can wipe out the cherished values of patients, thus conflicting with the health professional's primary responsibility to serve the best interests of the patient.[20] Case 42 ("Grandma or the House," p. 262) illustrates the dilemma we face here. Physicians, responding one by one to the patient's multiple medical problems, initiated intervention upon intervention. The patient's family began to view this as a hopeless effort that the patient would not have wanted and that was conflicting with cherished values of the patient and her family.

The situation caused by this interventionist tendency is ironic indeed. The hope offered by increased technology is a sunny invitation to reflect on all the good things science and machines bring us. With respect to medical technology, improved quality of life and longevity are its primary goals. In its proper uses, it can serve these goals effectively. Yet as even popular culture such as television and movies demonstrate, medical technology applied blindly often leads to increased human suffering. It can also lead to dramatic conflicts with patients and families. Professional and clinical ethics can therefore be seen as a footnote to the larger problem in society of aiming our technology to good human ends.

The language surrounding the withholding and withdrawing of treatment is often fuzzy and confusing, language such as "merely prolonging dying," or talk of "extraordinary" or "heroic" measures. This language causes some laypersons and professionals alike to charge that withholding and withdrawing technology is tantamount to killing people on the basis of quality of life decisions.[21] When cardiopulmonary resuscitation technology beckons, a decision to withhold it becomes emotionally laden. It seems that we are withholding a chance for a "resurrection."[22] For dying persons, this often may not be the case. We may, instead, be avoiding what the title of one excellent short film terms a "Detour"[23] on the journey toward death.

The most plausible single basis on which to withhold or withdraw treatment is burdensomeness, the proportion between the disvalues of medically indicated treatment and its benefit to the patient in his or her particular circumstances.

A good example of apparent attempts to stop within particular circumstances is the data that Neu and Kjellstrand discovered in a retrospective review of deaths among long-term dialysis patients. In one Minneapolis hospital 704 of 1766 dialysis patients from 1966 to 1983 had died. By chart review, 155 had died because dialysis had been stopped, not because of other intervening lethal complications. Stopping dialysis is not "unusual"; overall one of eleven patients withdrew or were withdrawn from dialysis, one of six over sixty years of age.[24] This data is important for a decision a new patient faces in starting dialysis.

Other examples of medically based data abound. After a bone marrow transplant, among patients who are placed in an intensive care unit when they develop a pneumonia, none survived after being on the respirator for as long as four days.[25] Withdrawing the respirator after four days may therefore be medically indicated. Similarly, patients with an "overwhelming burn injury" (a mean total body surface area of 86 percent) need not be given fluid resuscitation since such treatment is futile.[26] It is important to note that the decisions not to initiate or to terminate treatment are, as Zawacki notes in an accompanying editorial, "judgments of value, not of biological fact." They ought to be the basis of a dialogue between physicians, patients, and families in which values are clarified.[27]

In this respect, several ethicists and physicians have called for a more comprehensive set of advance directives (as we have), since evidence exists that cardiopulmonary resuscitation and respiratory technology is too often applied without any hope of benefit.[28] Fidel Davila, for example, has developed "patient care categories" as a type of advance directive that controls not only CPR but other interventions as well.[29] Some have argued that physicians ought to have the right to withhold CPR for reasons of medical contraindication.[30] Since each case is different, the role of the physician in directing and advising the dying patient is underscored.

There is no obligation to employ treatment measures that are futile. This principle emerges from the data presented above. It also can be derived from the duty to benefit a patient and not to harm him. Medically contraindicated treatment would not benefit the dying patient, and would produce harms such as unduly prolonging a dying process or creating economic burdens for the patient and his family.

Another pattern of bewitchment by technology is the tendency to focus narrowly on one specific aspect of the patient's condition and the standard technological approaches to that, without examining it in the larger context of the patient's overall quality of life and life prospects.[31] For instance, the neurologist in Case 35 (p. 252) insists on reinstituting the respirator because this is the "normal and usual" technique for adjusting dosage of seizure medication. He does not stop to ask whether the seizures *in this case* are an isolated, curable medical problem or one more tragic complication in a terminal progression.

In any event, greater control of technology on the front end will lessen the pressure for active euthanasia later. This is the responsibility of physicians and patients — or family members of the dying patient, if the patient is now incompetent. The enthusiasm, optimism, and devotion to preserving life by physicians must be balanced by ethical concerns, dialogue with patient values, and a consideration of health care resources and burdens on the patient and family.[32]

Professional Axioms:

1. The patient should be treated as a whole person within the least threatening technological environment possible. Home care for terminally ill persons is preferable to hospital care in this respect, since it provides "an opportunity for quiet and privacy, dignity and family closeness."[33]

2. The primary guiding principle of therapy ought to be the patient's chosen values, not the latest technology or chemotherapy ("ceph du jour").[34] Naturally, it is a duty to try to convince the patient

about what might be his or her best interests. In the end, however, the patient's own choices and/or values must establish the basis for all decisions about treatment.

3. These values should be discussed frequently, both before and during treatment, in order to ascertain if the values themselves have changed order of priority in the patient's mind.[35] This axiom supports the Treatment Decision Status (TDS) protocols discussed briefly in the previous chapter.

4. The impact of any technique or intervention on the body of the patient is usually thoroughly discussed. But its impact on the patient's values often is not. This is also important.

5. No assumption should be made that technological intervention is equivalent to compassionate care (although it *can* be as an act within, as it were, a parenthesis of such care). The care of any patient involves personal extension of the caregiver to the patient.

6. Quality of life should be properly and scientifically assessed (and from the patient's point of view), so that patients and families can make informed judgments about therapies and their side effects.

7. Data about longevity often precipitates quality of life parameters. Patients should be told this when making decisions about their care.

8. There is no need to offer useless treatment.

Life-prolonging decisions. The paradigm goal of therapy is to eradicate the disease.[36] There are no ethical problems with such a goal, unless the goal is unattainable, as it is in so many cases. Once that is the case, other values ought to come into play in the relationship of healer and patient.[37] One cannot assume that the patient automatically endorses secondary goals of palliation and comfort care. Most patients affirm these secondary goals, but they should be spelled out in detail, with side effects clearly articulated. This is the point of our slight disagreement with the AMA Council on Ethical and Judicial Affairs, as explained in note 1.

All therapy ought to be patient-driven and patient-derived. This means that the goals of therapy are derived from the particular physical and mental status of unique individuals, and they should be adjusted on the basis of the values of those patients. Experienced health professionals are aware of the importance of patient values in deciding to prolong life. This is particularly true of elderly patients.

Treatment decisions therefore must take into account the quality of life the patient may have, the impact of the intervention on that quality, and the physical and mental well-being of the patient. Most importantly, the patient's value system should be honored. Duties that derive from these reflections are the following.

Professional Axioms:

1. The autonomy of the patient may lead the patient to conclusions at odds with considered medical advice.[38] The health professional should support these conclusions as far as his or her own conscience allows.[39]

2. As far as possible, decisions to prolong life should also be respected, within the bounds of economic justice.[40]

3. Family reports and values can be used to construct a value history of the patient (as noted in Chapter Four) so that the method of making decisions in the past can function, by substituted judgment, to guide decisions in the present for patients who become incompetent during treatment.[41]

4. As patients become more and more dependent upon health care providers during their illness, the responsibility to respect their values does not diminish. Indeed, it might be argued that it increases because, as their vulnerability increases, not to respect them does double damage to their dignity.[42] (a) The first part of the damage is that of stripping persons of their values. Since values are the fundamental basis of decisions made throughout life, not to respect their wishes at this point in their lives is tantamount to denying validity to their life.[43] (b) The second part of the damage occurs to the spiritual struggle for maintaining one's self-respect. Indifference to what matters to the patient leads to an internal destruction of the courage and determination needed to continue to make one's own decisions about one's life.[44]

5. Life prolongation decisions should always be discussed in terms of the statistical curve, as presented above (p. 126). A decision to accept some course of technical or chemotherapeutic intervention should be presented as a possibility of moving one's position on a statistical curve in either a favorable or unfavorable direction.[45] The intervention should never be presented solely as a possible benefit to the patient. Experience shows that it may not be rewarding at all.

6. Sometimes patients refuse to make out a living will, or designate any action that might withhold or withdraw treatment. Insofar as medical treatment continues, it should do so on the basis of medical indications. Patients should be warned, however, that not to decide is to decide:

Not to make a living will, designate a surrogate decision maker, or withdraw artificial intervention systems is to decide to abdicate responsibility.

It is to relegate the burden of decision making to someone (physician, hospital, committee, court) far less qualified to make it, and refuse to accept our ability and responsibility... to share in the rational determination of our destiny.[46]

These patients should be advised that, as we pointed out in the previous chapter, advance directives can be employed to communicate the wish to prolong life as well as desires to limit life-sustaining treatment.

The right to die. There is no firmly established right to die either discovered in the Constitution by courts or created through legislation. But there is a constitutional right to privacy, which has traditionally been regarded as establishing the freedom of each individual to decide for himself or herself what interventions to approve or disapprove. Beginning as early as 1914 with the case against New York Hospitals, and Chief Justice Cardozo's famous dictum that "every human being of adult years and sound mind has a right to determine what shall be done with his own body,"[47] the right of consent (and refusal) has been derived from the Constitution itself and from the common law right of self-determination.

Recently, in a set of dramatic court cases, most of them having to do with the provision of food and water for persons in comatose or related incompetent states, this right has been carved out against the equally important duty of health professionals to preserve life. Recall that in the case of Karen Ann Quinlan (Case 20, p. 230), the Supreme Court of New Jersey determined that, given the patient's poor prognosis, the state's interest (and, by derivation, the health professional's interest) in preserving life must yield to the patient's right of self-determination.[48] Acting contrary to her own wishes, as these were expressed by her parents (her surrogate decision makers), was seen as an unlawful bodily invasion.

In the case of Claire Conroy (Case 50, p. 274), an elderly woman locked in a fetal position in a nursing home and suffering from advanced diabetes and senility, the New Jersey Supreme Court again stated firmly that persons who become incompetent do not by that fact lose their right to determine their own treatment. A surrogate expresses their wishes instead, if there is sufficient indication as to what those would have been. In Ms. Conroy's case, her nephew wanted to convince the court that she would not have wanted a nasogastric feeding tube. He was not entirely successful in this regard. The court indicated some doubt that they would have ruled to withdraw feeding in Ms. Conroy's case. Since she died prior to the decision, they did not rule on the specific case but merely set out guidelines for making such a decision in future cases of this type.[49]

By no means is the principle of self-determination about medical treatment confined to the state of New Jersey. The California Supreme Court has upheld a similar view in the case of Bartling[50] and the case of Bouvia (Case 51, p. 275).[51]

When the wishes of the patient cannot be reliably ascertained (using substituted judgment supported by clear and convincing evidence, the test which the Conroy court called the "subjective test"[52] and which we, in Chapter Three, called "presumed voluntary" euthanasia), the Conroy court suggested two alternative bases upon which decisions can be made for incompetent patients. The second of these tests is the "limited objective test." This test is a combination of presumed wishes of the patient, as established by the surrogate and health providers on the basis of a lower standard of evidence than is required in the subjective test, and a judgment of proportionality of the proposed treatment or intervention and its impact on the patient:

> when there is some trustworthy evidence that the patient would have refused the treatment and the decision-maker is satisfied that it is clear that the burdens of the patient's continued life with the treatment outweigh the benefits of that life for him.[53]

The third test, the "pure objective test," is a form of medical indications policy that applies when there is no trustworthy evidence as to what the patient would have wanted. According to this test, the patient must receive treatment unless the treatment is disproportionate to the outcome and its use constitutes cruelty by prolonging pain and suffering:

> The net burdens of the patient's life should clearly and markedly outweigh the benefits that the patient derives from life. Further, the recurring, unavoidable and severe pain of the patient's life with treatment should be such that the effect of administering life-sustaining treatment would be inhumane.[54]

The right to die should therefore be seen, in the legal context, as a convenient shorthand phrase for the right of privacy and self-determination as applied by dying patients to their current treatment decisions. Patients who have expressed preferences for a DNR order, or have asked not to be a burden on others during the dying process, or have asked not to be kept alive on machines, are all articulating a right to privacy, a right to have their wishes respected. They do not want their bodies invaded by medical technologies they have foresworn. It is extremely important not to strip such persons of their most profound values as they die in our presence.[55]

Over one hundred court cases over the past thirteen years have tested the right of privacy and self-determination with respect to the withholding or withdrawal of care, including medically delivered fluids and nutrition (for selected examples, see Appendix III.) With overwhelming frequency, these courts have affirmed the right of families and surrogates to make the decision.[56] With over 10,000 persons in hospitals and nursing homes in the United States suffering from persistent vegetative states, why must families have to go to court to get treatment removed that keeps persons in death-deferred states? Why have physicians and health administrators been unwilling to accept the responsibility given them by the courts and public opinion polls?

Some clearly defined duties arise from these considerations:

Professional Axioms:

1. Decisions that hasten death are legally and morally acceptable in certain situations.

2. Patients should determine their own treatment, regardless of the condition of their mind or body: "The voluntary choice of a competent and informed patient should determine whether or not life-sustaining therapy will be undertaken."[57]

3. When there is a conflict between the patient and health care providers, the patient's autonomy, coupled with the patient's own interpretation of his or her best interests, takes precedence over the health providers' beneficence (desire to act in the patient's best interests).[58]

4. When the patient becomes incompetent, a surrogate (usually a family member) should make decisions for the patient. These decisions should be based on substituted judgment, that is, on what preferences the patient possessed in the past, now applied to the matters at hand.[59] As noted, the Conroy court called this the "subjective test." Lately it has been suggested that substituted judgment rules be dropped in favor of a presumption, unless otherwise proved, that the family may make decisions for the incompetent patient. This would constitute a legal initiative that would recognize families as appropriate decision-makers without the burden of proving what, if any, wishes of the patient would govern treatment in the absence of explicit instruments like the living will or other advance directives.[60] In effect, legislation supporting this view would constitute "presumptive advance durable power of attorney" by assigning such power to family members ahead of time. This approach

is consonant with the view of the family we set out in Chapter Four.

5. If a conflict develops between the surrogate and the managing health care provider about the wishes of the patient or what might be in the patient's best interests, all health providers, including nurses, should be present and consulted at clinical care conferences or clinical ethics consultations, so that a consensus can be reached if at all possible. However, if the disagreement persists despite all such efforts to resolve it, health providers have a duty to act in the best interests of the patient in the presence of doubt about the surrogate's competence and/or reliability.[61]

6. If this conflict cannot be resolved, and the appeal to the hospital ethics committee has already taken place, then appeal to the court system for a guardian is inevitable. If this course is chosen, the guardian, too, must act in the best interests of the patient.[62] At this point, the only duty of health providers must be to follow the decisions made by a duly appointed guardian, unless these clearly violate the law.

7. The judgment of proportionality between treatment and outcome, necessary to the limited and pure objective tests suggested by the Conroy court, should include detailed consultation with the entire caregiver staff. As we noted in Chapter Two, the judgment of proportionality, the benefits/burdens calculus, is left deliberately vague, so that each individual case must be judged on its own merits. To draw the conclusion about disproportionality between intervention and outcome, a judgment of balance based on previous experience and the concrete experience with this particular patient is required. The patient's current condition and previous responses are of particular importance in reaching this sophisticated judgment. Nurses and other health professionals can offer essential data for such a decision by the physician and patient and/or family.

8. The primary duty for "ensuring that morally justified processes of decision-making are followed" lies with physicians.[63] As we have argued, this duty also includes personal involvement with the dying person and explicit discussion of that person's values as far as possible in connection with advance directives. Physicians should never find themselves in the bind of continuing medically contraindicated care to dying patients.

Treatment modalities. As we saw in Chapter Three, not all forms of treatment are created equal. These distinctions are upheld in the thinking of physicians and other health care professionals. Jonsen, Siegler, and Winslade describe the stages by which physicians tend to withdraw or withhold aggressive therapeutic efforts. These might be made into a normative progression of steps, rather than just descriptive ones. To them we will add double-effect euthanasia and (in the following section) assisted suicide:

1. The withdrawal of experimental therapy, such as extracorporeal membrane oxygenator or cardiac assist balloon pump.

2. The DNR decision, the decision not to perform CPR.

3. The discontinuation of breathing support, such as a respirator.

4. The discontinuation of agents that artificially maintain blood pressure and cardiac output.

5. The decision not to intervene in the face of infections with antibiotic treatment.

6. The decision to discontinue unusual forms of alimentation, such as tube feeding or parenteral hyperalimentation.

7. The decision to reduce fluids to a maintenance or even, at times, a below-maintenance level.[64]

All of the above steps qualify as passive euthanasia, the withholding or withdrawing of treatment to allow an underlying disease to take its course. The next step is more active, but may still be ethically defended in certain situations.

8. The decision to control pain even if the medication given with this intention will hasten death or even cause it. Although one may intend death in this action (as the final relief of suffering), one does not intend to cause that death. It is an accompanying effect of action aimed at relief of pain.

Although it may appear to be splitting hairs to draw this distinction, it is nonetheless important for both patients and physicians to make clear that physicians never directly kill their patients.

It is difficult to classify the action of injecting morphine before removing a patient from the respirator "to control the discomfort of trying to breathe" (see Case 52, p. 276) or, even more thorny, injecting curare to prevent the discomfort by suppressing the attempt itself. Could this be interpreted as an extension of double-effect euthanasia, since the direct goal is not death itself? It seems clear that injecting potassium chloride (as in Case 3, p. 211) could *not* be brought under this classification. This latter seems clearly to be active euthanasia.

Professional Axioms:

1. When patients suffer terminal, irreversible illness, the duty to prolong life is overridden by a duty not to prolong dying and/or a duty to relieve suffering.[65]

2. This duty requires attention to the patient's explicit wishes about all interventions, not just the major ones like CPR.[66]

3. Comfort care should have pain control as its major objective, although value priorities of the patient should determine how aggressively this is carried out.

4. Controlling pain is a final duty we have to the dying patient, even if it means that we also kill the patient in our efforts.[67] As we have seen, this is called double-effect euthanasia. If the physician's intent is to relieve suffering with a morphine injection, it is justified.[68]

5. In general, one ought to prefer a step that is numerically lower on the progression cited in this section to one that is numerically higher.

Assisted suicide and euthanasia. It is very difficult for health professionals to acquiesce in decisions that they think are fundamentally and morally wrong.[69] Nurses are sometimes portrayed as having serious reservations about withdrawing or withholding food and water from senile and dying patients, once the doctor and family decide on this course of action. But many patients, physicians, and health administrators share such reservations.

The entire question of assisting at the "suicide" and "euthanasia" of some patients is even more telling. We asked in the introduction to this chapter whether the moral obligation to reduce pain and suffering developed in Chapters Two and Three has sufficient weight to impel those who object in conscience. Some of the conflict can be cleared up through a proper understanding of terminology. All of it is emotionally loaded. It is imperative to use it correctly. Even then, ethical problems persist.

A next step along the progression initiated in the previous section might be:

9. The decision to assist in a suicide. Here the distinction between involuntary and voluntary assisted suicide is important, where the voluntariness in question is, not that of the patient, but that of the health professional.

The term "assisted suicide" has entered the bioethics catalogue through the Elizabeth Bouvia case in California (Case 51, p. 275). Bouvia suffered from multiple sclerosis and severe arthritis that required pain control. She could not take care of even her most elemental needs. She entered a hospital in order to starve herself to death while still maintaining her pain control. The public and professional debate about her care and the proper decisions was synopsized in the term "assisted suicide." To help Bouvia die was seen by health professionals as assisting in her suicide attempt, even though the Appeals Court in California mandated that her physicians and the second hospital she entered were required to do just that. The physicians and doctors felt that they were being coerced to assist in Bouvia's suicide. Further they judged that her underlying disease was not in a terminal phase.

But what about voluntary assisted suicide in the form of a request by a patient in a terminal and painful condition for sufficient medication to take her own life? What should a physician do? Ten of the twelve authors of the Wanzer article cited earlier argue that it may not be immoral for physicians to help such persons die:

> all but two of us (J.V.E. and E.H.C.) believe that it is not immoral for a physician to assist in the rational suicide of a terminally ill person.[70]

The co-authors of this article note that assisted suicide does not follow from the principle of flexible care for the dying they had advocated, and suggest further "wide and open discussion."[71]

We suggest that all the normative withholding steps should be taken before any physician entertains the request for assisted suicide. The guidelines developed by Dutch physicians for implementing active euthanasia require that all other efforts have failed to control pain and suffering.[72] Such occasions are extremely rare. Furthermore, we would find it difficult to conceive of a situation in which double-effect euthanasia, a step to take prior to assisted suicide, had failed.

Perhaps the best context in which to consider assisted suicide is when a patient is not hospitalized where double-effect euthanasia can be implemented. In this regard, then, assisted suicide might possibly be justified as a kind of double-effect euthanasia in which the physician does not directly administer the pain control, but prescribes a sufficient amount to be lethal if taken with the intent still to control pain. In a letter to the editor of the *American College of Surgeons Bulletin*, responding to an article by one of us (D.C.T.), George Crile of the Cleveland Clinic suggests, "When a physician prescribes a medication that is intended, in overdose, to provide an 'assisted suicide,' he should *not* say, 'If things get too bad, take all of this at once.' Instead he should say, 'This medicine is toxic; if you take all of it at once you will surely die.'"[73] In this way, by describing but not necessarily judging the action, the physician protects the intent to control pain while offering a message of compassion.

By contrast to these last two steps, and to recap, passive euthanasia is the provision of a kind death through permitting an underlying terminal process to take its course. Thus, one can withhold or withdraw treatment that might prolong life, but that life is terminal. Thus one is actually only prolonging the dying process. Withholding or withdrawing is intentional, of course, as we explored in Chapters Two and Three, but the intent is to let a disease continue. As the President's Commission noted, "The mere difference between acts and omissions never by itself determines what is morally acceptable. Acceptability turns on other morally significant considerations."[74]

Although some ethicists see no moral difference between inaction and active euthanasia, there is a difference in the sense that one does not directly kill the patient through a new intervention, as in active euthanasia, and the intent is not to kill but to let a person die from an underlying disease. These are the types of other morally significant features referred to by the President's Commission. Our discussion in Chapter Three pointed this out, with the caution about not making too much out of the distinction between active and passive euthanasia. However, passive euthanasia permits health professionals to affirm their commitment not to kill patients, but to provide relief from suffering.[75] As a Swiss physician indicted for murder for withholding fluids and nutrition from elderly and dying patients said: "The great interest in letting people die naturally is an uprising of plain common sense. I think in the end passive euthanasia will be victorious."[76]

Professional Axioms:

1. At present there is no legal duty to provide active euthanasia, although we have argued that in some very specific circumstances, there may be a moral duty to do so. However, the next step in the national debate about active euthanasia might be the development of a right of patients not to suffer unduly during the dying process. Health professionals should be involved in this national discussion. We leave this discussion for our final chapter, and turn now to the primary value of the doctor-patient interaction.

THE HEALING TASK

The most important value in treating patients is healing. It is for this reason that patients come to doctors, and that doctors extend their expertise to patients.

Quite often, healing involves a cure. But during the dying process this no longer becomes possible. The sheer impossibility of a cure creates enormous pressures on those who misidentify their health care vocation with curing patients, rather than healing them. Much of the reason for inappropriately applied technology to the dying stems from this misidentification of the role of the health professional. Recall our discussion at the start of this chapter about appropriate goals of medicine.

But what is healing? Healing is fundamentally a personal extension of one human being to another. It is a capacity that is shared. The dying person may heal the healer as much as the healer heals the dying person. Another way of putting this is that the dying become part of a healing community. We noted the importance of family and hospice in this regard in the previous chapter.

We have and will use the phrase "personal extension" to describe how health professionals must get involved in the lives of those they care for, without losing their objectivity. What does this phrase mean? It can be best described by using the words of Arthur Kleinman, M.D., a medical anthropologist, speaking about approaching patients with chronic illness:

> When you are with a sick person in a crisis, a window is opened, figuratively. That window gives a physician a view not only of the crisis, but of the person's life. In the past, we [medicine] have closed the window as rapidly as we fixed the crisis. But there's lots of important information and understanding that can come by looking carefully, diligently, through that window over a long period of time that can help in the care of the chronically ill patient.[77]

Caring for patients in crisis, therefore, to use Kleinman's word again, "imbeds" physicians in the lives of patients. This makes medicine a moral enterprise, since the physicians become engaged with the lives and values, the choices and abhorrences of individuals, who like themselves, share in a fundamental human nature.[78]

Andrew Weil, M.D., has devoted much of his life to a scholarly examination of alternative modes of healing, especially of drugs. His first book, *The Natural Mind*, explored the role drugs play among traditional groups in their vision of healing and higher consciousness.[79] He is often accused of being soft on drugs.[80] Part of the controversy lies in his exploration of nontraditional views of healing. In his work *Health and Healing*, he examines a variety of healing systems. Common to them all, he holds, and in fact what enables each to work for individual patients, is belief. The patient and the healer must both believe in the system proposed. The practitioner's successful experience with a treatment procedure ignites a belief in the patient that sets into motion that patient's own healing response. This parallels the way drugs "ignite" our nervous system. The entire process of healing triggers the nervous system in ways that are still not fully understood.[81]

The interaction just described must take place within a communal context as well: "A feeling of connectedness is an important aspect of well-being. People who don't have that sense tend to feel much more lonely and despairing."[82]

Weil is Harvard-trained. He reserves his most scathing critiques for allopathic, interventionist, and expensive health care. A similar suggestion for healing has recently been proposed by a Yale surgeon, Bernie Siegel, M.D., who invites his patients to visualize their white blood cells as killer cells out to attack their cancer or, if they find the military imagery uncomfortable, to substitute some alternative picture.[83] And Norman Cousins, in a book written from his own experience, suggested that humor itself can help heal, something that has recently been confirmed in studies of therapies in Sweden.[84] Belly-laughs may assist just like chemotherapy.

Even if healing is a value, it cannot be used to override patient requests not to prolong life. The reason is that a patient has a right to life, but can waive that right and turn it over to others for a sufficient reason (see Chapter Two, p. 20). Thus the patient makes a judgment about his or her own quality of life. Even if a physician were to properly identify the healing task with a personal engagement with the patient, the physician must stand ready to bracket out his or her own judgments about the patient's quality of life as an essential feature of healing. It sounds ironic. But it is the case that to heal sometimes means to back off and allow an individual, however wrongheadedly, to make her own decision. Doing nothing can be a duty too.[85] It is especially difficult for professionals dedicated to the value of human life to back off in this way and let someone die. This very disengagement may be the voice of love and healing, however. Put another way, it is the patient who decides what constitutes a benefit. As Fenella Rouse puts it: "The patient is permitted to ask, 'What do I want?' and the question for physicians is 'What does this patient want, regardless of what others, even a majority, would choose?' "[86]

Recall our discussion in Chapter Two on the patient's own judgment of his or her quality of life (see p. 20). All such judgments occur in a context of extremely low probability for prolonging life. The patient must accept "second best," a short time of decent quality of life in exchange for the risk of an even earlier death. Physicians, meanwhile, try to "hold out hope" within the hopeless context.[87] They do this by offering a balance of medically indicated treatments gauged against the patient's quality of life.

Some of the strategies physicians use to "hold out hope" are interesting. One, Mark Siegler calls "the hanging of crepe." This approach, similar to that of Pascal's wager, is to predict the worst possible scenario, the bleakest, most pessimistic prediction of the patient's outcome to lessen the family's grief when the end does come. This is a "no-lose" strategy that also seems to comfort the caregiver. In the end, though, physician-patient-family communication requires greater compassion and less candor. Though this strategy may appear at the outset to be truth-telling in its most extreme form, it is actually an attempt to manipulate the feelings of the patient and family about outcomes. Siegler favors prognostication instead, since it adheres more closely to the truth.[88]

Butheil, Bursztajn, and Brodsky counsel identifying with the patient's and family's fantasies about getting better, and then gradually convey the truth that they are indeed fantasies, through language such as "I wish it were possible. ... " This language also conveys an alliance with the patient, since the physician then shows empathy with the dreams of the patient and family at the same time he or she demonstrates leadership in facing the reality that it isn't going to be so. Capping the bond created can be explicit language promising continuing partnership in the relationship even if the outcome is bad in statements such as "I'll be with you every step of the way."[89] This kind of reassurance does not create false promises as long as the personal engagement of which we spoke is still present, nor does it try to manipulate the natural processes of grief, despair, and mourning that occur when loved ones pass on.

Reassurance is an essential part of that personal extension. As Neil Kessel observes, it is restorative. It tells the patient that he or she can bear whatever comes with the help of the physician. It is the contract between them. It creates fortitude in both the doctor and the patient.[90] Although doctors are taught to be detached and objective, this stance can be a retreat that isolates them from the realities of human encounter that are essential to the relationship to the dying.[91] It parallels, and may even contribute to, the identification of caring with technological and other objective interventions. It may even contribute to the notion that it is compassionate to inject patients rather than take the more difficult course of entering their pain and suffering and trying to heal them.

WHY DOCTORS SHOULD NOT PERFORM
ACTIVE EUTHANASIA

About 25 percent of doctors surveyed in one questionnaire in California said they would support voluntary active euthanasia if it were legalized. And yet the concerns of many physicians that we avoid any semblance of Nazi atrocities is legitimate, particularly if society becomes more economically distressed than it is today.

There are at least seven distinct positions doctors and ethicists take regarding physician-assisted deaths, ranging from the most direct to the least. They are worth examining here and summarize our arguments in this chapter:

Direct, public, even involuntary: Physicians ought to assist in bringing about a good death for persons who cannot make decisions for themselves, or for those who have, for one reason or another, been declared enemies of society, or have been condemned to death. This is the position of those who support physicians assisting at deaths by lethal injection for condemned murderers (at least those who are reluctant to die) in states like Texas or Illinois,[92] or who support the "patient advocate" role to such an extent that they would argue that physicians have a duty to kill people who are suffering and can no longer do anything about their condition. Recall the prosecution of Dr. Herman Sander in the early 1950s. He was accused of injecting one of his dying patients with a dose of air. The murder trial was sensational. He was acquitted by the jury on the grounds that the patient was already dead when he injected her. On behalf of the Euthanasia Society in America, Dr. Charles Francis Potter stated shortly after the trial: "We maintain that what is morally right should be made legally right or else all respect for law will be gone. It would seem that the greatest single factor acting against legalized euthanasia may be the willingness of many doctors to act compassionately on their own."[93] Judging from the California survey noted above, Dr. Potter was right. Note that Dr. Sander allegedly engaged in involuntary euthanasia.

We will examine the dangers of this position in the last section of the next chapter. For now, however, consider how a physician of the last century argued that a physician has a duty to take the life of incompetent persons. Adolph Jost put it in the context of a duty to society and state as well:

In the case of mental patients, this right (personal decision) reverts back to the state, and the diagnosis "incurability" is sufficient in itself to justify a mercy killing.[94]

Direct, public, but voluntary only: Physicians ought to bear the responsibility of putting people out of their misery. The health care system creates many problems with advanced disease because of prior interventions. **The patient can turn to no one else in society who bears the responsibility and authority of dispensing lethal drugs. Guidelines should be developed and legalized.** This is the position of the Hemlock Society and a number of physicians.

Direct and private: Physicians ought to bear the responsibility of putting people out of their misery, but this ought to be done only after all other possibilities have been exhausted. Then a private decision should be made between the doctor and the competent patient. **This decision will vary from patient to patient. No external, governmental, or legislative intervention is required.** This is what is requested by the patient in Case 16 ("Mr. Meissner's Request," p. 226). This is also the position favored by many in the Netherlands. Officially, it is illegal to induce death. But most physicians have not been prosecuted for inducing death for compassionate reasons. The lack of prosecution creates ambiguities in the law and in public policy that probably cannot be tolerated in this country. But physician-friends confide in us that several times during their practice they have induced death through injections in order to bring the relief to patients that only death could provide. In this decision, the goal was to induce death in order to relieve pain, not the opposite (which would have been double-effect euthanasia), to relieve pain without directly intending the death accompanying this relief.

The fact that this sort of action brings considerable legal jeopardy in the United States is seen by some as healthy — it ensures that such an action will be undertaken only in cases in which the physician would be willing to defend her or his actions before a jury. Others, of course, deplore this "chilling" effect.

Modified direct: Physicians should bring about death, but not through direct lethal injections. Patients do not really understand the consequences of some of the high technology interventions that are brought to bear on their care. While not supporting active euthanasia, the president of Johns Hopkins Hospital, Robert Heyssel, M.D., was quoted in regard to this arrogance:

I think there's a good deal of arrogance in modern medicine, perhaps at the expense of people. I really do wonder whether Barney Clark or

Schroeder or Hayden fully understood what the artificial heart would mean to them.[95]

Those who hold this position only wonder out loud whether or not physicians should be able to, in Kenneth Vaux's words, "open the door on death," as much as they can now, with their technology, close that door:

The fact that we can do so many things to sustain living or prolong dying, as the case may be, leads many in our society to dread ending their life in a technology-driven hospital. It also leads a large percentage of citizens to gradually accept not only passive euthanasia by allowing the withholding of essentials like food and water but also to entertain the taboo possibility of taking active initiatives to end terminal suffering.[96]

Indirect: Physicians can never directly induce death, nor can any individual morally intend the death of another. However, one can will and act on that will to reduce the pain and suffering of persons to such an extent that death follows (double-effect euthanasia), or withdraw inappropriate care. We have examined this view in some detail already.

Physician as friend. This position complements some of the above-named positions. We will develop it below. In brief, this position holds that even if active, direct euthanasia should become a legal reality in the United States and elsewhere, physicians themselves should not be the ones authorized to carry out the deaths through direct interventions. The position is based on the healing task of physicians and the importance to all patients, not just the dying patient, of the doctor-patient relationship.[97]

A stronger version of this position has been enunciated by Leon Kass, M.D., who notes a primary impediment within the very doctor-patient relationship to any use of active euthanasia, whether or not it may be legalized.[98] This position will figure in an important argument in the final chapter, and will not be further discussed here.

Drs. Gaylin, Kass, Siegler, and Pellegrino are concerned that if physicians were to "take matters into their own hands" and kill patients, not only is this a moral evil, but physicians will lose forever their public trust. Hence no physician should ever use active, direct euthanasia.[99]

We argue on the basis of friendship with the patient that doctors should not kill patients. The notion that doctors should not perform euthanasia only because of the way it would impact negatively on the public's perception of physicians is weak. It is not the public's perception, but rather inherent moral principles that are important in resolving this problem.

Physicians should not directly take the lives of their patients, though they should help them in the many other ways discussed above. The reason we object to physicians killing their patients goes beyond professional codes and legal restraints. In all other forms of sanctioned (as opposed to violent and emotional) killing, the person to be killed is made into an enemy or is said, as in capital punishment, to have lost his or her "innocence." Even then, training people like soldiers and executioners to kill takes real work. When soldiers come upon one another as persons rather than as enemies (finding a young "enemy" eating K-rations in a foxhole, for example), they have tremendous difficulty killing each other. Even injecting convicted criminals requires a great deal of impersonality — one pushes several of a number of buttons in a box alongside another person, in a room hidden behind the victim. One does not see the convict at all.[100]

A physician thinking of active euthanasia is faced with a patient who is not an "enemy" or a "criminal," but a friend, who has trusted him or her. If it is difficult even to kill enemies and criminals, how much more difficult to kill someone who has trusted in you? There is no social construct available for this action. Research suggests that physicians who have actively euthanized patients have found it repulsive in just this sense. This is confirmed by an interview with Dr. Borst-Eilers of the Netherlands, who said: "The few doctors I know who have done euthanasia tell me they were miserable for months afterwards. Our doctors are not going to go around killing too easily."[101] Yet, as Weinfeld notes, the meaning of euthanasia is: "Someone wishing to kill you normally is your enemy; anyone preventing it is your friend. However, there are situations when the opposite is true: he who wishes to kill you is your most precious friend, and anyone preventing it is your worst enemy."[102]

CONCLUSION

"The care of the dying is an art.... The concept of a good death does not mean simply the withholding of technological treatments that serve only to prolong the act of dying. It also requires the art of deliberately creating a medical environment that allows a peaceful death," say Wanzer and his co-authors.[103] All medical treatment should be guided by patient values. These values can be ascertained either through dialogue about treatment modalities, interventions, and their consequences, or through the expressed wishes of patients or their surrogates. A balance should be struck between always following patient wishes and traditional health care paternalism, in which patients had little or no say over their treatment. The best way to strike this balance is through advance directives and intensive dialogue with the patient or surrogates about the patient's values throughout the course of treatment. The care of the dying patient in this way can become a truly fiduciary responsibility. Health care providers can salvage their traditional obligation to preserve life through a commitment to the preservation of the meaning of the patient's life.

Conflicts about treatment are difficult to resolve. But mechanisms are being developed for making ethical decisions. The rise of hospital ethics committees is one such mechanism, whose impact on physician decision-making is just now being explored.[104] Ethics committees can carefully chart relationships between physicians, nurses, patients, and families. They then can construct workable models for ethical decision-making in the clinical setting.

Institutions should support mechanisms like this by guaranteeing the protection of the conscience of all individuals caring for patients, with the right to withdraw without prejudice to one's job, and without abandoning the patient, as an essential feature of such policies.

Earlier the importance of reaching a consensus was stressed. This is difficult to accomplish in individual cases, but not impossible. The best way to approach ethical quandaries as presented in cases is through a process of moral reasoning that does not require that all participants think alike about ethical theory. All that is required is that, in working through the decision, the participants, the health providers, and in most cases, the family, work through each step so that they can more clearly ascertain exactly where they might disagree, if at all. It is our experience that often disagreements vanish under the discipline of more rigorous thinking about the decision that an ethical workup offers.[105]

NOTES

1. The Council on Ethical and Judicial Affairs of the American Medical Association acknowledges a two-value goal: "The social commitment of the physician is to sustain life and relieve suffering" (*Current Opinions — 1986*, § 2.18). As we argue below, we would contend that this is not broad enough.

2. James Walter, "The Meaning and Validity of Quality of Life Judgments in Contemporary Roman Catholic Medical Ethics," *Louvain Studies* 13 (Fall 1988).

3. Walter, "Quality of Life," p. 4 in ms. Author's emphasis.

4. Eugene Kennedy, "It's Over, George: 'Debbie' Is Too Dubious to Support Serious Debate," *Chicago Tribune*, February 19, 1988, sec. 1, 17. The "George" referred to in the title is the editor of the *Journal of the American Medical Association*, George Lundberg, M.D., with whom one of the authors (D.C.T.) talked about the piece. One of the debates that occurred with regard to the publication of this article was whether or not journals could encourage anonymous publication of articles like this. Was Doctor Lundberg acting responsibly when he and the editorial board decided to publish this article? A grand jury subpoena was sought to obtain the name of the author, since it was widely viewed that a crime had been committed by the resident in question. See: Howard Wolinsky and Tom Brune, "JAMA's Jam," *The Quill*, May 1988, 25–32.

5. Edmund D. Pellegrino and David C. Thomasma, *For the Patient's Good: The Restoration of Beneficence in Health Care* (New York: Oxford University Press, 1988), pp. 1–67.

6. Stephen M. Shortell and Edward F. X. Hughes, "The Effects of Regulation, Competition, and Ownership on Mortality Rates among Hospital Inpatients," *New England Journal of Medicine* 318, no. 17 (April 28, 1988), 1100–1107; see also Michael Millenson, "Study Links Hospital Cost Cuts, Deaths," *Chicago Tribune*, April 28, 1988, sec. 3, 1. In the same issue of the *New England Journal* there is a study suggesting that early hospital discharge in a selected group of heart attack patients does not adversely affect mortality: Eric J. Topol, Keren Burek, William W. O'Neill et al., "A Randomized Controlled Trial of Hospital Discharge Three Days after Myocardial Infarction in the Era of Reperfusion," *New England Journal of Medicine* 318, no. 17 (April 28, 1988), pp. 1083–1088.

7. Egilde P. Seravalli, "The Dying Patient, the Physician, and the Fear of Death," *New England Journal of Medicine* 319 (December 29, 1988), 1728.

8. Ibid.

9. H. Tristram Engelhardt, Jr., "Advance Directives and the Right to Be Left Alone," in C. Hackler, R. Moseley, and D. E. Yawter, eds., *Advance Directives in Medicine* (New York: Praeger, 1989), pp. 141–154.

10. See Howard Brody, "Hope," *Journal of the American Medical Association* 246, no. 13 (September 25, 1981).

11. See E. D. Pellegrino and D. C. Thomasma, *The Predicament of Illness: Religious Reflections on Being Ill and Being Healed* (New York: Continuum, forthcoming), chapter on Hope.

12. See the issue of *Journal of Medicine and Philosophy* devoted to clinical trials: Kenneth Schaffner, ed., "Ethical Issues in the Use of Clinical Controls" 11, no. 4 (November 1986), entire issue.

13. See Howard Brody, *Placebos and the Philosophy of Medicine* (Chicago: University of Chicago Press, 1980).

14. The procedure whereby scientific data about a drug's effectiveness is

slightly abrogated in favor of getting the drug into the hands of persons with AIDS has been hotly debated.

15. Carol McMillen Moinpour, Polly Feigl, Barbara Metch, Katherine A. Hayden, Frank L. Meyskens, Jr., John Crowley, "Quality of Life End Points in Cancer Clinical Trials: Review and Recommendations," *Journal of the National Cancer Institute* 81, no. 7 (April 5, 1989), 485–495.

16. On the former, see Case 42 ("The Family Felt Betrayed," p. 262); on the latter, see Case 44 ("R. B.'s Leg Condition," p. 265).

17. David C. Thomasma, "Philosophical Reflections on a Rational Treatment Plan," *Journal of Medicine and Philosophy* 11 (1986), 157–165.

18. Sidney Wanzer, Daniel Federman, S. James Adelstein, et al., "The Physician's Responsibility Toward Hopelessly Ill Patients: A Second Look," *New England Journal of Medicine* 320 (March 30, 1989), 844–849.

19. Ibid., 845; cf. S. E. Bedell, D. Pelle, P.L. Maher, P. D. Cleary, "Do-Not-Resuscitate Orders for Critically Ill Patients in the Hospital: How Are They Used and What Is Their Impact?" *Journal of the American Medical Association* 256 (1986), 233–237.

20. Hans Jonas, "Technology and Responsibility: Reflections on the New Task of Ethics," in his *Philosophical Essays: From Ancient Creed to Modern Man*. Englewood Cliffs, N.J.: Prentice-Hall, 1974.

21. Philip Boyle, O.P., "Merely Prolonging Dying," *Ethical Issues in Health Care* (a newsletter of the Center for Health Care Ethics, St. Louis University Medical Center) 7, no. 5 (January 1986), 1–2.

22. Kathleen Nolan, "In Death's Shadow: The Meanings of Withholding Resuscitation," *Hastings Center Report* 17 (October/November 1987), 9–18.

23. Phoenix Films, *The Detour* — available from Phoenix Films, 13-A Jules Lane, New Brunswick, N.J. 08901.

24. S. Neu and C. M. Kjellstrand, "Stopping Long-Term Dialysis," *New England Journal of Medicine* 314 (1986), 14–19.

25. S. J. Denardo, R. K. Oye, P. E. Bellamy, "Efficacy of Intensive Care for Bone Marrow Transplant Patients with Respiratory Failure," *Critical Care Medicine* 17 (1989), 4–6.

26. J. Hammond, C. G. Ward, "Decision Not to Treat: 'Do Not Resuscitate' Order for the Burn Patient in the Acute Setting," *Critical Care Medicine* 17 (1989), 136–138.

27. B. Zawacki, "Tongue-tied in the Burn Intensive Care Unit: Editorial," *Critical Care Medicine* 17 (1989), 198–199.

28. Linda Emmanuel, "Does the DNR Order Need Life-Sustaining Intervention?" *American Journal of Medicine* 86 (January 1989), 87–90; R. M. Wachter, J. M. Luce, J. Turner, P. Volberding, P. C. Hopewell, "Intensive Care of Patients with the Acquired Immunodeficiency Syndrome: Outcome and Changing Patterns of Utilization," *American Review of Respiratory Disease* 134 (1986), 891–986; M. S. Ewer, M. K. Ali, M. S. Atta, R. C. Morice, P. V. Balakrishnan, "Outcome of Lung Cancer Patients requiring Mechanical Ventilation for Pulmonary Failure," *Journal of the American Medical Association*

256 (1986), 3364–3366; G. E. Taffet, T. A. Teasdale, R. J. Luchi, "In-hospital Cardiopulmonary Resuscitation," *Journal of the American Medical Association* 260 (1988), 2069–2072; N. J. Farber, S. M. Bowman, D. A. Major, and W. P. Green, "Cardiopulmonary Resuscitation (CPR), Patient Factors and Decision Making," *Archives of Internal Medicine* 144 (1984), 2229–2232; M. W. Charlson, F. L. Sax, C. R. MacKenzie, S. D. Fields, R. L. Braham, and R. G. Douglas, "Resuscitation: How Do We Decide?" *Journal of the American Medical Association* 255 (1986), 1316–1322; R. M. Wachter, M. Cooke, P. C. Hopewell, and J. M. Luce, "Attitudes of Medical Residents Regarding Intensive Care for Patients with the Acquired Immunodeficiency Syndrome," *Archives of Internal Medicine* 148 (1988), 149–152.

29. Fidel Davila, "Beyond DNR: Patient Care Categories as Advanced Directives," *Hospital Ethics* 5, no. 2 (March/April 1989), 1–4.

30. "Charges of CPR 'Overuse' Debated by *Medical Ethics Advisor* Readers," *Medical Ethics Advisor* 5, no. 4 (April 1989), 45–49.

31. Glenn C. Graber, Ph.D., Alfred D. Beasley, M.D., and John A. Eaddy, M.D., *Ethical Analysis of Clinical Medicine: A Guide to Self-Evaluation* (Baltimore: Urban & Schwarzenberg, 1985), p. 186.

32. F. D. Moore, "The Desperate Case: CARE (Costs, Applicability, Research, Ethics), Editorial," *Journal of the American Medical Association* 261 (1989), 1483–1484.

33. Wanzer et al., "The Physician's Responsibility Toward Hopelessly Ill Patients: A Second Look" (1989), 845.

34. Edmund D. Pellegrino, "Towards a Reconstruction of Medical Morality: The Primacy of the Act of Profession and the Fact of Illness," *Journal of Medicine and Philosophy* 4 (1979), 44.

35. David C. Thomasma, "Ethical and Legal Issues in the Care of the Elderly Cancer Patient," *Clinics in Geriatric Medicine* 3 (August 1987), 541–547.

36. Glenn C. Graber, Ph.D., Alfred D. Beasley, M.D., and John A. Eaddy, M.D., *Ethical Analysis of Clinical Medicine: A Guide to Self-Evaluation* (Baltimore: Urban & Schwarzenberg, 1985), pp. 118–123.

37. Edmund D. Pellegrino and David C. Thomasma, *For the Patient's Good: The Restoration of Beneficence in Health Care* (New York, Oxford University Press, 1988).

38. Eric Cassell, "The Nature of Suffering and the Goals of Medicine," *New England Journal of Medicine* 310 (1984), 955–959.

39. Graber, et al., *Ethical Analysis of Clinical Medicine: A Guide to Self-Evaluation*, pp. 167–178.

40. President's Commission for the Study of Ethical Problems in Medicine and Biomedical & Behavioral Research, *Making Health Care Decisions: Introduction and Part I* (Washington, D.C.: U.S. Government Printing Office, 1983).

41. Laurence McCullough, "Medical Care for Elderly Patients with Diminished Competence," *Journal of the American Geriatrics Society* 32 (1984),

150; W. Marriner, "Decision Making in the Care of the Terminally Ill Incompetent Patient," *Journal of the American Geriatrics Society* 32 (1984), 739.

42. Edmund D. Pellegrino and David C. Thomasma, *A Philosophical Basis of Medical Practice* (New York: Oxford University Press, 1981), chapter 7.

43. Jay Katz, "Limping Is No Sin: Reflections on Making Health Care Decisions," *Cardozo Law Review* 6 (1984), 245.

44. Joanne Lynn, "Brief and Appendix for Amicus Curiae," *Journal of the American Geriatrics Society* 32 (1984), 9156.

45. David C. Thomasma, "When Healing Involves a Risk to Life: Risky Medical Procedures and Experimentation," *New Catholic World* 230 (July/August 1987), 163–167.

46. Charles Meyer, *Surviving Death: A Practical Guide to Caring for the Dying and Bereaved* (Mystic, Conn.: Twenty-Third Publications, 1988), p. 33.

47. *Schloendorff v Society of New York Hospitals*, 211 NY 125, 105 N.E. 29, 1914.

48. *In re Quinlan*, 70 New Jersey 10, 355 A. 2d. 647, 1975.

49. *In re Conroy*, 486, A 2d, 1209, New Jersey, 1985.

50. *Bartling v. Superior Court of California*, 2 Civil No. B007907, 1984.

51. *Elizabeth Bouvia v. Superior Court*, State of California for the County of Los Angeles, Superior Court No. C.583828, April 16, 1986.

52. *In re Conroy* at 1229.

53. *In re Conroy* at 1232. Compare the statement of the AMA Council on Ethical and Judicial Affairs: "Life should be cherished despite disabilities and handicaps, except when prolongation would be inhumane and unconscionable" (*Current Opinions — 1986*, § 2.16).

54. *In re Conroy* at 1232.

55. Glenn C. Graber, Alfred D. Beasley, and John A. Eaddy, *Ethical Analysis of Clinical Medicine* (Baltimore: Urban & Schwarzenberg, 1985), pp. 184–185. The authors found at least fifty considerations relevant to decisions about terminating treatment.

56. Society for the Right to Die, "Right-To-Die Backgrounder," *News from the Society for the Right to Die*, January 1989, 1.

57. President's Commission for the Study of Ethical Problems in Medicine and Biomedical and Behavioral Research: *Deciding to Forego Life-Sustaining Treatment* (Washington, D.C.: U.S. Government Printing Office, 1983).

58. President's Commission for the Study of Ethical Problems in Medicine and Medical and Behavioral Research, *Making Health Care Decisions: Introduction and Part I* (Washington, D.C.: U.S. Government Printing Office, 1983).

59. Laurence McCullough, "Medical Care for Elderly Patients with Diminished Competence," *Journal of the American Geriatrics Society* 32 (1984),

150; R. Steinbrook, Bernard Lo, "Decision Making for Incompetent Patients By Designated Proxy," *New England Journal of Medicine* 310 (1984), 1598.

60. Howard Brody, "Ethics of Treatment Refusal: Saying What We Mean in Court," *Medical Humanities Report* (Winter 1989), 2.

61. Edmund D. Pellegrino, "Toward a Reconstruction of Medical Morality: The Primacy of the Act of Profession and the Fact of Illness," *Journal of Medicine and Philosophy* 4 (1979), 44; David C. Thomasma, "Ethical Judgments of Quality of Life in the Care of the Aged," *Journal of the American Geriatrics Society* 32 (1984), 525; Edmund D. Pellegrino and David C. Thomasma, *For the Patient's Good: The Restoration of Beneficence in Health Care* (New York: Oxford University Press, 1988).

62. M. Fowler, "Appointing an Agent to Make Medical Treatment Choices," *Columbia Law Review* 84 (1984), 985.

63. President's Commission for the Study of Ethical Problems in Medicine and Biomedical and Behavioral Research, *Deciding to Forego Life-Sustaining Treatment: Ethical, Medical, and Legal Issues in Treatment Decisions* (Washington, D.C.: U.S. Government Printing Office, 1983), p. 4.

64. Albert Jonsen, Mark Siegler, William Winslade, *Clinical Ethics* (New York: Macmillan, 1982), p. 35.

65. P. Ramsey, *The Patient as Person: Explorations in Medical Ethics* (New Haven: Yale University Press, 1970).

66. L. Schneiderman and J. Arras, "Counseling Patients to Counsel Physicians on Future Care in the Event of Patient Incompetence," *Annals of Internal Medicine* 102 (1985), 693.

67. S. H. Wanzer, S. A. Adelstine, R. E. Cranford, et al., "The Physician's Responsibility toward Hopelessly Ill Patients,"*New England Journal of Medicine* 310 (1984), 955.

68. Beth Wilson, "Letter from Dying Woman's Killer Draws Legal, Ethical Fire," *Knoxville Journal*, February 29, 1988, A2–A3. The article contains quotes by Graber and John Burkhardt, M.D., Chairman of the AMA Council on Ethical and Judicial Affairs. The discussion centers on intention of any double-effect action.

69. David Jackson and Stuart Youngner, "Patient Autonomy and Death with Dignity: Some Clinical Caveats," *New England Journal of Medicine* 301 (1979), 404–408.

70. Wanzer et al., "The Physician's Responsibility" (1989), 848.

71. Ibid.

72. The Central Committee of the Royal Dutch Medical Association, "Vision on Euthanasia," Utrecht, The Netherlands, 1986.

73. George Crile, Jr., "Euthanasia," Letter to Editor, *American College of Surgeons Bulletin* 74, no. 3 (1989), 2.

74. Albert R. Jonsen, "A Concord in Medical Ethics," *Annals of Internal Medicine* 99 (August 1983), 263; President's Commission for the Study of Ethical Problems in Medicine and Biomedical and Behavioral Research, *Deciding to Forego Life-Sustaining Treatment: Ethical, Medical, and Legal*

Issues in Treatment Decisions (Washington, D.C.: U.S. Government Printing Office, 1983), pp. 62–73.

75. American Medical Association: Statement of the Judicial Council. New Orleans, La., March 1986.

76. Urs Haemmerli, M.D., went to speak to a new member of the Zurich City Council in 1975 about the needs of the elderly when that member became head of the Department of Health. She had been sensitive to those issues during her campaign, and he went as chief of medicine of a 700-bed Triemli hospital, to fill her in and discuss issues further. While there he spoke of how physicians sometimes should do nothing, and related how he even withheld fluids and nutrition from some dying patients. He was shocked when police came to his house one morning in January 1975. He was arrested and jailed on a complaint from the new head of the Department of Health! See "Swiss M.D. Tells of Indictment," *Euthanasia News* 2, no. 1 (February 1976), 1, 3.

77. Michael Weinstein, "The 'Human Side' of Chronic Illness," *ACP Observer* 8, no. 11 (December 1988), 10–11.

78. Edmund D. Pellegrino and David C. Thomasma, *For the Patient's Good: The Restoration of Beneficence in Health Care* (New York: Oxford University Press, 1988).

79. Andrew Weil, *The Natural Mind* (New York: Houghton Mifflin, 1972).

80. More recent works explore the assortments of plants and drugs traditional societies and our own use to attain a state of well-being: Andrew Weil, *The Marriage of the Sun and the Moon* (New York: Houghton Mifflin, 1980); and Andrew Weil with Winifred Rosen, *Chocolate to Morphine* (New York: Houghton Mifflin, 1983).

81. Andrew Weil, *Health and Healing* (New York: Houghton Mifflin, 1983). This book was reviewed by the epitome of an allopathic publication, *New England Journal of Medicine*, as being courageous in addressing "issues and ideas whose time has come." (See a summary of Weil's views by Bill Thomson, "A Radical Look at Health and Healing: Andrew Weil, M.D., Tells Why Alternatives Work," *East West Journal* [March 1985], 32–37).

82. Ibid., 37.

83. Bernie Siegel, *Love, Medicine and Miracles* (New York: Harper & Row, 1986), 152–156, 227–235.

84. Norman Cousins, *Anatomy of an Illness as Perceived by the Patient* (New York: W. W. Norton, 1979).

85. See the Haemmerli discussion, *Euthanasia News* 2, no. 1 (February 1976), 1, 3.

86. Fenella Rouse, "Legal and Ethical Guidelines for Physicians in Geriatric Terminal Care," *Geriatrics* 43, no. 8 (August 1988), 69.

87. David C. Thomasma and Jurrit Bergsma, "Patients and Incurable Cancer: Autonomy, Decision-Making, and Quality of Life," submitted to *Social Science in Medicine*.

88. Mark Siegler, "Pascal's Wager and the Hanging of Crepe," *New England Journal of Medicine* 293 (October 23, 1975), 853–857.

89. Thomas G. Butheil, Harold Bursztajn, and Archie Brodsky, "Malpractice Prevention through the Sharing of Uncertainty," *New England Journal of Medicine* 311, no. 1 (July 5, 1984), 49–51.

90. Neil Kessel, "Reassurance," *Lancet*, May 26, 1979, 1128–1133.

91. Louis Borgenicht, "Richard Selzer and the Problem of Detached Concern," *Annals of Internal Medicine* 100 (1984), 923–934.

92. The American Medical Association has condemned the use of physicians in this task, even if they only prepare the lethal medication but do not actually deliver it. Yet physicians have always assisted at such events by certifying the death of the condemned person.

93. As quoted in Ruth P. Smith, "Remarks by Ruth P. Smith at SRD's 50th Anniversary Celebration," Society for the Right to Die, December 7, 1988, p. 5.

94. A. Jost, *Das Recht auf den Tod*. 1895, as quoted in H. Lauter and J. E. Meyer, "Active Euthanasia without Consent: Historical Comments on a Current Debate," *Death Education* 8 (1984), 89–98.

95. Editor, "The Editor Talks with the President of Johns Hopkins Hospital," *Johns Hopkins Magazine* (February 1986), 15–20.

96. K. Vaux, "If We Can Bar the Door to Death, Can't We Also Open It?" *Chicago Tribune*, February 10, 1988, 1, 23.

97. Edmund D. Pellegrino and David C. Thomasma, *A Philosophical Basis of Medical Practice* (New York: Oxford University Press, 1981).

98. Leon Kass, "Arguments Against Active Euthanasia by Doctors Found at Medicine's Core," *Kennedy Institute of Ethics Newsletter* 3, no. 1 (January 1989), 1–3, 6.

99. Willard Gaylin, Leon Kass, Edmund D. Pellegrino, and Mark Siegler, "Commentaries: Doctors Must Not Kill," *Journal of the American Medical Association* 259 (1988), 2139–2140.

100. L. Gonzales, "The Executioners," *Chicago* 37 (March 1988), 91–95, 180–185.

101. A. Otten, "Fateful Decision: In the Netherlands, the Very Ill Have Option of Euthanasia. *Wall Street Journal*, August 21, 1987, sec. 1; 1, 6.

102. J. Weinfeld, "Active Voluntary Euthanasia — Should It Be Legalized? *Medicine and Law* 4 (1985), 101.

103. Wanzer, 1989, 846.

104. Michael Weinstein, "Ethics Committees Changing Medical Habits," *ACP Observer* 8, no. 11 (December 1988), 1, 14.

105. David C. Thomasma, "Training in Medical Ethics: An Ethical Workup," *Forum on Medicine* 1, no. 12 (December 1978), 33–36; James Drane, "'Ethical Workup' Guides Clinical Decision Making" 69 (December 1988), 64–67.

Chapter Six _____

EUTHANASIA AND SOCIETY

Now is a good time to return to the five fundamental problems that contribute to the growing trend toward active euthanasia. A list of these problems inaugurated our first chapter (see p. 1). We return to them now to see if we have made any progress toward resolving them. This analysis will form the basis of this chapter. Our point of view will shift from the individual patient, the patient's family, and the medical profession, the points of view of the previous chapters, to the point of view of society itself.

The five problems dealt with the rise of modern medical technology, the control of pain and suffering, the response of compassion, the distinction between active and passive euthanasia, and the possible right to die. They will be explored in the following four sections: Victimization by Technology; Suffering and Public Responsibility; Compassion; and Social Euthanasia and the Nazi Experience.

VICTIMIZATION BY TECHNOLOGY

Nowhere is victimization by technology more apparent than in the application of medical technology and its various interventions to the dying patient. Not surprisingly, studies have confirmed that it is not the technology but the care persons receive that determines their well-being and, in the case of the dying patient, the protection of their human spirit to the end.[1]

The constant increase of medical technology, and the new choices that it brings to the dying process, is one major factor in social pressure for legalizing voluntary active euthanasia. The fact that society does not seem to control the apparently mindless application of medical technology to human lives, especially to defective newborns, the aged,[2] and dying patients, is a central piece of the argument for legalizing euthanasia. How can this technology be directed to good human ends? How can it be directed away from causing increased pain and suffering for patients and their families (and sometimes for their health providers)?

But is it really the case that society does not already try to control the application of medical technology for good human ends?

Take the case of Daniel McKay (Case 39, p. 256). Although the means he employed raises questions about classifying this case as active euthanasia (as opposed to murder), some of its features help uncover social restraints on professional judgments. McKay, recall, was a veterinarian. One would expect that he would be more familiar than the average person with the ways in which medicine today attacks life-threatening disorders. His son, who was to be named John Francis, was born with myriad anomalies — including a hairlip, cleft palate, webbed hands, and heart and lung deformities. McKay did what most of us would do. He pleaded with the doctors and nurses in the birthing room for a consideration of extramedical values, his own and presumably those of his wife, against the immediate decision to put the child in an incubator and try to keep him alive. Although we are not privy to the content of his argument, only that it was reportedly highly emotional, we can imagine that he spoke of the needless suffering of his child and of the uselessness of modern technology in changing anything for the better. When these arguments were ignored, he killed his son by smashing his head on the delivery room floor.

McKay was brought to trial twice. As soon as the second mistrial was declared, the assistant state's attorney announced that the state was going to make a third effort to convict McKay of murder. Some political wrangling took place behind the scenes, since the then state's attorney general, Richard Daley, son of the late mayor of Chicago, had a son born with spina bifida; the son spent the two years of his life mostly in a hospital before he died.

Associate Judge Will Gierach, who tried the case, pointed to the problem of considering this act of euthanasia equivalent to murder:

If they [the jury] were dealing with somebody who was going out and committing crimes every week and they felt it was their duty to the citizens to put him away because of his danger to the community, that would be a different question. But here you are not dealing with that question. You are dealing with an isolated event, an event which is as much a tragedy for the accused and his family as it is for society. At some point, you have to temper justice with mercy and with compassion and with humanity.[3]

The crux of the problem was that the jurors, most of whom thought he was guilty, could not reach a unanimous agreement that he was

160   EUTHANASIA AND SOCIETY

probably not in full control when he did this act. Some wanted a
verdict of guilty but mentally ill, others, a verdict of not guilty by
reason of insanity. McKay is a prominent member of his community,
a volunteer firefighter and the town's only veterinarian. Among letters
sent to his attorney in support of his action (or better, in support of
understanding his action), came one from a woman who said that she
strangled her defective newborn when doctors left her alone in the
delivery room. Other issues were whether the hospital was remiss in
not removing a distraught father from the delivery room, where he
had begged doctors not to use heroic measures to save his son.

The argument for understanding and mitigation is counterbal-
anced by at least three factors, factors supported by society itself.
First, despite our analysis in the previous chapter, many physicians
still see their obligations in terms of prolonging life, especially in
medical settings that do not permit of extensive evaluation, like the
birthing room. This is not to say that what we are calling the victimization by technology process might not happen in other, less
technologically intensive settings than surgical suites and emergency
rooms. We are only saying that the physicians in the McKay case
acted on the default mode of society and their profession. They presumed that society would support their efforts to try to preserve the
life of the newborn infant over those of a distraught father. The first
principle of directing technology to good human ends, therefore, is
*the default mode in emergency situations is to attempt to save the life
of the patient, no matter in what condition that patient may be.* This
is an important condition for the practice of emergency medicine,
and one that citizens would clearly support if ever there were a referendum. It is a rational, but normally unexpressed, principle for
protecting the lives of others in any society.

The second default mode presumably used by the physicians in
the McKay and other similar cases is that *the default mode in dealing with patients who are temporarily or permanently incapacitated is
to presume in favor of prolonging their lives.* One could think that
this principle is derived from the doctrine of informed consent. The
informed consent doctrine requires that no procedure be done on
a person without full information about the procedure and its side
effects, and without a free consent to that procedure and the risks
and benefits it entails. Since the McKay infant (and all other infants)
cannot speak for themselves, a decent human society (one may think)
would direct its life-saving technology toward saving the lives of such
vulnerable beings, even in the face of objections of parents. Presumed
consent leads to the rights of physicians to treat children in this way.

It is further supported by what is called in Illinois the "forty-eight hour rule." This rule provides immediate authorization to physicians to treat children when child abuse is suspected, until they can gain court orders to do so. For forty-eight hours, they become legal guardians for the child. As can be seen, this social principle on the face of it causes problems for an unrestricted view of our arguments for the principle of the family as a value unit in Chapter Four.

The third social principle is more explicitly contained in laws and regulations governing the disabled. In our society, the rights of the handicapped are especially protected, since in the past these persons have been subject to inconsistent protection of their rights as persons and as citizens. The best expressions of these rights as they pertain to the McKay case are the "Baby Doe regulations,"[4] and the statement of the New Jersey Supreme Court *In re Conroy*[5] (see Case 50, p. 274).

The Baby Doe regulations require that physicians treat defective newborns unless those newborns suffer from a terminal disease. Even in those instances, strict guidelines exist governing the range of discretion allowed physicians. The intent of the controversial regulations is to protect the newborn's constitutional right to life against prejudicial judgments regarding its incapacities.

Recall the Conroy case concerned an elderly woman, Claire Conroy, who had become incompetent through senility and multiple diseases. The court stated that persons have a right to control their own treatment decisions, and *that they do not lose this right when they become incompetent*. Impaired persons are protected by society. This principle cuts both ways. It can mean, as it did in the Conroy case, that others must speak for her values not to have her life prolonged unduly. But it also means that incompetent patients, such as the McKay infant, do not lose the right to the previously stated default modes simply because they are impaired. Prejudice about their care is ruled out.

These three social principles, the two default modes and the principle of personal control, are evidence that society does attempt to direct medical technology to good human ends. In cases of incompetency, the individual is protected as well. Surrogates must express treatment choices on the basis of the expressed or presumed values of the patient. This is impossible to do for infants, so society acting *in loco parentis* adds a presumption for the right to treat that severely limits the rights of parents and physicians to withdraw care.

But does not admitting this fact, that society does indeed direct medical technology to good human ends, just beg the question? Proponents of active euthanasia stress strict conditions for its use as well, among them the presence of terminal illness and voluntariness. By considering the McKay case as we have we can more clearly see that the real pressure for active euthanasia from the point of view of society does not come from society's *neglectfulness* regarding medical technology, as some proponents argue. Rather it comes from inappropriate applications of the default modes and principles just enunciated to cases of competent, dying patients. There is a further problem. Note that Dr. McKay presumably pleaded for his son on the basis of extramedical values. He argued that he and his wife had a right to a voice in the decision about treatment (the argument that the family is the fundamental unit of value), and that the values they expressed should be used to override the three principles just described. The reason he became more distraught was that his view was ignored.

In addition to the right of the patient to decide his or her own treatment, a right supported by living will legislation and court decisions, nonmedical values of patients must also be respected in treatment decisions.[6] Not every person accepts the medical care presumptions noted above. This is a good example of why general and abstract principles cannot always be applied in particular cases. It supports the thesis we develop, that a more flexible social policy is required, one that is sensitive to individual, clinical realities. At the heart of this policy is a requirement that the individual's and family's wishes must take precedence over policies of a state or institution in right to die cases.[7] Such policy would, in effect, delegate to the triad of physicians, families, and health providers the decisions that must be made in such cases on behalf of the individual. As Michael Nevins, M.D., said of the Jobes case:

> ... physicians should feel comfortable that they're free of liability so long as they are acting in good faith and guided by the patient's family and wishes.[8]

Recall the case of Rudy Linares ("I've Got a Gun"; see Case 40, p. 258). The Linares boy, Samuel, one of four children of a family on welfare, swallowed a balloon at seven months old while at a birthday party. The uninflated balloon lodged in his posterior pharynx, blocking the area around the epiglottis and closing off both the esophagus and trachea. Sammy's father, Rudy, tried to remove the balloon, but couldn't. He was rescued but his brain was irreversibly damaged. He had been in a persistent vegetative state since August 1988. His father and mother frequently asked about removing the boy from a respirator upon which he was dependent. The doctor in the case assured the family that the boy could not last long. However, he did. Then in April 1989, when Sammy was fifteen months old, the father shut off the respirator himself, but was restrained by health professionals, and it was turned back on. Prior to that incident, he had asked how long the boy would live off the respirator, and was told about four minutes. On Wednesday, April 26, 1989, after months of pleading, Rudy Linares disconnected the respirator from his son, put his son in his arms, and counted the minutes. He held off beseeching health professionals at gunpoint. After borrowing a stethoscope to listen for his son's heartbeat and determining that he was dead, he turned over his gun. Although charged with murder, the grand jury refused to indict him. Richard Scholz, one of three public defenders assigned to the Linares case said:

> We feel this situation should not be in any way considered a murder. It is a situation where medical technology has outstripped the ethics regarding what is a life and what is not.[9]

The case was complicated by the fact that the physician, while ambivalent, was sympathetic to the family's plight. So was the hospital, which agreed in principle that the technology ought to be removed, but argued that "Illinois law must be clarified regarding parental rights in coma cases."[10] When the case hit the Chicago media, not one ethicist could be found who would not have "quietly pulled the plug." But the *Chicago Tribune* found that hospital lawyers would rather go to court. The problem is that it would have cost the Linares family from $10,000 to $30,000 to hire a lawyer for that purpose, money which as welfare participants they did not have, and would have taken an immense amount of time away from their family.[11] Public sympathy for Linares was immense. A *Chicago Sun-Times* poll showed thirteen-to-one support for no indictment for Linares. It seems obvious that a national policy explicitly giving the right to families and doctors to withdraw useless therapy would have broad support.

One of the most telling features of the Linares case was the bad advice given to the doctor and the family by the hospital lawyer. Ron Cranford, asked to address the question of whether hospital lawyers should be members of hospital ethics committees, seemed to respond with prescience about the Linares case when he said:

> ... they [the hospital lawyers] are the enemy, they are the ones giving ultra-conservative legal advice that is often wrong. Some of the very reasons you form a committee [are] because of the extremely poor legal advice given by house legal counsel.[12]

For the most part, legal rather than moral concerns govern this advice. Although the supreme courts of many states have made determinations that clarify the role of the family, in some states that has not happened.

In the final analysis, then, the default principles governing medical care discussed above are part of the problem. Although they are designed to direct medical technology to good human ends, they are sometimes taken out of context and applied to persons for whom that protection by society can become an immense burden. At that point, most citizens would want support withheld or withdrawn. As Kenneth Vaux said about the Linares case, "When a human being is irretrievably brain dead it's wrong to keep him alive, a punishment to keep forcing breathing into the lungs that no longer function on their own."[13]

SUFFERING AND PUBLIC RESPONSIBILITY

Many people in our society do not feel supported in their struggles to act in a loving and supportive way toward family members who are suffering. In Chapter One we mentioned Geraldine Sagel, the mother of a dwarf she had cared for in her home for fifty-one years. She herself was eighty-one years old at the time she attempted to murder her son. In a wheelchair in court she said: "I was afraid he would be on the mercy of the world, and I think that you can understand that, your honor...I love him too much."[14] She suffered from poor eyesight, hearing loss, and emphysema. As her health failed, she became obsessed with what would happen to him. Her plan was to kill him, and then herself. But the gun jammed after the first shot that only wounded him. She then took an overdose of pills. The event was discovered by a neighbor who had not seen her for several days. The son, "Butch," was functional, but never learned to read and write. He could do some everyday chores. The neighbor found out that he had been shot when he complained to her that his shoulder hurt. Sagel's perception that society would not support her son in a loving way was based on years of experience.

Leona Anderson, seventy, of Norridge, mentioned in Chapter Four, stabbed her terminally ill husband fifty times in a mercy killing. Her husband, William, seventy-seven, was dying of cancer. She then stabbed herself in the abdomen, but survived when a neighbor came upon the carnage and called an ambulance. Is this kind of euthanasia justified? The woman is now confined to a mental hospital. The couple talked about his medical problems and his pain the night before her actions. William apparently said to her that he wished they were both dead.[15]

These two examples of home-based loneliness and desperation add to those institutional ones we have examined regarding the difficulties people have getting life-prolonging technology removed from loved ones in hospitals and nursing homes. In both instances, something is missing in the community that would support the burdens these caregivers experience. In an unrelated case, Martin Klein had to go to court to obtain the right to abort a fetus in his wife, Nancy, thirty-two. Nancy had suffered brain damage in a car wreck, and doctors had advised that her chances for recovery, however dim, would be better without the pregnancy. Mr. Klein struggled with the decision, because the couple wanted the baby. A two-week legal battle with anti-abortionists ended at the New York Supreme Court. After a judgment granting him the right to make this decision, he said:

> It's been a major battle. I am tired and wounded. I want to go on with my life. No other family should ever have to go through what we have gone through.[16]

By this he meant not only the terrible trauma of the accident and a decision to abort a desired pregnancy to possibly save his wife, but also the uncertainty and legalism that surrounded a moral decision.

Given the scope of the problem just explored, do we not have a greater responsibility to dying persons than in the past to address the results of the success of our medical technology? In Chapter Five we argued that the goal of medicine is not life-prolongation, per se, but the assistance in achieving the patient's personal and social values. How does that goal transcribe into social responsibility?

Although the state's interest in the protection of human life and the protection of the conscience and values of the health professional are very important, these have almost always been seen by the courts as of secondary interest when dealing with terminally ill patients. Thus, in the landmark case of Karen Ann Quinlan (Case 20, p. 230) who suffered a vegetative state from a drug overdose, the State of New Jersey Supreme Court judged that the interests of the state in protecting her life could no longer prevail over her guardians' wishes that she not be kept alive in such a condition, *given her poor prognosis.*[17] The same court decided nearly a decade later, in addressing *In re Conroy*[18] (Case 50, p. 274) that prior expressions of the wishes of the patient should be given a prominent place in these decisions. Another way of putting this judgment is that medical technology, in this case, the respirator, is optional in supporting the life of a patient

(a) when it is judged useless, and the patient would be better off dead; and (b) when the patient's wishes about further treatment are known, either directly or through surrogates. (These are the same conditions we arrived at in Chapter Two.) Since the time of the Quinlan decision, advances in medical ethics and in significant case law and legislation have made it clear that the patient's right of self-determination and constitutional right of privacy support his or her decisions about care almost absolutely. Controversy arises over the two points just noted, namely, whether or not the treatment is really useless and whether or not an incompetent patient has actually stated wishes about the current problem.

With respect to the former point, a national conservative group called "Citizens United Resisting Euthanasia" asked that a Catholic order, the Knights of Columbus, withdraw its support of a workshop for Catholic Bishops held from January 30 to February 3, 1989 in Dallas on medical ethics issues because two Dominican priests, Fr. Kevin O'Rourke, O.P., and Fr. Philip Boyle, O.P., both from the St. Louis University Medical Center, "support euthanasia." Actually both priests, who are medical ethicists, support the withholding and withdrawing of medically useless therapy, including fluids and nutrition. This position is common among medical ethicists.[19] The basis of the position is that withholding and withdrawing fluids and nutrition from comatose patients is permissible if such treatment is burdensome, representing an intervention disproportionate to the outcome. But in the opinion of the conservatives, such withholding and withdrawing constitutes "starving people to death," or active euthanasia. Said Earl Appelby, executive director of the anti-euthanasia group:

> We find the idea of starving people to death immoral and we will oppose it in every way.[20]

At least a part of the conservative position fails to draw the proper distinctions between active and passive euthanasia. When people are dying they don't eat big meals. One of the sophisticated treatment decisions physicians face with dying patients is the balance between nutrition and pain control that reduces appetite and creates constipation. Dying people starve sometimes. When nutrition and hydration is withheld from dying persons or persons in end-stage dementia, they soon slip into a coma. The comatose person feels no pain. This is nature's way "for the end of life to be a state that is free of pain, fear, and suffering...." Thus, as Judy Ahronheim, M.D., notes, "death in these situations is not 'gruesome,' 'cruel,' or 'violent' as some right-to-die opponents stridently claim."[21]

The fact that one may withhold nutrition and hydration at the patient's request makes it possible to place the type of death a patient may undergo in the patient's own hands, and not in the control of the enthusiasms of others. But this is not the only point. Commenting on the Cruzan case in Missouri (see Case 21, p. 233), Fr. O'Rourke contends that the cost of artificially feeding a comatose patient is a misuse of resources because it is expensive and ineffective. The costly procedure in Nancy Cruzan's case prolongs life in a person unable to meet life's spiritual goals and represents no gain.[22]

However, some persons are concerned that by establishing criteria for the removal of life-support systems from comatose and brain-damaged people, we are setting up economic rather than moral criteria that will permit us to control the "cost" of living too long. The specter of Nazi society is raised in such concerns, and deserves explicit discussion later in this chapter.

After a decade of hard-fought legislative and court battles, it seems fair to say that society, through the appellate and supreme court cases in individual states, does now offer explicit protection against the inappropriate application of medical technology that is judged to be useless to the outcome of not only dying patients, but any competent adult.

Unfortunately, the results vary from case to case and from state to state. California, perhaps as a result of its historical role as the last frontier to which people escaped from other locales, underlines a more individualistic, libertarian approach to extraordinary cases. Massachusetts, New Jersey, and New York emphasize the role of society more than California has; while protecting the right of patients to refuse treatment, they have generally instituted recommendations that society's voice be heard, through institutional ethics committees (Quinlan), through the state's ombudsman office (Conroy); and they have also indicated reluctance to coerce institutions to remove feeding tubes against their own "conscience" (Brophy). (See Appendix III for selected court cases.)

In America's heartland, few cases have been heard. But Missouri's Supreme Court in Cruzan effectively diminished one's right to die if one does not propose explicit advance directives about virtually every contingency, something most individuals would be hard pressed to do. A case currently being adjudicated in Illinois gives rise to similar concerns:

Sidney Greenspan suffered a stroke in 1984 and has lain comatose ever since. His family argues that that fate would not have befallen him twenty years ago. But now medical technology keeps him alive against his wishes. The public guardian's office in the state of Illinois argues in conjunction with the family that Mr. Greenspan repeatedly told his family that he would not want to be kept alive on life-support systems or in a nursing home in the condition he now suffers. His directives were quite explicit in this regard.[23]

In a previous case regarding Virginia T. Prange, seventy-four, the 1st Appellate Court gave the public guardian the right to substitute his judgment for his charge and remove all artificial means of keeping alive a person in a vegetative state. For the first time in Illinois, the court held that a nasogastric feeding tube was among life-sustaining technologies a person could refuse.[24] Upon review, the Illinois Supreme Court simply vacated the case.

In the Greenspan case, the public guardian's office also argued, as do many ethicists and courts in other states, that the provision of food and water through a medical device, like a tube, constitutes nutrition and hydration, an optional medical treatment.[25] Yet the Illinois Supreme Court is concerned that withdrawal of this basic support, not the underlying disease, will "kill" the patient. Hence the case, like others before it in other states, seeks to clarify whether food and water supplied through a feeding tube constitutes a medical treatment; whether it can be withdrawn if death is imminent; when exactly death should be considered imminent; and whether its withdrawal or the underlying disease (in this case the results of the stroke) contribute to the death?[26]

What is needed is uniform legislation in each state regarding the right to die similar to the efforts made to construct uniform legislation about the definition of death. Perhaps someday a constitutional amendment will make it a federal right to die without the imprecations of technology.

Let us look in more detail at the problems and concerns raised by the specter of the "right to die." The following cases attest to these concerns.

Cases involving rights of others. A young woman (Angela Carder) has leukemia. After a period of treatment, she is in remission. She then decides to become pregnant. This decision is made against all medical advice, since the radiotherapy and chemotherapy she has received for her leukemia are considered possible high risks for fetal development. During her pregnancy, she is discovered to have tumors in her lungs, considered to be metastases from her original cancer or its treatment. Her gynecologist agrees with her not to try to save the baby, just now approaching twenty-two weeks, a time when an effort can be made to rescue the fetus, with about a 5 percent chance for survival after one year.

But the hospital overrides this physician's decision and seeks a court order to save the baby, even though the mother is dying. The mother at first refuses to have a caesarian because of the very high risk that she would die from it; she later relents, and then changes her mind again just before slipping into her final coma. The court order comes through, and the caesarean is done. The mother dies as a result of the operation. The baby died one day later.

This case demonstrates that inappropriate application of medical technology still can occur, especially when it comes to the thorny issue of saving the lives of unborn children, even against the wishes of the mother. Here, however, the presumed principle is to try to save the life of a vulnerable human being when the life of the mother is in its last days. One goes for the possible life over the certain death. Yet how does this action differ from the intent to bring about a death in order to save a person from pain and suffering? In this case, the death is brought about indirectly through the operation whose goal is to save the baby. In the latter instance, death is brought about indirectly by increased pain control dosages. There is little moral difference in the relation of the action to the death; but there is a significant difference in the fact that, in the latter case, the patient's wishes are being honored whereas, in the former case, the action is forced on the patient against her will.

Analogous involuntary actions occur in the lives of mothers who are drug dependent, especially those addicted to cocaine. Babies born of drug-dependent mothers now number almost 10 percent of all live births. Some of these babies are very damaged (a lack of eyes is seen in babies born of cocaine-addictive mothers); all are born drug-dependent themselves. Conservatives argue that if mothers were found feeding newborns concoctions of cocaine and milk, they would be accused of child abuse, and the babies taken from them. Therefore, the rights of others, the unborn children in this instance, require that the mothers be jailed or otherwise restrained from further harming the unborn. Depriving these women of their liberty is serious enough; but forcing Angela Carder and other mothers like her to undergo the invasive procedure of caesarean section is a deep breach of her right to privacy and self-determination.

Cases involving previously expressed wishes. Earlier we discussed the Missouri case (Cruzan, see Case 21, p. 233) and the O'Connor case in New York (Case 22, p. 234). Both of these cases involved persons who expressed prior wishes governing their care should they become comatose or otherwise incompetent. But the statements they made were not considered specific enough to cover continued interventions of medically-delivered fluids and nutrition. Saying that one did "not want to be kept alive on machines" does not directly correlate with being kept alive through the less burdensome interventions of fluids and nutrition delivered through nasogastric or gastric tubes.

In such cases the "rights of others" are considered to be the rights of the victims of accidents, the rights of the comatose or medically incapacitated. The concern, of course, is that we not become a society like the Nazis, which regularly dispatched those who did not qualify or meet standards of the vision of the new society. We will examine this fear about Nazi society shortly.

Cases involving newborns.   Euthanasia of defective newborns comes as close to our fears of Nazi society as any other medical action. Without the protections noted in the Baby Doe regulations, many citizens fear that killing such infants through foregoing life-sustaining procedures or withdrawal of food and water is equivalent to actions done by the most vicious regimes in Western civilization. The case of Baby Boy Miller (Case 41, p. 259) illustrates the thorny dilemmas that can arise in this area, as do the situations in which Daniel McKay (Case 39, p. 256) and Rudy Linares (Case 40, p. 258) took drastic action.

COMPASSION

Where are we so far in our argument? We started with one component of the argument *for* voluntary active euthanasia, that society does not adequately protect dying persons from applications of medical technology and other unwanted medical interventions. We saw that, in fact, society does direct medical technology to good human ends (in some instances), and that this direction protects the rights of the incompetent and disabled from capricious decisions by others. But in that analysis we were able more clearly to perceive that the real objection to social directions of medical technology concerns inappropriate applications of that technology to the dying. The dying person is then victimized by its power over his or her extramedical values.

Then we saw that struggles to establish the constitutional right of privacy over one's own body and therefore the right to refuse treatment have resulted in decisions that support passive euthanasia, the withholding or withdrawing of life-support measures, including fluids and nutrition, from terminally ill patients. The grounds for such withholding and withdrawing are the wishes of the patients and families and the benefits/burdens calculus. The former are either directly or indirectly expressed, through living wills, advance directives, or the durable power of attorney, or through the stories and information passed on to physicians and other caregivers by the patients' families. The latter measures the proportion between the intervention and the outcome on the patient's quality of life and/or longevity. These are, at least in part, medically-based judgments. For this reason, at the very least, clinical flexibility needs to be part of any policy governing euthanasia. Recall the flexible treatment argument developed in Chapter Five ("Duties of Health Care Providers to the Dying," p. 129) and supported by the theoretical argument in Chapters Two and Three.

The upshot of all this is that active euthanasia should not be needed. And yet we learned from other cases that problems still exist in protecting the dying from the enthusiasms of others.

On the one hand, a society that condones active euthanasia is one that is in danger of seriously undermining its commitments to the value of human life. This is especially true of our violence-prone society. On the other hand, a society that condones overturning the values and wishes of its citizens, especially during the dying process, and strips them of their fundamental rights as human beings to control their lives, also seriously undermines its commitments to the value of human lives. The middle ground between these two extremes is a process of bringing about death through a therapeutic plan, a process discussed in the final chapter. Yet, if using passive means alone cannot bring about a control of pain, then this process fails to express our compassion for the dying person.

What social policy should we have to support or control the possibility of active euthanasia in cases in which pain control proves ineffective? As we have argued in Chapter Three, voluntary active euthanasia can only be morally justified in a limited instance. But if it is morally justified in such an instance, does this mean that there is a social obligation to protect that justification? And what should the outlines of that social obligation be?

The August 20, 1987, issue of the *Chicago Tribune* contained two letters to the editor that most clearly display the fundamental rift in our society between autonomy and paternalism in the matter of respect for life.

Joseph Addante proposed that society should legalize suicide so that those suffering from incurable diseases, like AIDS, or old people "rotting away in nursing homes" could choose euthanasia. This is wholehearted support for individual decision-making and autonomy, not far removed, if at all, from the sentiments of those who established the euthanasia societies in Europe and America between the wars.

By contrast, Jane Hoyt argued that persons in a permanent vegetative state are actually to be regarded as disabled persons. They should receive the protection of the state against family members who wish to dispatch them. Further she argued that "while respecting autonomy, we have an affirmative duty to eliminate the reasons why a person would want to die instead of pressing on with life. In other words, while respecting autonomy, our society should protect disability rights. When informed competent persons request death, their wishes should not be protected." This is a form of social paternalism.

Is there a way out of this impasse?

Persons who suffer from a terminal illness that is judged by physicians to be irreversible should have their constitutional right to privacy protected by social policy. One form of this policy already in place in most states is living will legislation. Another is durable power of attorney. These instruments permit persons to state ahead of time what they do and do not want done in case they become incompetent. It is an act of extreme belligerence not to respect these and other competent wishes. Not to respect such wishes has also been declared unconstitutional in most states, as we saw in the sketch of court decisions above.

When persons have failed to express these wishes explicitly, the law should provide for their loved ones to automatically act as their surrogates — unless there is evidence of estrangement, ill-will, or cupidity. Physicians and families now act in this manner informally. When a disease is thereafter judged "hopeless," that is, that no intervention can reverse its course or improve the patient's present condition, then the family, acting in the best interests of the patient, can order the care stopped. Sometimes this is done on the basis of constructing a value history of the patient: "Grandpa was always so independent. He hated hospitals. He would not have wanted to be hooked up to these machines." In any event, there is no moral requirement to press on in the face of hopelessness.

This is the crux of the Nancy Ellen Jobes case that prompted Ms. Hoyt's concerns. Jobes, who lay in a nursing home in a near vegetative state, could not recover. There was no intervention that would change her condition. She had been arrested by our modern technology in a near-death condition. She was not so much disabled, as Hoyt argued, as impeded from dying.

Failure to make the distinction between interventions that can make a difference in the outcome and interventions that cannot makes it appear that active euthanasia is now endorsed by the supreme courts of such states as New Jersey, Massachusetts, and California. Clearly this is not the case, despite conservative efforts to paint it so.

While some persons suffering from a terminal illness as defined above could conceivably be counted as disabled, the normal meaning of that term applies more precisely to those who suffer a chronic but not immediately terminal condition. When persons in this condition state a wish to die, social paternalism may be an important step to take while we seek social support systems to address their needs. Recall our concerns in Chapter Four about friends who helped Kenneth Wright in his wheelchair shoot himself (Case 47, p. 271). Unfortunately, in many cases, we cannot eliminate the causes that impede some people's desire to live. Often these causes are rooted in the chronic disease itself.

What should we do, then, after we have tried our best to eliminate the conditions that cause some persons to want to die, and those persons still express that wish? In the case of Elizabeth Bouvia (Case 51, p. 275) in California, the appeals court opted in favor of respecting autonomy and allowing her wish to die to be unimpeded by the conscience of physicians and hospitals. Because Bouvia was so disabled by both disease and intense pain, not to feed her constituted assisted suicide. This case raises the question about anyone judging the quality of life of another. The best judge of that is the patient himself or herself. Yet we do not live as islands. We are part of a social fabric that owes us compassion and care.

It is at this juncture that the concerns Hoyt expresses trump the ideal of a wholesale respect for patient autonomy. In the end, the dispute is a metaphysical one about the nature of human beings and their relationship to society. The best solution is a set of carefully structured conditions under which patient autonomy during the dying process would be protected, while distinguishing this process from conditions under which a wish to die would *not* be respected. We would also bear in mind our arguments about the nature of healing in the previous chapter and the personal extension to the dying that transcends technologically defined care. So far, there is nothing alarming in the way we have argued about these issues, and in the way the courts have generally analyzed these conditions.

Our proposal in the final chapter builds on that analysis.

SOCIAL EUTHANASIA
AND THE NAZI EXPERIENCE

We asked at the outset of the first chapter whether there is any moral difference between acts of commission and acts of omission. We have seen since that there is, but that the distinction sometimes is important and sometimes not, from a moral point of view. Now we must consider such acts on a broader scale. How does omission, not providing care to persons who need it, relate to the act of commission, killing undesirables, such as was done in Nazi Germany?

Some of the methods we currently use to limit access to health care may make it seem that we are with great subterfuge carrying out a pogrom against the poor, the elderly, and other undesirables in society, comparable in scope and intent to that done under the Nazis in Germany or under Stalin in Russia. In the first chapter, we called this a form of social euthanasia. (For a conceptual analysis of this category of cases, see p. 294). Recall the statistics. About 38 million (by the turn of the century, this may reach 50 million) uninsured and underinsured in the United States cannot get access to health care. If a poor person needs an angioplasty to stay alive, and cannot receive it, while others who can pay are able to receive it, then we have socially euthanized that person. If the DRG reimbursement system goes bankrupt in a state and hospitals that care for the poor in the inner city can no longer survive, they close. And access for the poor person covered by Medicaid, but who has a stroke while working in a shop in the inner city, is effectively denied. It takes the ambulance twice as long to get her to an emergency room as it might for a comparable person who suffers a stroke in an affluent suburb near a highly technical hospital. Consider, in this connection, the case of euthanasia by transfer (see Case 53, p. 276), as well as cases of "dumping."

Recall the paradigmatic case of a bad death that inaugurated Chapter Two, the death of Bobby Bright, the convenience-store clerk who was murdered. Analogously, the paradigmatic case of bad euthanasia, euthanasia that gave that word a bad name, was the Nazi experience. The Nazi initiatives were so gruesome that the "Mythology of Nazi Euthanasia" functions as a social impediment to any and all efforts to address the problems created by modern technological medicine. As Robert Jay Lifton notes in the Foreword to his important study of the Nazi physicians, he was reminded of Albert Camus's injunction that we be neither victims nor executioners, and that therefore we avoid creating the kinds of social structures that lead us into one or the other.[27] It is this lesson that can be learned from what he calls "carefully examined past evil."[28]

Let us look more carefully at what the Nazi doctors did. As Lifton demonstrated, the Nazi doctors did bureaucratic things. He discovered thousands of memos, letters, documents, that discussed the most efficient means of euthanizing certain citizens, arguing about the best methods. They set up a bureaucracy of evil, without ever seeming to question the fundamental premises upon which this evil rested. Lifton holds that at the heart of the Nazi enterprise was a boundary that was crossed between healing and killing:

> My argument in this study is that the medicalization of killing — the imagery of killing in the name of healing — was crucial to that terrible step.[29]

Sadism and viciousness among camp guards and certain types of personalities the Nazis attracted are not sufficient reasons to explain wholesale genocide. The latter enterprise is too vast for that. It had to be clothed in more gentle terms of healing. In fact, it had to be turned to the "faceless, detached bureaucratic function originally described by Max Weber, now applied to mass murder."[30] Lifton reports interviews with psychiatrists who had to treat disorders among those troops who had to kill persons face-to-face. Distancing through bureaucracy and through gassing were essential features of medicalized killing, without which it probably could not have been done on such a vast scale.

Note our argument in the previous chapter that on the basis of friendship with patients, physicians should not do direct euthanasia. This argument is strengthened, it seems to us, with the findings of Lifton.[31] But it is also strengthened by the number of mercy killing cases involving nurses.

Most recently in Vienna, in the spring of 1989, four nurses were indicted for murdering forty-nine elderly patients at Lainz hospital. At first the nurses began euthanizing helpless patients seventy-five years old or older. After a short time, these "mercy" killings, actually involuntary euthanasia cases, turned to troublesome patients. The methods used were drug overdose, smothering, or pouring water down a patient's nose and drowning her.[32] The patients were all seriously ill. Yet the nurses are being likened to concentration camp guards and were called by the citizens, "The Death Squad of Lainz." It is easy to consider how our natural animal compassion may override other considerations in cases like this.

Evil is banal, in the end.[33]

Look at some of the original Nazi initiatives.

The path toward euthanasia and genocide began with an initiative developed by the party in 1933, five months after gaining power. It was called a "Law on the Prevention of Hereditarily Ill Offspring." This was a compulsory sterilization law, not unlike others in the United States. It is estimated that between 200,000 and 300,000 mentally retarded and genetically misfit persons were sterilized without their consent. The precedent was thereby established to "heal" persons without their or their family's consent.

A few months before World War II, a "Children Action" was inaugurated. This "Action" was a party rule, not something enacted by elected authorities. It was simply signed by the Führer. According to this action:

1. The Government Committee for the Scientific Registration of Hereditary and Congenital Diseases was established to look like a research organization.

2. Compulsory reporting forms were created.

3. All physicians and midwives were to report "all severe cases of idiocy, mongolism, microcephalic disorders, hydrocephalia, deformed extremities and paralysis."

4. Three physicians, without seeing the patients, would vote plus or minus on the reports.

5. If unanimously minus, the child was ordered placed in one of twenty-one "pediatric wards" around the country.

6. There they were euthanized without parental knowledge or consent.

It is estimated that 5,000 children were killed by this method.

The first day of World War II, another action was initiated, this one called "The Committee for the Study of Mental Hospitals." The steps were similar. If a patient at a hospital was unable to work after five years there, he or she was reported to a committee of three physicians and a leader. Again without interviewing the patient or family, a judgment was made, and the patient was sent to one of six secret, guarded hospitals to be gassed. Families were never told of the location or fate of their loved one. This action, unlike others, became known. Churches protested, and it was the only action halted, in 1941. The secret sites were turned over for use in the "Final Solution" instead. But the killing of such patients did not stop. "Wild euthanasia," euthanasia not considered truly kind (like gassing), was practiced instead. It consisted of starving the patients to death. A total of 80,000 to 100,000 persons were killed this way.[34]

These initiatives were based on thinking that paralleled that in other countries between the wars, that parallels now our current thinking about the need for euthanasia.

The key phrase that captures the Nazi initiatives is "Die Vernichtung des lebensunwerten Lebens," literally, "The Reduction to Nothing of Life-unworthy Life," or "The Elimination of Valueless Life." This phrase is not far from our own concerns to halt lives that are not worth living any longer. But our concerns stem from DRGs running out. Our current society does not suffer economically as much as the Germans did between the wars. It is not yet a distressed society. Calling meaningless existence, ballast existence, two physician authors pondered the question of prolonging such lives:

> The question of whether the expense of maintaining these categories of ballast existence is in every aspect justifiable was not an urgent one in former times of prosperity. Today conditions are different and we have to consider it.[35]

It makes sense to be concerned about allocating resources to lives, like those of the mentally defective or the increasingly aged Alzheimer's victims in nursing homes, when other goods and services in society suffer. Remember that during the depression in Germany, it took a wheelbarrow full of money at one point to buy an apple. Why would one want to continue to prolong lives in institutions at greater expense than providing schooling and other needs of healthy citizens?

The turn in reasoning from concern about individuals suffering, and their voluntary efforts to relieve that suffering by requesting euthanasia, to involuntary euthanasia, comes about through both a concern about the common good (reducing heavy medical expenses on society) and a concern for the emotional burdens on families and caregivers. Note this latter kind of reasoning from the same authors:

> The incurable mental defectives, those either born that way, or, in cases of general paralysis, those who have become so, have no will to live or die. Therefore there is no actual consent to be killed, nor is there a real will to live which would have to be broken. Their lives are absolutely worthless, but they don't find them intolerable. For their family and for society they are a terribly heavy burden.[36]

The reasoning that placed external value on human lives, and calculated that those lives no longer had value, is extremely dangerous. This contributes to our caution about direct, active euthanasia, in the absence of voluntariness. It also should contribute to cautions about putting in place public policies that permit active, direct euthanasia, even if voluntary, if there are other measures in place that can properly address the suffering and pain of individuals. Having such measures in place during times of prosperity will not be a cause of concern; but when a depression hits, and the DRGs run out even faster than they do now, or when our society approaches overload in the coming century as gerification continues, then will we behave any differently than the Nazi's?

CONCLUSION

We have examined how society protects vulnerable citizens from both the capricious decisions of others and, sometimes, from the misapplication of life-prolonging technology during the dying process. The key element in this protection is voluntariness. Recall that the very purpose of establishing the right to die is to help dying persons regain some *control* over the dying process. Even if voluntary active euthanasia is permitted, we argued, society places itself at risk in time of economic depression of disvaluing human beings and subjecting them to a death they did not choose. In itself this is no reason not to pursue legalization of euthanasia, but it is a source for immense caution.

Balancing the effort to provide dying persons with control over their dying with the disputed and controversial methods to be used to respect the value of human life, while simultaneously controlling pain and addressing suffering, is a herculean human task.

At this point we can see that promoting euthanasia is not a simple act of honoring the wishes of patients, of honoring their autonomy. Many other values are involved.

It is time now to propose a workable solution for the present age.

NOTES

1. "Hospital Study Finds Care Disparity," *Chicago Tribune*, March 10, 1986, sec. 1, 8. The federally funded study showed that among thirteen hospitals and 5,000 patients some intensive care units saved three times as many lives as others, and that the staff's attitude was more important than the technology in saving lives.

2. Office of Technology Assessment, *Life-Sustaining Technologies and the Elderly* (Washington, D.C.: U.S. Government Printing Office, July 1987).

3. Andrew Fegelman, "2d Mistrial for Dad in Newborn's Death," *Chicago Tribune*, October 10, 1987, sec. 1, 1, 7.

4. There were several versions of these rules, all of which were struck down by federal courts: 47 *Federal Register* (June 16, 1982), p. 26027; 48

Federal Register (March 7, 1983), p. 9630; 48 *Federal Register* 129 (July 5, 1983), pp. 30846–30852; 49 *Federal Register* 6 (Thursday, January 12, 1984), pp. 1622–1654. Finally, the matter was addressed by federal legislation: Public Law 98–457 ("Child Abuse Amendments of 1984"); and procedures for implementing this law were developed by regulations: 49 *Federal Register* 238 (December 10, 1984), pp. 48170–48173; 50 *Federal Register* 72 (April 15, 1985), pp. 14893–14901.

5. In *re Conroy.*

6. Edmund D. Pellegrino and David C. Thomasma, *For the Patient's Good: The Restoration of Beneficence in Health Care* (New York: Oxford University Press, 1988).

7. Thomas Swick, "NJ Court Backs Patient's Right to Refuse Care; Ruling Parallels Brief Submitted by ACP Chapter," *ACP Observer* 7, no. 7 (July/August, 1987), 2. The Nancy Ellen Jobes case discussed in this article was widely viewed as a victory of the individual over institutions.

8. Ibid.

9. Mike Gallagher, "No Charges in Life-Support Case," *USA Today*, May 19, 1989, 3A.

10. Ibid.

11. J. L. Griffin and W. Grady, "Hospital in Center of Storm: Life-Support Controversy Follows Death of Infant," *Chicago Tribune*, April 28, 1989, 1, 1, 24.

12. "Lawyer on Ethics Committee Can Represent Involved Parties Later," *Medical Ethics Advisor* 4 (August 1988), 113–115.

13. Kenneth Vaux, as quoted in "Linares Case Highlights Ethical Dilemma," *Illinois Medicine*, May 26, 1989, 8.

14. Robert Enstad, "Attempted Murder Called Act of Love," *Chicago Tribune*, October 8, 1987, sec. 2, 4. See also "Judge Sentences Geraldine Sagel to 30 Months' Probation," *Chicago Tribune*, February 15, 1988, sec. 2, 1.

15. Terry Wilson, "Bond Cut in Mercy Killing Case," *Chicago Tribune*, February 2, 1989, 2, 4.

16. "Woman in Coma Has Abortion: Patient Stable After Operation That Caused Legal Fight," *Chicago Tribune*, February 12, 1989, 1, 4.

17. *In the Matter of Karen Ann Quinlan*, 70 N.J. 10, 355 A.2d 647 (1976).

18. In *re Conroy.* For a sketch of the three "tests" proposed by the court in Conroy, see p. 136 above.

19. Pamela Schaeffer, "Workshop on Ethics Stirs Furor," *St. Louis Post-Dispatch*, January 15, 1989, 1, 5.

20. Ibid.

21. Judith Ahronheim, "Starvation — A Physician's View," *SRD Newsletter*, Spring 1989, 1, 7.

22. "Workshop," 5.

23. William Grady, "High Court Hears Right-to-Die Arguments," *Chicago Tribune*, January 28, 1989, 2, 3.

24. Katherine Schweit, "Ruling Broadens Right to Die," *Law Bulletin*, 1, 10. This article was about Prange.

25. Joanne Lynn, ed., *By No Extraordinary Means* (Bloomington, Ind: Indiana University Press, 1987).

26. Grady, "High Court Hears Right-to-Die Arguments."

27. Robert Jay Lifton, *The Nazi Doctors: Medical Killing and the Psychology of Genocide* (New York: Basic Books, 1986), p. xiii.

28. Ibid.

29. Ibid., p. 14.

30. Ibid., p. 15.

31. Ibid.

32. Joseph A. Reaves, "Killings in Hospital Stir Nazi Nightmares," *Chicago Tribune*, April 16, 1989, sec. 1, 8.

33. Hannah Arendt, *The Human Condition* (Chicago: University of Chicago Press, 1958); *On Violence* (New York: Harcourt, Brace, Jovanovich, 1970).

34. All data is taken from H. Lauter and J. E. Meyer, "Active Euthanasia without Consent: Historical Comments on a Current Debate," *Death Education* 8 (1984), 89–98. This is also the source for the quotations from Binding and Hoche cited below.

35. K. Binding and A. Hoche, *Die Freigabe der Vernichtung lebensunwerten Lebens*, 1920.

36. Ibid.

THE TREATMENT OF SUFFERING

The terrible "problem of suffering" is regarded by the Bible not so much as a problem to be explained...but as an inscrutable existential fact.
—Thomas Merton[1]

It is clear that there is a broad range of euthanasia practiced in the United States, some forms of which are more acceptable than others.[2] We discussed these in each of our chapters. At the very least current public discussion of the issue means that both the medical profession and the public have taken their heads out of the sand and are facing the problems of maintaining human life in the midst of suffering.[3] Robert Veatch once characterized death in American society as "an immoral power to be driven from the community like the Salem witch."[4] The very places that death happens testify to our inability to confront it. In 1937, only 37 percent of Americans died in hospitals. Today the figure is closer to 80 percent.

Because of the trap of high technology that can keep persons in a state of deferred death, a surgeon, John Wrable, M.D., argued in *American Medical News* that active euthanasia would be a humane way to end human suffering.[5] He urged:

Euthanasia is a realistic alternative to the extraordinary measures being used today to keep patients alive, and it's cost effective...because it reduces the terminally ill patient's hospital stay and stops the use of expensive machines.[6]

Dr. Wrable argues for both withholding and withdrawing and active euthanasia. He also brings to bear on the subject the problem of cost. In a subsequent interview he noted that three patients in 1988 asked him for active euthanasia; "One was a forty-four-year-old woman who was paralyzed from the neck down with cancer, and she said to me, 'John, just put me to sleep. They do it to animals, don't they?' " Wrable wonders how the medical profession can condone passive euthanasia while condemning active euthanasia.[7] Patrick Nowell-Smith, president of the World Federation of Right-to-Die Societies, claims that to maintain moral validity for the distinction between active and passive euthanasia is "irrational, perhaps even immoral."[8]

Greater openness about and widespread discussion of active euthanasia seems to have begun about 1983. Before then, in the United States, thinkers such as James Rachels, Marvin Kohl, Daniel Maguire, and Eike-Henner Kluge had proposed in the early 1970s that it would be moral and should be made legal to take direct, positive action to induce death.[9] Richard Brandt examined the rule against killing and concluded that the real moral weight of that rule was not harming another. He argued that not all killing harms people.[10] But in 1983, Dutch physicians began to discuss their real problems and challenges in their practice, giving examples such as that of a twenty-nine-year-old patient suffering end-stage diabetes out of control and in great pain, a fifty-eight-year-old woman with colon cancer, an eighty-five-year-old woman with cancer of the jaw and neck, a sixty-four-year-old woman with melanoma and eye cancer, and a forty-six-year-old woman with metastases to bone from breast cancer.[11]

These case descriptions, rather than astute philosophical discussion, drove home the need for doctors to reconsider their duties; and this reconsideration gradually produced a more sophisticated understanding of the conditions under which euthanasia could be practiced.[12] Most likely the fabled Dutch openness to ideas helped the process along. Dutch physicians are no more or less enamored of killing their patients than physicians anywhere else. But there is no question that the Dutch medical and nursing societies are farther along than in any other country. Both national societies recently adopted strictly controlled guidelines for active euthanasia; these are based on the rights of individuals — not only do they have a right to life but also a right to pursue happiness. They allow mercy killing on a patient's well-considered request in cases of unacceptable suffering.[13]

In 1984 in Nice, before an annual meeting of the Federation of Right-to-Die Associations, five French doctors issued an ultimatum while admitting that they helped their patients to die. The time had come, they affirmed, "to respond to the demand for a better quality of this last period of life and for a death which prevents suffering and preserves dignity."[14]

In the United States the more public discussion of euthanasia began with the desperate actions of families toward senile elderly loved ones. We mentioned Roswell Gilbert, a seventy-six-year-old retired electronics engineer, who killed his wife, Emily, by shooting her through the head while she sat on the couch. Gilbert took matters into his own hands after fifty-one years of marriage. Emily had suffered from Alzheimer's disease since 1973, and from osteoporosis. Her spinal column was severely collapsing. He did not want her to continue life as a "suffering animal." Gilbert is one of the few mercy killers who is still in jail, since he refused to be contrite about his action. As Roger Rosenblatt in *Time* pointed out, "the matter of mercy killing is getting rough and out of hand." In Ft. Lauderdale, a man seventy-nine shot his sixty-two-year-old wife in a stairwell of a hospital. In 1981, in San Antonio, a man sixty-nine shot his seventy-two-year-old brother in a nursing home. In 1985 a man put two bullets through the heart of his three-year-old daughter who was comatose after a freak accident.[15] No wonder the grand jury refused to indict Rudy Linares for simply withdrawing the respirator from his son.

Independent of the many philosophical, theological, social, and political questions about voluntary active euthanasia is the most pressing one of all: is euthanasia the best way to support suffering, dying persons?

For some, the constant pain of the dying, and the lack of any hope, cause a tremendous feeling of frustration and anxiety. They see active, voluntary euthanasia as the only possible alternative to continued pain and suffering.[16] When the California initiative was inaugurated, an initiative that would have put legalization of active euthanasia on the ballot so voters could establish a statute directly, circumventing the elected legislature, a group was formed that called itself Americans Against Human Suffering.[17] Basic compassion was the motive of the organization.

If compassion drives our desire to put people out of their misery, it is difficult to understand the position of organized religion against active euthanasia from the standpoint of compassion and personal autonomy. Is religion in favor of suffering? Does it have an ancient interest in maintaining the human condition of "sinfulness"? The standard religious viewpoint is:

> It is never an act of mercy to the individual as such to take away his life when it is truly human. Human life has intrinsic value and should not be taken by another human even if the victim requests it. God alone holds the right to give and take life.[18]

Yet does not the new control over dying presented by medical technology make human beings co-creators with God over life and death?

And does not this technology require a new kind of responsibility for human life and death?

In our pluralistic society, most citizens do not seem to share this religious view, at any rate (however true or false it may be). An early poll showed that 62 percent of those questioned would support some form of Human and Dignified Death Act.[19] When euthanasia is no longer taboo, patients do request active euthanasia. One study in the Netherlands would indicate that it is the cause of about 2 percent of all deaths that occur in general practice there.[20] However, the distinction between active and passive euthanasia in the Netherlands has been dropped in all official documents: "In the eyes of the law acts of omission and commission directed at hastening of death are the same."[21] To draw that distinction may seem to be splitting hairs, since the intent to provide a dignified death is the same in both instances. But the data about how frequently active euthanasia is requested in the Netherlands is suspect without the distinction. And Dutch physicians have continued to say that "the distinction is not juridically relevant, but it is enormously important in medical practice."[22]

For others, the lack of personal engagement during the dying process is viewed as a temptation to seek an easy way out, death by injection. This is seen as avoidance of more difficult personal tasks.[23] The British Medical Association issued an eighty-page report on euthanasia in 1988, arguing that active euthanasia is morally wrong and utterly unacceptable. The report argues that patients seldom request euthanasia, when they do it should be viewed as a cry for help, and active euthanasia is not a relevant option in view of adequate terminal care.

At issue is whether doctors must respect the individual autonomy of patients who request euthanasia, or whether such patients' autonomy is limited by the distress of the dying process and thus may/must be discounted.[24] In October of 1987, physicians from forty-one countries met in Madrid for the annual meeting of the World Medical Association. They drafted a statement that decries active euthanasia, even if it is the patient's wish. The statement said in part:

> Euthanasia, the act of ending the life of a patient through a deliberate action, even on his request or that of a relative, is contrary to all ethics. This does not prevent the doctor to respect the will of the patient to let the natural death process follow its course in the terminal stage of the illness.[25]

Nor are these doctors "outliers" from others, including ethicists, in the United States. In contrast to the poll cited above, 45 percent of readers of *Medical Ethics Advisor* are strongly against legalizing active euthanasia, 12 percent are opposed generally, and 31 percent are undecided at present. Only 5 percent are currently in favor of legalization.[26]

When the physician and other caregivers in society approach a dying patient, is the option for terminating that life a part of the care to be offered? Patients have complications that require compassionate care that borders on killing, yet (as we argued in the previous chapters) physicians especially have a traditional duty to respect the life of patients. If the physician or other caregiver is committed to preserving the life of the patient, is there an alternative to active euthanasia that will not neglect the suffering of that patient?

Even though we argued in our third chapter that the positive duty to promote benefits to persons may permit voluntary euthanasia as a moral good, our other chapters have detailed the sweat and tears of doctors, family members, and society that suggest extreme caution in implementing any social policy that encourages direct and active euthanasia.

CURRENT SITUATION

The current situation can be characterized by four key elements, the first two set against the second two. These are presented as a summary of the conflicts discussed throughout our book.

The incredible power of modern medicine to prolong life would stun even the most farsighted proponent of the right to voluntary active euthanasia during the period between the world wars. We pointed out some of the thinking in Europe at and before this time in the previous chapter. At the origin of the current United States Society for the Right to Die, for example, many prominent Protestant clergymen supported active euthanasia as a means for persons to maintain some control over their dying process. On January 17, 1938, a headline of the *New York Times* proclaimed: "For Mercy Deaths — New Group Formed to Fight for Legalization of Ending Agony of Incurably Ill." The founder and president of the group was Dr. Charles Francis Potter, a Unitarian minister. The goal of the group, later to become the Euthanasia Society of America, was based on the belief "that with adequate safeguards it should be made legal for *incurable* sufferers to *choose* immediate death rather than await it in agony." The board and advisors was loaded with liberals — Harry Emerson Fosdick, Margaret Sanger, Havelock Ellis, Julian Huxley, Somerset

Maugham, and H. G. Wells were among them, as was the head of the American Cancer Society.[27]

All the arguments presented by these leaders would only be intensified by the experience of families and caregivers with the real sufferings of some patients during the dying process today. So many of the members of the original board were active in other fields, such as planning one's family, that it is clear their commitment to active, voluntary euthanasia stemmed from the right of persons to make a choice. This choice was seen as a way to preserve human dignity. Dr. Potter is quoted in the newspaper article as saying:

> The problem of euthanasia is one which sooner or later confronts every practicing physician. Perhaps the time has come to forget the Commandment "Thou Shalt Not Kill," and listen to Jesus — "Blessed Are the Merciful." There is no logical argument against euthanasia. Most opposition is based on *misunderstanding* of the proposed procedure.[28]

Obviously, the misunderstanding was greater than Dr. Potter believed. Once the Germans instituted the reprisal for a shooting of a Nazi diplomat by a Polish Jew in Paris, the reprisal that went by the code word *Krystallnacht*, everything changed. Prior to the awareness that the modern state was capable of immense violence, almost 46 percent of the population in New York was in favor of a bill that would legalize euthanasia. But not only did the word "euthanasia" acquire a negative and belligerent coloring from the Nazi experience; citizens rightly became reluctant to center so much power over human life in the hands of the state, however well-meaning.

Even so, a major effort was launched in 1952 to draft an Amendment to the U.N. Declaration of Human Rights to include "The Right of Incurable Sufferers to Voluntary Euthanasia," signed by more than 2,500 British and American clergy, physicians, scientists, and lawyers. Eleanor Roosevelt, then chair of the Human Rights Commission, decided against supporting it at the time precisely because of Nazi genocide that continued to be revealed after the Second World War.[29] Nevertheless, the natural offshoot of this movement came in 1954 with the publication by Joseph Fletcher of *Morals and Medicine*, a book that argued for the right to control reproduction, the right to control parenthood, and the right to control death through euthanasia.[30]

Dramatic advances have occurred in underlining the rights of patients — not only their rights to determine the treatments they desire and do not desire during the dying process, but also the development of the right to choose treatments at any time during life. The efforts of the Society for the Right to Die in sponsoring and supporting legislation and court deliberations have been outstanding. The living will, and other advance directives, including the durable power of attorney, all point to eventual further clarification of these rights, for example, what impact they will have on long-term care settings.[31] What is important to note is that the underlying motivation for the development of such instruments, as Alice Mehling points out, is the prevention of suffering.[32] It would make sense to extend these rights to even greater control over the dying process.

The kind of suffering that nevertheless continues was outlined in detail by Steven Miles, M.D., associate director of the Center for Clinical Medical Ethics at the University of Chicago. Dr. Miles was a guest lecturer at a chronic care hospital, where he was asked if he wanted to see "the feeding wards." There he observed a long corridor of two wards, each with eighteen beds.

On each bed, a still lump was covered by a blanket. These patients were in the final stages of devastating progressive brain diseases. They no longer spoke, or moved, or recognized their attendants. Pumps stood at the head of each bed from which plastic tubes carried a creamy liquid under the blankets. A single nurse sat at a desk in the corner. The wards were quiet.

Miles asked his tour-guide whether these patients were involved in their treatment plans. The answer was no. They had progressively stopped eating and feeding tubes were inserted after they had become incompetent. "Are their families involved in their care?" he asked. Again, the answer was no. "Families get discouraged by this kind of situation and stop coming after a while." Then Miles asked whether there was any review of whether this kind of treatment ought to be stopped. His companion was stunned by the question. "Oh no, that would be unthinkable!" he said.[33]

Although we normally do not consider painless and somnolent treatment like this a kind of suffering, it is. The patient's lives are prolonged without the dignity of choice governing their treatment, either their own or their family's. We have argued that the family ought to have the power to determine what is in the best interest of loved ones caught in this progressively deteriorating state. Withholding and withdrawing seem far more humane than the occasional, but desperate, acts of killing described throughout this volume.

By contrast, the emphasis upon personal autonomy in medical ethics is coming under greater scrutiny today. Concerns about the Libertarian society implied by this emphasis has led many thinkers to counter autonomy with the need for beneficence as well. The implications of conflicts about medical ethics and ethical theory for active euthanasia include (a) the increased role of the health provider's values in caring for the dying patient, (b) greater attention to the *relation* between physician and patient, rather than exclusive focus on the needs and wants of the individual patient alone, and (c) questions about the kind of society we ought to be.

Since the mid-1970s the right of individuals to control their dying process has led to support for passive euthanasia.[34] The history of the argument goes back farther than that, of course.[35] While courts have been open to recognizing a right to passive euthanasia, state legislatures have effectively proscribed active euthanasia or mercy killing by implicitly characterizing it as first-degree murder. Motive and consent ought to diminish the harshness of this judgment, and often do in actual cases. Because of the increased control over the dying process that modern medicine affords, a greater sense of the balance between individual autonomy and medical, ethical, and religious values is required in today's society.[36]

Further contrast to the first two points comes from physicians' concerns about either the perceptions of the community about physicians being involved in voluntary active euthanasia,[37] or more profound arguments about the traditional physician commitments to the value of human life. Thus Leon Kass presents a thoughtful articulation of what is owed a dying patient by the physician. He argues that humanity is owed humanity, not just "humaneness" (i.e., being merciful by killing the patient). Kass argues that the very reason we are compelled to put animals out of their misery is that they are *not* human and thus demand from us some measure of humaneness. By contrast human beings demand from us our humanity itself. This thesis, in turn, rests on the relationship "between the healer and the ill" as constituted, essentially, "even if only tacitly, around the desire of both to promote the wholeness of the one who is ailing."[38] This is still a majority view among physicians, perhaps as large as 75 percent.

For most, the traditional principles of respect for the patient's well-being (beneficence),[39] respect for autonomy, maintaining the integrity of the health professional, and balancing justice and equity,[40] are the predominate concerns. Studies have shown that physicians employ more than biomedical data in evaluating whether a patient is dying. They also take into account the important features of human interaction and the proportion between therapeutically available interventions and the possible outcome.[41] Such interactive concerns tend to present counterpressures to a straightforward honoring of patient wishes and autonomy when someone requests active euthanasia.

Additional concerns about euthanasia revolve around the distinction between active and passive, as we noted in Chapter Three, and the duties and rights that would arise if active euthanasia would ever be legalized. Recall that philosophers such as James Rachels hold that the distinction between active and passive is of no moral importance.[42] One reason is that when one has a clear responsibility for the welfare of another and when it is within his or her power to save that person, the moral difference "between killing and letting die seems most negligible."[43] From the point of view of intention, Helga Kuhse has argued that it is a myth that letting die is not the intentional causation of death.[44] Natalie Abrams also argued that the good outcome of active euthanasia is superior to passive.[45]

Yet there are intuitive reactions that do make moral sense of the distinction. For one thing, the distinction permits physicians to preserve the intention of mercy without directly taking the life of the patient in light of their traditional commitments to preserving life. This is not hypocrisy or hair-splitting. It is one thing to intend death and do it, and another to intend death and let it happen. But more important than this intuitive concern is the difficulty many physicians and laypersons have of establishing a right to active euthanasia. As Peter Williams has argued, rights have a "demand quality." That is to say, a right is not a right unless it obliges others to meet needs. If there is a right to be killed, then there must be identifiable individuals who have a duty to kill. "In a nutshell," he argues, "rights are prima facie justifications for acts in accordance with them. The assertion of a right is the assertion of a sufficient reason for action."[46]

Critical to the establishment of a right to active euthanasia in our society would be not only its function in justifying action, but also the moral sentiments that would surround neglect of such rights. We can already see the charge that those opposed to active euthanasia are in favor of cruelty, pain, and suffering of dying persons. Even though the Hemlock Society guidelines for active euthanasia respect the right of physicians who oppose active euthanasia not to perform it, if it were legalized, the moral sentiments of society would increasingly and negatively judge such individuals. This is surely another part of the intuitive protection of the distinction between

active and passive euthanasia even Dutch physicians find important.

In sum, radical conservatives and radical liberals seem to agree
that there is no distinction between killing and letting die. The former
view all forms of euthanasia as equal and equally abhorrent. The
latter view all forms of euthanasia as equal and equally moral, even
required. In the middle of these two camps are those who wish to
preserve the distinction either with respect to the act or with respect
to intention. The former agree that there is no distinction between
intending the death of a suffering person by using active or passive
euthanasia, but the actions themselves are distinct, one direct killing,
the other letting an underlying disease take its course. The latter
hold that the actions of killing and letting die may be morally the
same, but the intentions between passive and active euthanasia are
distinct; the intent of passive euthanasia is the mercy and not the
death, while the intent of active euthanasia is the death as a means
to the mercy. Each of these positions has subtle differences within
it as well.

Even if active euthanasia becomes one of a number of important
ways society benefits its members, difficulties still exist about giving
such power to individuals in our own quite violent and life-degrading
society.

TECHNOFIX SOCIETY

The greatest concern of those opposed to active euthanasia is the cre-
ation of a new sort of Nazi society. Commentators point out that
Germany between the wars had many enlightened groups, similar to
those present in the U.S. today. Among these groups were physicians
and laypersons interested in fostering voluntary active euthanasia.
When this idea was taken by the Nazi party and imbedded in initiatives to eliminate the retarded and other genetically and (later)
racially impure persons, it was, of course, an aberration. But the
misuse by political power of a technology available in medicine and
the reasoning of active euthanasia are dangers in all modern states.

For the U.S. the danger exists in the economic sphere. Will it be
easier to use a simple method of dispatching those persons whose care
costs too much,[47] or who are now considered to be a burden on society, like the aged and the poor, than to address their suffering, which
sometimes is overwhelming even for the most dedicated caregivers?
As Joseph Cardinal Bernadin noted in an address on euthanasia at
the University of Chicago Hospital, "We cannot accept a policy that

would open the door to euthanasia by creating categories of patients whose lives can be considered of no value merely because they are not conscious."[48]

The "technofix" solution is not only easier to conceptualize and implement than the more difficult processes of human engagement, but is also "suggested" by technology itself. The training and skills of modern health professionals are overwhelmingly nurtured within a bath of technological fixes. By instinct and proclivity, all persons in a modern civilization are tempted by technical rather than personal solutions to problems. This is the real issue for Cardinal Bernadin, for example, who poses this question:

> What would we be suggesting to one another and to our society, if, seemingly with the best of motives, we were to say that those who are sick, infirm, or unconscious may be killed? How could we allege that such actions would not affect us individually and collectively?[49]

Such actions are a form of "privatizing life," denying its social and communal dimensions as both a private and public good.

Therefore the concerns of disvaluing human life through technical responses to human suffering should not be dismissed as hopelessly conservative and neurotic. Disagreements about treatment strategies are often less a matter of principle than of assessment of the facts in the case.[50] The overbearing experience of the twentieth century is one in which persons have been put at the mercy of technology. Caution about this reversal of the creative process is not only justified, but important in developing any social policy and legislative process.

The proper kinds of caution can be seen from the reaction of physicians, members of the Hemlock Society, and the lay public to the "It's Over, Debbie" case published in *Journal of the American Medical Association* (reprinted as Case 1, p. 208). Concerns were expressed about the lack of feeling on the part of the resident who dispatched Debbie with an overdose of morphine. There was no engagement with her, her values, or her suffering (except to eliminate it as easily as possible). Annoyance at the interruption of the schedule of the resident was expressed. The resident did not try to find out what Debbie meant when she said, "Let's get this over with." Nor did he discuss the values of the patient and the family with the other, unidentified person in the room. Nor, most damagingly, did he try to contact the managing physician. All of these problems portrayed in a vivid way the dangers of the "technofix" mentality drummed into the heart of all of us.

THE RIGHT NOT TO SUFFER

The movement toward voluntary active euthanasia rests on the following principles:

Autonomy. A person has a right to do what he or she pleases with the body. In constitutional terms, this is the right of privacy. It is extremely important to maintain this right in our day. If any person is deprived of this right, as have been mothers of unborn children at the hands of medicine and courts (see above, pp. 168–169), then the state will gradually acquire the right to dispatch those of us who no longer count. This will most likely take the form of compassionate euthanasia for the sick, elderly, retarded, and the aged, as a means for our society to cut unnecessary health care costs. Alternatively — and no less unwelcome — the political imperialism might take the opposite extreme of forbidding any life-shortening limit to treatment, even when the patient explicitly requests it.

A person should not have to suffer unduly at the hands of a rampaging modern medical technology. Uwe Reinhardt has suggested that the modern American health industry is the fourth largest country in the world.[51] The right to control one's own destiny should be seen, in light of this remark, as a major civil rights effort in facing the power of modern medicine.

When a person decides that continued life is meaningless, that decision ought to be respected. No one else has a better sense of the value and meaning of one's own life than that individual.[52] In the second chapter we developed the argument that our duty is to benefit the dying person. If that person consigned his or her life over to us for euthanasia, it was with the judgment that the life was no longer worth living. This is not a judgment we want to consign to the state, given the experience of Nazism. So it ought to be centered in the individual who makes this judgment.

These arguments are for the most part valid. They can be met by a social policy that ensures, through double-effect euthanasia, that no one will suffer pain unduly, and that all other suffering will be eliminated as far as possible.

An important distinction must be drawn here, however. The distinction should be between pain and suffering. Persons ought not to have to suffer pain; but all dying involves a kind of suffering that cannot entirely be taken away. As Eric Cassell has argued, suffering is distinct from physical distress. The former is undergone by persons, and the latter by the body.[53] Since persons experience suffering, personal engagement by health providers and caregivers is essential to relieve it.[54]

Pain control is not only required but possible.[55] In this regard, the focus should turn to the obligations of the community and away from rights of patients. The patients cannot control the pain entirely on their own; we must assist them in this effort.

This social policy might be called a right not to suffer (within the confines of medical treatment). But the policy can be articulated better as an obligation on the part of the community to control the pain and address the suffering of dying. This is how Liebeskind and Melzack put it on behalf of the International Pain Foundation:

We are appalled by the needless pain that plagues the people of the world — in rich and poor nations alike. By any reasonable code, freedom from pain should be a basic human right, limited only by our knowledge to achieve it.[56]

Let us look at the outlines of a proper social policy for the control of suffering before expanding our notions about planning for death.

OBLIGATIONS TO RELIEVE PAIN AND SUFFERING

As Eric Cassell has argued, the primary obligation of physicians and other caregivers to the dying patient is to control the suffering and pain of that person.[57] This position was taken in our earlier chapters. In all respects, Cassell also argues, confrontations about the person's right to make treatment decisions within this context are "ugly," if they do not take into account the structure of that person's life and value choices.[58] This obligation includes, as Dame Cicely Saunders indicates (from her long association with the hospice movement), an obligation to address the spiritual suffering that patients experience.[59] Although modern medicine offers many means for pain control, it is an irony, perhaps stimulated by the overwhelming sense of responsibility for the lives of patients, that physicians are reluctant to use the means at their disposal to control pain.[60]

Balancing the duty to control pain and suffering with the wishes of patients and the good of society can be extremely difficult. As Edmund D. Pellegrino, M.D., says, "Relief of pain is the least disputed and the most universal of the moral obligations of the physician. He can be excused for not being able to cure his patient, but not for failing to relieve the suffering that accompanies illness."[61]

Yet many persons complain that their pain and suffering was not addressed during the dying process.[62] We have already seen how families suffer when their loved ones suffer. Even though most persons who are dying do not wish to commit suicide, a "way out" of pain is ever on their mind. They tend to hoard their pain medications, foregoing relief at this time so that when things get too bad they have something ready for it. This means that their fears about future pain force them to submit to present pain.

Furthermore, the engagement of doctors and health care providers with dying patients has a dangerous dimension. Doctors can impose their own values about suffering and bearing pain that can be entirely inappropriate.[63] Thus, even though the control of pain may be a moral requirement of medicine, its application to individual cases may vary to such an extent that real pain is simply not controlled.[64] Evidence exists that this is more often the case than is realized.[65]

Why is there so much seeming reluctance to control pain, and more importantly, to address the deeper suffering that goes with dying? Perhaps one reason is that we have no common language about pain. Since each person experiences it differently and at different levels of intensity, it is very difficult to manage it properly. Physiologically speaking, pain control can vary over the hours, with widely divergent swings. On top of that, the experience of pain is an interpreted experience, interpreted by the patient with all the values and meaning of life the patient brings to dying. It is a subjective experience, subjectively interpreted, yet "read" by compassionate others through the actions and reactions of the body and the words of the patient.[66] Additionally, even if a physician is proficient in the understanding and application of analgesics to pain control, this proficiency must be worked out through a therapeutic plan with the patient so that the latter's values and goals can still be respected. The person suffering and dying must be protected as a person, as a being who can still pursue goals. Simply avoiding imposing one's values on the vulnerable and dependent person who is dying is not enough. Enhancing that person's values is also required.[67] Thus, the personal extension or personal engagement of which we spoke dovetails into the duty of beneficence discussed in Chapters Two and Three. This goes quite clearly beyond technofix solutions.

Yet in practice, balancing this duty and the desire to address the pain and suffering of dying people creates some of the most exquisitely difficult dilemmas physicians face. Consider, for example, Case 25 ("The Quadriplegic Surgeon," p. 237) as paralysis is often not considered a "terminal" illness, even though it does eventually lead to death. Clearly this patient "suffers" though he may not be in pain. Not only must physicians and other health providers address this suffering, they must meet it head-on as a challenge to their own personal and social values.

Furthermore, as our examination of hospice principles showed, the commitment of modern medicine to engaging persons and their spirits on the level of biosocial interdependence is strongly impeded in modern society by technological barriers. Technology influences training. It makes people think that the only intervention into the lives of others must be through technological means, rather than interpersonal ones.

If the focus turns to the obligation of caregivers to control pain and address suffering, this requires a rethinking of the goals of modern medicine, especially during the dying process. The goal of medicine in this instance must be to assist persons to accomplish (however small) some life-plans, a point we made in Chapter Five (see p. 143).[68] One way of rethinking these goals is to introduce a duty not to prolong dying at the point when a patient:

1. suffers from the effects of a terminal illness, however long that illness may take to play out its course.

2. judges, on the basis of his or her own self-worth and attendant quality of life judgments that the life he or she now lives is no longer of meaning, or has given advance directives in this regard.

3. has left no advance directives, the family and caregivers agree that the condition of the patient is such that the terminal illness is now in its imminent phase, and the patient is no longer able to participate in the spiritual and material goods of human life.

Finally, a rethinking of the nature of the human community is required in any social policy stressing the obligation to address suffering. This requires, at the very least, the kind of thinking that informs the hospice movement.[69] The community must become a community of healing, even in the presence of death. Saunders refers to this as "friendship for each individual person in pain."[70]

One of the difficulties we experience in addressing suffering and controlling pain of the dying is that we suffer from a dysfunctional notion of the community. In Chapter Five we encountered the problem of reaching out to the dying patient, of breaking through the barriers in our own minds that suggest that we ought to "leave the dying alone," since it is such an individual and private act. This is not an authentic human response to the agony of another person. As Erich Loewy puts it:

> ...when we deny community, when we see in community merely an entirely voluntary and fluid association of entirely free individuals or claim that individuals do not emerge from and, therefore, are obligated to each other and to community by more than merely their autonomy, we end up with individuals free to starve to death in the street.[71]

Another way of putting this is to note that a morally significant aspect of all beings is their capacity to suffer.[72] But even more remarkable is the moral significance of the capacity of *human* beings to heal. Animals feel pain and can sympathize, but they cannot heal effectively beyond the most elemental licking of sores. Only humans can heal. This capacity grounds a view of human society as capable of being a community of healers.

Background for this reflection comes from the debate about whether mere membership in a certain class of species confers generic moral properties. In the past, the natural law theory held that individual membership in the human race conferred on that individual certain inalienable rights, and by consequence, such an individual became "someone whose freedom and well-being ought to be regarded as having ultimate value."[73]

However, the movement to establish animal rights, or at least to address animal suffering, directly attacked species-specific moral properties. Peter Singer, for example, argues that "if a being suffers, the fact that it is not a member of our own species cannot be a moral reason for failing to take its suffering into account."[74] Singer attacks speciesism as the illogical reasoning and prejudice that creates moral supremism among humans. A similar position is taken by Diana T. Meyers, who says: "...the implication that individuals possess certain rights because they are members of a select species sanctifies a conceptual muddle. Individuals qualify for rights as individuals, not as members of a species."[75]

From this movement we can extract the importance of suffering as a moral category, as Erich Loewy does, without taking a stand on species-specific moral standing as such. Yet it seems obvious to us that certain rights, rights such as free speech, freedom from interference in thinking, and the like, *are* applied to a specific species, the human species, as a class, as a form of life, not just individually. In this we agree with Morton Winston. [76] It would not make sense to predicate these freedoms of other species of animals.

In like manner, if suffering contains a moral quality, that of obligating others to care about that suffering, so too does healing. And healing is an action of human beings, not other animals. (We have to be careful here. Owning a pet, like a dog, is supposed to be beneficial in the recovery from serious illness. Petting the dog can lower blood pressure. But is this the dog's healing effect on us, or our own sensors reducing the blood pressure?) Hence, we think that the capacity to heal itself is a primary and fundamental moral quality of human beings as a species. As such it can be expected of one another. The obverse is also true. It is a duty as a member of the species to heal, not only other members, but also, as we do, members of lower species as well.

Perhaps this aspect of human life is most jeopardized, in the view of many, by a social policy permitting voluntary active euthanasia. Will human persons neglect the admittedly difficult task of addressing suffering, and their own capacity to heal, by too quickly dispatching others who are clearly suffering pain and the loss of self-worth and the meaning of life? How much easier it is to give someone a shot than to engage them personally, with all the time and energy it takes for that engagement. We are a society of rapid fixes.

CLINICAL METHODOLOGY: THERAPEUTIC PLANNING FOR DEATH

Planning to bring about death is an alternative to active euthanasia (direct killing) that may be sufficient in all but the most extreme cases in bringing about a good death. Its chief components would be the following:

1. Death should be seen as a kindness for some dying people.

2. Inducing or bringing about death can be a virtuous and moral act, especially if done in conjunction with the wishes of the patient. Recall the arguments presented in the second and third chapters about intention and motivation. There we established that if benefiting the dying patient were a prima facie duty, then sometimes aiming them at death would be a good much to be preferred to continued suffering and pain.

3. Death planning would accept the explicit goal of active euthanasia — a merciful and painless death for the patient — while using passive means to carry out this goal. Among such means would be withholding and withdrawing of technological care at the patient's request, including antibiotics or fluids and nutrition, and the like.

4. Far greater care would be taken than is often the case today at

controlling pain and suffering, not just physical pain, but also psychological and social suffering. The double effect would be used to make a commitment to the patient that he or she need not suffer, even if adequate pain control would shorten life.

5. When and if active euthanasia is permitted by society, the therapeutic plan process leading to death could be proposed as an alternative to active euthanasia that pays attention to fears and concerns of patients who do not wish to go quickly "into that dark night." Evidence exists that very few dying patients want to be dispatched early.[77]

6. Managing the patient's course to lead to death requires a rethinking of the goal of medicine. Medicine's aim in a technological age should be to preserve life as a conditional value, that is, a good that permits us to pursue higher values, such as love, work, contributions to society, travel, friendship, and the like. When patients themselves, or their surrogates, inform us that their lives no longer possess these meanings, it is a cruelty to prolong their lives at all costs while ignoring their statements. The values such patients articulate should be part of the therapeutic plan. When these values can no longer be achieved, then preserving life loses its importance in the therapeutic plan. In its place is bringing about a kind death for the patient.

Recall how in Chapter Two we discussed the importance of digging behind the expressed wishes of patients. Donald C. (Case 19, p. 229), seemed clear about his wish to die. But the psychiatrist was able, through extensive personal engagement, to ascertain the real values Donald possessed, values about controlling the outcome of his own life. Thus, while straightforward acknowledgement of individual wishes seems to be good on the surface, a prudential caveat is required. People do not always know what they want, nor express what they want clearly. The most important feature of a clinical management plan is the personal and spiritual encounter between the caregiver and the dying person.

LEGISLATIVE AND PUBLIC POLICY POSSIBILITIES

Among legislative possibilities are:

1. Seek to establish an obligation of caregivers to dying patients that establishes the latter's right not to suffer severe pain and to have their suffering addressed.

2. Establish legislation that holds all physicians harmless who,

while meeting these needs of dying patients, with the proper documentation, induce their death through double-effect euthanasia.

3. In effect, legalize all forms of passive euthanasia, including
double-effect euthanasia.

4. Continue to support the traditional commitments of health
providers to the value of human life as an important component
of a life-oriented human society. Leon Kass's argument that medicine possesses its own intrinsic ethic through a devotion to others is
essential in this regard.[78]

5. If occasionally voluntary active euthanasia is deemed necessary
by physicians and their individual patients (when all other methods
have failed), continue the present method of adjudicating each case
on its own merits, if it does come to the attention of legal authorities.
In almost every case that has been brought to court, the health professional guided by motives of compassion has been acquitted on one
or another technicality. This experience parallels that in the Netherlands, where killing or active euthanasia still carries a penalty in the
law. It is widely assumed that active euthanasia is legal in the Netherlands. It is not. But Dutch physicians are immune from prosecution
if they follow strict guidelines set down by court judgments in three
judicial tiers, district courts, appeals courts, and the supreme court.
At the heart of these guidelines is the requirement that all other means
of controlling pain have been exhausted, the patient makes repeated
and voluntary requests, and two physicians concur with the appropriateness of the request.[79]

6. Require that all health professional caregivers who work with
seriously ill patients are trained in appropriate methods of pain-
control, and that certification examinations include this educational
requirement.[80]

7. Require that persons dealing directly with dying patients be
required to be board certified by the American Academy of Pain
Management itself.[81]

8. Establish accredited pain management centers at major medical centers throughout the country, so that psychiatrists, psychol-
ogists, anesthesiologists, physiatrists, and physical and occupational
therapists can all assist patients who are dying and in pain. At present,
most pain centers concentrate on chronic musculoskeletal pain, but
their skills can also be put to use for controlling other forms of pain
as well.

9. Establish enabling legislation that would designate as a surrogate or substitute decision-maker the family member, next of kin,
or extended family person (not necessarily related) who most prox-

imately cared for the patient as the legally valid surrogate in the absence of any documentation. As a default mode, this proximate caregiver would be empowered to act on behalf of the patient with his or her managing physician. In cases of elderly persons without families in nursing homes or in what Miles called the "feeding wards," the default surrogate might even be the nurse.

10. Before entrance into any long-term care facility, or before being cared for in any service of a hospital dealing with seriously ill persons (intensive care unit, the hematology/oncology ward, cardiology, kidney dialysis, etc.), legislation ought to provide the necessity for a discussion of the wishes of the patient or family caregivers regarding technological interventions and life-prolonging actions. This discussion may be mandated by law or social policy, without requiring individuals or families to execute specific instruments like a living will or a durable power of attorney for health care. Individual institutions and services, of course, may wish to consider requiring some sort of instrument.[82] Minimally, all admissions might be required to have a place on a form for "designated decision maker" should the patient become incompetent.

11. Throughout the text we spoke of the assistance that can be given by hospital ethics committees and ethics consultants in an ethics consult service. In some instances, like the Linares case discussed several times in this book, calling for the assistance of the committee or an ethics consultant might have avoided an overly legalistic response that might come naturally from the hospital attorney. Enabling legislation might be passed that would designate the family unit and physician (unless there be evidence of dysfunction in the family, or abusive tendencies), upon consultation with a second, external physician, to make decisions about withdrawing inappropriate care from the incompetent family member, even if it is a child. Discussion with the ethics committee or ethics consultant might be part of this legislation.

The increased debate about active euthanasia in our society should be welcomed. It will force the medical profession, ethicists, the legal system, and churches to provide better responses to the questions posed at the beginning of Chapter One.

CONCLUSION

At this time, there is little need for active euthanasia if more attention is paid to controlling pain and suffering, if more attention is paid to the patient's value system, if much firmer responses are made to patient requests to die, and if plans are made with the patient and family about the best way to bring about a kind and merciful death. These are all big "ifs." Dutch physicians surveyed on a senior Fulbright research fellowship independently and unanimously indicated the need for far greater attention to the psychosocial aspects of caring for the dying patient.[83] In other words, the proper care of the dying requires a kind of loving community our society finds so elusive.

Arthur Dyck, in his *On Human Care*, observed that in the early days of the discussion of the principle of beneficence by Frankena and Ross, "Do no harm" was considered virtually equivalent to "Do not kill."[84] Today, however, the problem has become one of interpreting beneficence from the point of view of the harm to the patient from intractable suffering and the community's obligation to address that suffering in its most profound and intimate ways.[85]

Keeping a person alive at all costs is a form of biological idolatry. This idolatry denies the finitude of human existence in favor of a Faustian adventure at the expense of the dying person.[86] If that person wishes to participate in this adventure, he or she may sign on, of course. But at present, the default mode should not be the assumption that care can be delivered only by high technology medicine. Personal healing is a ministry of persons, not of technology. The dying person in our society deserves at least all our human capacity to heal.

NOTES

1. Thomas Merton, *Opening the Bible* (Collegeville, Minn.: Liturgical Press, 1983), p. 56.
2. David C. Thomasma, "The Range of Euthanasia," *Bulletin of the American College of Surgeons* 73, no. 8 (August 1988), 4–13.
3. "Active Euthanasia Gaining Acceptance as Topic for Debate," *Medical Ethics Advisor* 5, no. 3 (March 1989), 29–35. This issue contains the latest proposed Dutch guidelines for active euthanasia as well.
4. Robert M. Veatch, *Death, Dying and the Biological Revolution* (New Haven and London: Yale University Press, 1976), p. 5.
5. John Wrable, "Euthanasia Would Be a Humane Way to End Suffering," *American Medical News*, January 20, 1989, 31, 33.
6. *Ibid.*, 33. Ninety-five percent of Wrable's practice is in geriatrics.
7. "Active Euthanasia Gaining Acceptance as Topic for Debate," *Medical Ethics Advisor* 5, no. 3 (March 1989), 30.
8. Patrick Nowell-Smith, "A Plea for Active Euthanasia," *Geriatric Nursing and Home Care*, March 1987, 23.

9. Daniel Maguire, *Death by Choice* (Garden City, N.Y.: Doubleday, 1974); Marvin Kohl, "Voluntary Beneficent Euthanasia," in *Beneficent Euthanasia*, Marvin Kohl, ed. (Buffalo, N.Y.: Prometheus Press, 1975), pp. 134–135; Marvin Kohl, *The Morality of Killing* (New York: Humanities Press, and London: Peter Owen, 1974); Daniel Maguire, "Death and the Moral Domain," *Saint Luke's Journal of Theology* 20, no. 3 (June 1977), 197–216; Eike-Henner W. Kluge, *The Practice of Death* (New Haven and London: Yale University Press, 1975).

10. Richard Brandt, "A Moral Principle about Killing," in Marvin Kohl, ed., *Beneficent Euthanasia*, pp. 109–11.

11. E. G. H. Kenter, "Euthanasie in een huisartspraktijk," *Medisch Contact* 38 (September 23, 1983), 1179–1183.

12. E. G. Scholten, "Euthanasie ex lege artis?" *Medisch Contact* 46 (November 18, 1983), 1447–1448; W. C. M. Klijn, "Kanttekeningen bij een euthanasieverslag," *Medisch Contact* 6 (February 10, 1984), 183–184; D. J. Kruythoff, "Euthanasie een oplossing?" *Nederlands Tijdschrift voor Geneeskunde* 129, no. 15 (1985), 700–702.

13. "The View from the Netherlands," *Hospital Ethics* 4, no. 1 (January/February 1988), 14.

14. "5 French Doctors Admit to Helping Patients End the Misery," *Chicago Tribune*, September 21, 1984, 1, 12.

15. Roger Rosenblatt, "The Quality of Mercy Killing," *Time*, August 26, 1985, 74.

16. Joseph Fletcher, "The Courts and Euthanasia," *Law, Medicine and Health Care* 15 (1987/88), 223–230.

17. Derek Humphrey, "Legislating for Voluntary Active Euthanasia," *Humanist*, March/April 1988, 10–12, 47.

18. Norman Geisler, *Ethics: Issues and Alternatives* (Grand Rapids: Zondervan, 1971), p. 235.

19. Derek Humphrey, "Legislating for Active Voluntary Euthanasia."

20. A. P. Oliemans and H. J. G. Nijhuis, "Euthanasie in de huisartspraktijk," *Medisch Contact* 41 (1986), 691.

21. Henk Rigter, Els Borst-Eilers, H. J. J. Leenen, "Euthanasia across the North Sea," *British Medical Journal* 297 (December 17, 1988), 159.

22. Our translation of "het verschil is juridisch niet relevant, maar in de medische praktijk enorm groot." J. H. Mulder, "Euthanasie in de oncologie," *Medisch Contact* 38 (1983), 563–565.

23. Dr. Stein Husebo explicitly asks himself this question, examines some of the most powerful cases with which he has been associated, and concludes: "I emphasize, however, that in a very few situations, active euthanasia will be a caring thing for doctors to do." ("Is Euthanasia a Caring Thing to Do?" *Journal of Palliative Care* 4, nos. 1 and 2 [1988], 113–114); by contrast, Kenneth MacKinnon considers active euthanasia a cop-out: "Active Euthanasia: A "Cop-out"? *Journal of Palliative Care* 4, nos. 1 and 2 (1988), 110.

24. British Medical Association, *Euthanasia* (London: British Medical Association, 1988).

25. "Mixed Messages Heard Over Euthanasia," *Hospital Ethics* 4, no. 1 (January/February 1988), 14.

26. "Little Support for Active Euthanasia among Readers of *MEA*, Poll Shows," *Medical Ethics Advisor* 5, no. 3 (March 1989), 31.

27. See the historical sketch of the origins of the Society for the Right to Die presented to the board by Ruth P. Smith, "Remarks by Ruth P. Smith at the SRD's 50th Anniversary Celebration," December 7, 1988, New York, New York.

28. Ibid.

29. Ibid., p. 5.

30. Joseph Fletcher, *Morals and Medicine* (Princeton: Princeton University Press, 1979).

31. Fenella Rouse, "Living Wills in the Long-Term Care Setting," *Journal of Long-Term Care Administration* (Summer 1988), 14–19.

32. Alice Mehling, "Living Wills: Preventing Suffering or a Deadly Contract?" *State Government News* (December 1988), 14–15; Alice Mehling and Shirley Neitlich, "Right-to-Die Backgrounder," *News from the Society for the Right to Die*, January 1989.

33. Steven H. Miles, "When Medical Technology Replaces Caregiving," *Chicago Tribune*, February 17, 1989, 1, 23.

34. Douglas Walton, "Active and Passive Euthanasia," *Ethics* 86, no. 4 (July 1976), 343–349.

35. Gerald J. Gruman, "An Historical Introduction to Ideas about Voluntary Euthanasia: With a Bibliographic Survey and Guide for Interdisciplinary Studies," *Omega* 4 (1973), 87–138.

36. Linda A. Lacewell, "A Comparative View of the Roles of Motive and Consent in the Response of the Criminal Justice System to Active Euthanasia," *Medicine and Law* 6 (1987), 449–463.

37. W. Gaylin, L. Kass, E. Pellegrino, and M. Siegler, "Commentaries: Doctors Must Not Kill," *Journal of the American Medical Association* 259 (1988), 2139–2140.

38. Leon Kass, "Arguments against Active Euthanasia by Doctors Found at Medicine's Core," *Kennedy Institute of Ethics Newsletter* 3, no. 1 (January 1989), 1–3, 6. This article is a shorter version of a paper that will appear in *The Public Interest*.

39. E. D. Pellegrino and David C. Thomasma, *For the Patient's Good: The Restoration of Beneficence in Health Care* (New York: Oxford University Press, 1988).

40. As conveniently summarized by Fenella Rouse, "Legal and Ethical Guidelines for Physicians in Geriatric Terminal Care," *Geriatrics* 43, no. 8 (August 1988), 69–75.

41. Jessica Muller and Barbara Koenig, "On the Boundary of Life and Death: The Definition of Dying by Medical Residents," in Margaret Lock and

Deborah Gordon, eds., *Biomedicine Examined* (Dordrecht/Boston: Kluwer Academic Publishers, 1988), 351–374.

42. James Rachels, "Active and Passive Euthanasia," *New England Journal of Medicine* 292 (January 9, 1975), 78–80.

43. Joseph M. Boyle, Jr., "On Killing and Letting Die," *New Scholasticism* 51, no. 4 (Autumn 1977), 433–452.

44. Helga Kuhse, "A Modern Myth — That Letting Die Is Not the Intentional Causation of Death: Some Reflections on the Trial and Acquittal of Dr. Leonard Arthur," *Journal of Applied Philosophy* 1, no. 1 (March 1984), 21–38.

45. Natalie Abrams, "Active and Passive Euthanasia," *Philosophy* 53, no. 204 (April 1978), 257–263. For a critique of her position, see Richard A. O'Neil, "Abrams on Active and Passive Euthanasia," *Philosophy* 55, no. 214 (October 1980), 547–549.

46. Peter Williams, "Rights and the Alleged Right of Innocents to Be Killed," *Ethics* 87, no. 4 (July 1977), 385.

47. J. Daley et al., "Predicting Hospital-Associated Mortality for Medicare Patients," *Journal of the American Medical Association* 260 (December 23/30, 1988), 3617–3624.

48. Joseph Cardinal Bernadin, "Euthanasia: Ethical and Legal Challenge," address to the Center for Clinical Medical Ethics, University of Chicago Hospital, May 26, 1988, 16.

49. Ibid., 14.

50. Howard Brody, "Ethics of Treatment Refusal: Saying What We Mean in Court," *Medical Humanities Report*, Winter 1989, 2.

51. Uwe Reinhardt, "Health Care for America's Poor: The Economics of a Hot Potato," *Princeton Alumni Weekly*, February 27, 1985, 23–29.

52. Marcia Angell, "Euthanasia," *New England Journal of Medicine* 319, no. 20 (November 17, 1988), 1348–1350.

53. Eric Cassell, "The Nature of Suffering and the Goals of Medicine," *New England Journal of Medicine* 306, no. 11 (March 18, 1982), 639–645.

54. Marion Dolan, "Controlling Pain in a Personal Way," *Thanatos* 5 (Winter 1982), 5.

55. Marcia Angell, "The Quality of Mercy," *New England Journal of Medicine* 306, no. 2 (January 14, 1982), 98–99; Editorial, "Who Should Teach Pain to Medical Students?" *Pain Management* 4, no. 2 (September 1988), 2, 4; E. A. Mohide, J. A. Royle, M. Montemuro, et al., "Assessing the Quality of Cancer Pain," *Journal of Palliative Care* 4, no. 3 (1988), 9–15.

56. John C. Liebeskind and Ronald Melzack, "The International Pain Foundation: Meeting a Need for Education in Pain Management," *Journal of Pain and Symptom Management* 3, no. 3 (Summer 1988), 131–132.

57. Cassell, "The Nature of Suffering."

58. Eric Cassell, "Life as a Work of Art," *Hastings Center Report* 14 (October 1984), 35–37.

59. Dame Cicely Saunders, "Spiritual Pain," *Journal of Palliative Care* 4, no. 3 (1988), 29–32.

60. Health and Public Policy Committee, ACP, "Drug Therapy for Severe, Chronic Pain in Terminal Illness," *Annals of Internal Medicine* 99 (1983), 870–873; Daniel Goleman, "Physicians Said to Persist in Undertreating Pain and Ignoring the Evidence," *New York Times Health*, December 31, 1987, K, B5; "Judge Urges Allowing Medicinal Use of Marijuana," *New York Times*, September 7, 1988, A21.

61. Edmund D. Pellegrino, "The Clinical Ethics of Pain Management in the Terminally Ill," *Hospital Formulary* 17, no. 11 (November 1982), 1493.

62. Marcia Angell, "The Quality of Mercy," *New England Journal of Medicine* 306, no. 2 (January 14, 1982), 98–99.

63. Pellegrino, "The Clinical Ethics of Pain Management," 1496, therefore proposes that one moral requirement of pain control is that physicians not impose either their way of living or their way of dying on patients.

64. D. E. Boeyink, "Pain and Suffering," *Journal of Religious Ethics* 2 (1974), 85–98.

65. R. M. Marks, and E. J. Sachar, "Undertreatment of Medical In-Patients with Narcotic Analgesics," *Annals of Internal Medicine* 78 (1973), 178–181.

66. Jurrit Bergsma with David C. Thomasma, *Healthcare: Its Psychosocial Dimension* (Pittsburgh: Duquesne University Press, 1982).

67. Pellegrino, "The Ethics of Pain Management," 1496.

68. James Walter, "The Meaning of Quality of Life Judgments in Contemporary Roman Catholic Medical Ethics," *Louvain Studies* 13 (1988), 195–208.

69. Dame Cicely Saunders, "The Evolution of the Hospice," *The History of the Management of Pain*, pp. 167–178.

70. Ibid., p. 167.

71. Erich Loewy, "Comments at Session for Intergenerational Justice," Society for Health and Human Values Annual Meeting, April 1989, Little Rock, Ark., 1.

72. Erich Loewy, "Obligations, Communiites and Suffering: Problems of Community Seen in a New Light," *Bridges* 2, nos. 1 and 2 (1990), 1–16.

73. Morton E. Winston, "Species Membership and Moral Standing," *Contemporary Philosophy* 12, nos. 5 and 6 (1988), 20–23.

74. Peter Singer, "Not for Humans Only: The Place of Nonhumans in Environmental Issues," in Manuel Velasquez and Cynthia Rostankowski, eds., *Ethics: Theory and Practice* (Englewood Cliffs, N.J.: Prentice-Hall, 1985), p. 479; also see Singer, "All Animals Are Equal," *Philosophic Exchange* 1, no. 5 (Summer 1974).

75. Diana T. Meyers, *Inalienable Rights: A Defense* (New York: Columbia University Press, 1985), p. 116.

76. Winston, "Species Membership and Moral Standing," 23.

77. R. Kotulak, "Study of Terminally Ill Shows Most in No Hurry," *Chicago Tribune*, February 9, 1986, sec. 6, 5.

78. Leon Kass, "Why Doctors Must Not Kill," *The Public Interest* 94 (Winter 1989), 25–46.

79. Henk Rigter, Els Borst-Eilers, J.J.J. Leenen, "Euthanasia across the North Sea," *British Medical Journal* 297 (December 17, 1988), 1593–1594.

80. National Institutes of Health, "The Integrated Approach to the Management of Pain" 6, no. 3, Available from the U.S. Department of Health and Human Services, Public Health Service, NIH, Office of Medical Applications of Research, Building 1, Room 216, Bethesda, MD 20892.

81. Board Certification as "Diplomate," "Fellow," and "Clinical Associate" is available from the American Academy of Pain Management, 1320 Standiford Ave., Suite 136, Modesto, CA 95350.

82. S. H. Miles and M. B. Ryden, "Limited-Treatment Policies in Long-Term Care Facilities," *Journal of the American Geriatrics Society* 33 (1985), 707.

83. D. Thomasma and J. Bergsma, "Autonomy and the Cancer Patient," submitted to *Social Science and Medicine.*

84. Arthur Dyck, *On Human Care* (Nashville: Abingdon, 1977).

85. Richard M. Gula, "The Virtuous Response to Euthanasia," *Health Progress* 70, no. 10 (December 1989), 24–27.

86. Joseph Fletcher, "Medical Resistance to the Right to Die," *Journal of the American Geriatrics Society* 35 (1987), 679–682.

CASES

CASE 1	"It's Over, Debbie"

The call came in the middle of the night. As a gynecology resident rotating through a large, private hospital, I had come to detest telephone calls, because invariably I would be up for several hours and would not feel good the next day. However, duty called, so I answered the phone. A nurse informed me that a patient was having difficulty getting rest, could I please see her. She was on 3 North. That was the gynecologic-oncology unit, not my usual duty station. As I trudged along, bumping sleepily against walls and corners and not believing I was up again, I tried to imagine what I might find at the end of my walk. Maybe an elderly woman with an anxiety reaction, or perhaps something particularly horrible.

I grabbed the chart from the nurses' station on my way to the patient's room, and the nurse gave me some hurried details: a twenty-year-old girl named Debbie was dying of ovarian cancer. She was having unrelenting vomiting apparently as the result of an alcohol drip administered for sedation. Hmmm, I thought. Very sad. As I approached the room I could hear loud, labored breathing. I entered and saw an emaciated, dark-haired woman who appeared much older than twenty. She was receiving nasal oxygen, had an IV, and was sitting in bed suffering from what was obviously severe air hunger. The chart noted her weight at eighty pounds. A second woman, also dark-haired but of middle age, stood at her right, holding her hand. Both looked up as I entered. The room seemed filled with the patient's desperate effort to survive. Her eyes were hollow, and she had suprasternal and intercostal retractions with her rapid inspirations. She had not eaten or slept in two days. She had not responded to chemotherapy and was being given supportive care only. It was a gallows scene, a cruel mockery of her youth and unfulfilled potential. Her only words to me were, "Let's get this over with."

I retreated with my thoughts to the nurses' station. The patient was tired and needed rest. I could not give her health, but I could give her rest. I asked the nurse to draw 20 mg of morphine sulfate into a syringe. Enough, I thought, to do the job. I took the syringe into the room and told the two women I was going to give Debbie something that would let her rest and to say good-bye. Debbie looked at the syringe, then laid her head on the pillow with her eyes open, watching what was left of the world. I injected the morphine intravenously and watched to see if my calculations on its effects would be correct. Within seconds her breathing slowed to a normal rate, her eyes closed, and her features softened as she seemed restful at last. The older woman stroked the hair of the now-sleeping patient. I waited for the inevitable next effect of depressing the respiratory rate. With clocklike certainty within four minutes the breathing rate slowed even more, then became irregular, then ceased. The dark-haired woman stood erect and seemed relieved.

It's over, Debbie.

— Name Withheld by Request[1]

•

It is apparent from the text itself, that the resident intended to provide both comfort (give her rest) and death simultaneously. Would it have mattered if the resident only intended to provide comfort, and, as a double effect, did not will but knew ahead of time that death would result from depressed respirations? In other words, if the act were the same, would a slightly different motive have made any ethical difference?

Those who hold the doctrine of the double effect would argue that this act could be justified under certain circumstances.[2] The motive of the act would have to be to provide comfort, not to kill the patient. One would foresee that depressed respirations might take the patient's life, but this side effect would not be willed. Instead, physicians should become more aggressive about relieving suffering.[3]

For many, the action of this resident was unwarranted, and clearly murder. "It is not legal and it's not ethical to put a patient to death. Period," said Dr. John Burkhardt, a Knoxville family practice physician who was at the time chairman of the Council on Ethical and Judicial Affairs for the American Medical Association.[4] Even though the action may be merciful and compassionate, this view holds that physicians cannot be two things at once: both a healer and a killer. It is a violation of training, background, and, most importantly, commitment. Yet an objection to this point of view would be that the goal of medicine need not be just healing. It can be to provide comfort, or sufficient means (life) to pursue other ends.[5] Medicine might be seen as having a twofold objective: to preserve life and to relieve suffering. The two goals conflict in a case like this.

Others would rest their objection on more general rules than just professional commitment to preserve life, such as the rule against killing.[6] The distinction between active and passive euthanasia would be clearly drawn at this point.

Still others would object to the resident's action, not because it was inherently wrong, but because the process was not correctly followed. First, the author of the story was not Debbie's attending physician and would not have discussed her values with her over a period of time. Second, the resident may have mistaken her words to mean that she wanted to die, when she may have meant just that she wanted to have a procedure over with more quickly. This is very important. If active euthanasia is to be performed, then the patient's wishes must be unambiguously expressed.[7]

CASE 2   Anencephalic Heart Donor

On Friday, October 15, an hours-old baby boy was given a heart transplant. This operation was unprecedented in the Western hemisphere at the time for two reasons. First, it was unique because the surgery took place so soon after birth. The boy was born with congenital heart malformations called hypoplastic left heart syndrome. He was born at 12:45 p.m. and was operated on by 3:30 that afternoon. The reason it was possible to operate so quickly was that his heart defect was diagnosed by fetal echocardiography, a procedure that makes it possible to diagnose difficulties in fetuses as young as fourteen weeks old. A caesarean section was performed on the thirty-five-year-old mother as soon as a donor heart was known to be available. Dr. Leonard Bailey performed the operation at Loma Linda Medical Center, in California.

The second reason the operation was unprecedented was that the donor heart came from a baby born anencephalic. The heart was taken from the donor who was kept alive artificially for this purpose. Her name was Baby Gabrielle. Her parents decided to bear her to term, despite the fact that she had a severe brain malformation, so that her organs might help other babies live. The problem is that the baby was not totally brain-dead; some brain tissue, often a brain stem, is present in such babies, although this is insufficient to sustain life for very long. Thus, a form of active euthanasia took place in this case. It was an active euthanasia of an organism that is dying, kept alive artificially for the express purpose of salvaging organs.

At age seventy, Mrs. R. had become severely disabled by cardiac failure due to a damaged mitral valve. With her full and appropriate consent, she underwent a risky valve replacement, which initially went fairly well. However, within twelve hours after surgery, her cardiac output was clearly inadequate. Despite intensive care in the ICU, an adequate blood flow could not be sustained and an experimental cardiac assist device was implanted in her chest. Again, initially she seemed to improve as she was finally "waking up," though she remained moderately unresponsive. A few hours later, however, even with the assist device, her cardiac output again began to fail. No treatment arrested this downward spiral; everyone involved agreed that she would not survive. In addition to the cardiac assist device, Mrs. R. was on a respirator and had seven different tubes going into her body for fluids, medications, and monitoring.

Her surgeon, Dr. L., had remained in the hospital throughout the twenty-four hours since surgery. He talked with the family frequently and encouraged them to discuss their concerns, to visit the patient, and to call in other family members and their pastor.

Since Mrs. R. was vaguely aware and seemed quite uncomfortable, with her family's knowledge she was given morphine. Dr. L. turned off the cardiac assist device and stopped the medications regulating her blood pressure. Since she still seemed uncomfortable, jerking at intervals and furrowing her brow, Dr. L. gave her another dose of morphine. When that had no discernable effect, he asked a nurse to draw up 10 cc of potassium chloride. Then, within sight of most of the ICU staff, he injected it into Mrs. R.'s intravenous line.

Within minutes, she lay still and the cardiac monitor showed no heartbeat. Dr. L. turned off the respirator and went to tell the family that Mrs. R. was dead.

The ICU nurses and house staff were very concerned. Had Dr. L. behaved appropriately?[8]

CASE 4   Shirley Dinnerstein

Shirley Dinnerstein is a sixty-seven-year-old woman who suffers from a condition known as Alzheimer's disease.

This is a degenerative disease of the brain of unknown origin, described as presenile dementia, and results in destruction of brain tissue and, consequently, deterioration in brain function. The condition is progressive and unremitting, leading in stages to disorientation, loss of memory, personality disorganization, loss of intellectual function, and ultimate loss of all motor function. The disease typically leads to a vegetative or comatose condition and then to death. The course of the disease may be gradual or precipitous, averaging five to seven years. At this time medical science knows of no cure for the disease and no treatment which can slow or arrest its course. No medical breakthrough is anticipated.

The patient's condition was diagnosed as Alzheimer's disease three years ago, although the initial symptoms of the disease were observed as early as six years ago. She entered a nursing home four months following the diagnosis, where her (by that time) complete disorientation, frequent psychotic outbursts, and deteriorating ability to control elementary bodily functions made her dependent on intensive nursing care.

Four months ago, she suffered a massive stroke, which left her totally paralyzed on her left side. At the present time, she is confined to a hospital bed, in an essentially vegetative state, immobile, speechless, unable to swallow without choking, and barely able to cough. Her eyes occasionally open and from time to time appear to fix on or follow an object briefly; otherwise, she appears to be unaware of her environment. She is fed through a nasogastric tube, intravenous feeding having been abandoned because it came to cause her pain. It is probable that she is experiencing some discomfort from the nasogastric tube, which can cause irritation, ulceration, and infection in her throat and esophageal tract, and which must be removed from time to time, and that procedure itself causes discomfort. She is catheterized and also, of course, requires bowel care.

The Medicare program terminated assistance two months ago because, although she was hospitalized, her care was essentially custodial rather than oriented to treatment. The same care could be provided in some nursing homes, although a suitable placement has not been found. Most nursing homes would not have a team available capable of sophisticated resuscitation efforts in the event of cardiac or respiratory arrest.

Apart from her Alzheimer's disease and paralysis, she suffers from high blood pressure which is difficult to control; there is risk in lowering it due to a constriction in an artery leading to a kidney. She has a serious, life-threatening coronary artery disease, due to arteriosclerosis.

Her condition is hopeless, but it is difficult to predict exactly when she will die. Her life expectancy is no more than a year, but she could go into cardiac or respiratory arrest at any time. One of these, or another stroke is most likely to be the immediate cause of her death.

In this situation, her attending physician has recommended that, when (and if) cardiac or respiratory arrest occurs, resuscitation efforts should not be undertaken.

This decision was discussed with the patient's family (a daughter and a son), and they concur with the decision.[9]

| CASE 5 | Physician in an Overseas Hospital |

— Scene 1 —

A physician, aged sixty-eight, was admitted to an overseas hospital after a barium meal had shown a large carcinoma of the stomach.

He had retired from practice five years earlier, after severe myocardial infarction had left his exercise tolerance considerably reduced.

The early symptoms of the carcinoma were mistakenly thought to be due to myocardial ischemia. By the time the possibility of carcinoma was first considered, the disease was already far advanced. Laparotomy showed extensive metastatic involvement of the abdominal lymph nodes and liver.

Palliative gastrectomy was performed with the object of preventing perforation of the primary tumor into the peritoneal cavity, which appeared to the surgeon to be imminent. Histological examination showed the growth to be an anaplastic primary adenocarcinoma. There was clinical and radiological evidence of secondary deposits in the lower thoracic and lumbar vertebrae.

The patient was told of the findings and fully understood their import. He was not asked for, nor did he offer, any expressions of his wishes with regard to resuscitation or aggressive life support measures. His primary physician had indicated nothing about such decisions in the medical record.

In spite of increasingly large doses of pethidine, and of morphine at night, the patient suffered constantly with severe abdominal pain and pain resulting from compression of spinal nerves by tumor deposits.

On the tenth day after the gastrectomy, the patient collapsed with classic manifestations of massive pulmonary embolism and suffered cardiac arrest.

A staff physician happened to be on the unit when the arrest occurred. His first impulse was to order full resuscitation measures and to undertake an emergency pulmonary embolectomy.

But he hesitated a moment, wondering whether this was the right thing to do with this particular patient.

— Scene 2 —

The staff physician decided to proceed with resuscitation and emergency pulmonary embolectomy. The patient was successfully resuscitated and stabilized.

When the patient had recovered sufficiently, he expressed his appreciation of the good intentions and skill of his young colleague.

At the same time, he asked that if he had a further cardiovascular collapse no steps should be taken to prolong his life, for the pain of the cancer was now more than he would needlessly continue to endure.

He himself wrote a note to this effect in his case records, and the staff of the hospital were made aware of his feelings.

Two weeks after the embolectomy, the patient collapsed again — this time with acute myocardial infarction and cardiac arrest.

— Scene 3 —

His wish notwithstanding, the patient was again revived by the hospital's emergency resuscitation team.

His heart stopped on four further occasions during that night, and each time was restarted artificially.

The body then recovered sufficiently to linger for three more weeks, but in a decerebrate state, punctuated by episodes of projectile vomiting accompanied by generalized convulsions.

Intravenous nourishment was carefully combined with blood transfusions and measures necessary to maintain electrolyte and fluid balance. In addition, antibacterial and antifungal antibiotics were given as prophylaxis against infection, particularly pneumonia complicating the tracheotomy that had been performed to ensure a clear airway.

On the last day of his illness, preparations were being made for the work of the failing respiratory center to be given over to an artificial ventilator, but the heart finally stopped before this endeavor could be realized.[10]

CASE 6   Patient Ambivalence

An eighty-year-old man was admitted to the Medical Intensive-Care Unit (MICU) with a three-week history of progressive shortness of breath. He had a long history of chronic obstructive lung disease. He had been admitted to a hospital with similar problems four years earlier and had required intubation, mechanical respiratory support, and eventual tracheostomy. The patient remained on the respirator for two months before weaning was successfully completed. During the four years after discharge, his activity had been progressively restricted because of dyspnea on exertion. He required assistance in most aspects of self-care.

On admission, he was afebrile, and there was no evidence of an acute precipitating event. Maximum attempts at pulmonary toilet, low-flow supplemental oxygen, and treatment of mild right-sided congestive heart failure and bronchospasm were without effect. After four days of continued deterioration, a decision had to be made about whether to intubate and mechanically ventilate the patient. His private physician and the director of the MICU discussed the options with this fully conversant and alert patient. He initially decided against intubation. However, twenty-four hours later, when he became almost moribund, he changed his mind and requested that respiratory support be initiated. He was unable to be weaned from the respirator and required tracheostomy — a situation reminiscent of his previous admission. Two months later, he had made no progress, and it became obvious that he would never be weaned from respiratory support.

Attempts were made to find extended-care facilities that could cope with a patient on a respirator. Extensive discussions with the patient and his family about the appropriate course to follow revealed striking changes of mind on an almost daily basis. The patient often expressed to the MICU staff his wish to be removed from the respirator and said, "If I make it, I make it." However, when his family was present, he would insist that he wanted maximal therapy, even if it meant remaining on the respirator indefinitely. The family showed similar ambivalence. The patient was regularly the center of conversation at the MICU weekly interdisciplinary conference (liaison among medical, nursing, social-work, and psychiatric staff). There was great disagreement among MICU staff members concerning which side of the patient's ambivalence should be honored. Ultimately (after four and a half months on the respirator), the patient contracted a nosocomial pulmonary infection, became hypotensive, and experienced ventricular fibrillation. No efforts were made at cardiopulmonary resuscitation. In this difficult case, the concept of patient "autonomy" became impossible to define.[11]

CASE 7   Depression

A fifty-four-year-old married man with a five-year history of lymphosarcoma was admitted to the hospital intensive care unit for progressive shortness of breath and a one-week history of nausea and vomiting. Over the past five years, he had received three courses of combination-drug chemotherapy, which resulted in remission. His most recent course occurred four months before admission. On admission, x-ray examination of the chest showed a diffuse infiltrate, more on the left than on the right. Eight hours after admission, he was transferred to the MICU because of hypotension and increasing dyspnea. Initially, it was not clear whether these findings indicated interstitial spread of lymphosarcoma or asymmetric pulmonary edema. Physical findings were compatible with a diagnosis of congestive heart failure, and he was treated for pulmonary edema, with good response. His neurologic examination was normal, except for a flat, depressed affect. Deep-tendon reflexes were 2+ and symmetric. Laboratory examination revealed only a mildly elevated blood urea nitrogen, with a normal creatinine and a slightly elevated calcium of 11.8 mg per deciliter (2.95 mmol per liter). There were no objective signs of hypercalcemia. His respiratory status improved rapidly.

The patient refused his oncologist's recommendation for additional chemotherapy. Although his cognitive abilities were intact, he steadfastly refused the pleas of his wife and the MICU staff to undergo therapy. Over the first six days in the MICU with treatment by rehydration, his calcium became normal, his nausea and vomiting slowly improved, and his affect brightened. At that time, he agreed to chemotherapy, stating that, "Summer's coming and I want to be able to sit in the backyard a little longer." During this course of chemotherapy, the patient discussed his previous refusal of therapy. In his opinion, the nausea and vomiting had made "life not worth living." No amount of reassurance that these symptoms were temporary could convince him that it was worthwhile to continue his fight. Only when this reassurance was confirmed by clinical improvement did the patient overcome his reactive depression and concur with the reinstitution of vigorous therapy.[12]

CASE 8   Patient Who Uses a Plea for Death with Dignity
                                             to Identify a Hidden Problem

---

A fifty-two–year-old married man was admitted to the MICU after an attempt at suicide. He had retired two years earlier because of progressive physical disability related to multiple sclerosis during the fifteen years before admission. He had successfully adapted to his physical limitations, remaining actively involved in family matters with his wife and two teenage sons. However, during the three months before admission, he had become morose and withdrawn but had no vegetative symptoms of depression. On the evening of admission, while alone, he ingested an unknown quantity of diazepam. When his family returned six hours later, they found the patient semiconscious. He had left a suicide note.

On admission to the MICU, physical examination showed several neurologic deficits, bilateral ophthalmoplegia and bilateral cerebellar dysfunction. This picture was unchanged from recent neurologic examinations. The patient was alert and fully conversant. He expressed to the MICU house officers his strong belief in a patient's right to die with dignity. He stressed the "meaningless" aspects of his life related to his loss of function, insisting that he did not want vigorous medical intervention should serious complications develop. This position appeared logically coherent to the MICU staff. However, a consultation with members of the psychiatric liaison service was requested.

During the initial consultation, the patient showed that the onset of his withdrawal and depression coincided with a diagnosis of inoperable cancer in his mother-in-law. His wife had spent more and more time satisfying the needs of her terminally ill mother. In fact, on the night of his suicide attempt, the patient's wife and sons had left him alone for the first time to visit his mother-in-law, who lived in another city. The patient had "too much pride" to complain to his wife about his feelings of abandonment. He was able to recognize that his suicide attempt and insistence on death with dignity were attempts to draw the family's attention to his needs. Discussions with all four family members led to improved communication and acknowledgment of the patient's special emotional needs. After these conversations, the patient explicitly retracted both his suicidal threats and his demand that no supportive medical efforts be undertaken. He was discharged, to have both neurologic and psychiatric follow-up examinations.[13]

CASE 9   Patient Demands Out of Fear
                                        That Treatment Be Withheld or Stopped

---

An unmarried eighteen-year-old woman, twenty-four weeks pregnant and with a history of chronic asthma, was admitted to the hospital with a two-day history of increasing shortness of breath. She was found to have a left lobar pneumonia and a gram-negative urinary-tract infection. She was transferred to the MICU for worsening shortness of breath and hypoxia resistant to therapy with supplemental oxygen. Despite vigorous pulmonary toilet and antiasthmatic and antibiotic therapy, her condition continued to deteriorate. She was thought to require intubation for positive end-expiratory pressure respiratory therapy. Initially, she refused this modality of treatment. She was alert, oriented, and clearly legally competent. After several discussions with physicians, nurses, family, and friends, she openly verbalized her fears of the imposing and intimidating MICU equipment and environment. She was able to accept reassurance and consented to appropriate medical therapy. She showed slow but progressive improvement and was discharged eight days later.[14]

CASE 10   Family's Perception Differs
                           from Patient's Previously Expressed Wishes

A seventy-six-year-old retired man was transferred to the MICU
four days after laparotomy for diverticulitis. Before hospitalization,
he had enjoyed good health and a full and active lifestyle. He sang
regularly in a barbershop quartet until one week before admission.
The patient's hospital course was complicated by a urinary-tract infection, with sepsis and aspiration pneumonia requiring orotracheal
intubation to control pulmonary secretions.

Before intubation, he had emphasized to the medical staff his
enjoyment of life and expressed a strong desire to return, if possible, to his previous state of health. After intubation, he continued to cooperate vigorously with his daily care, including painful
procedures (e.g., obtaining samples of arterial-blood gas). However, he contracted sepsis and became delirious, and at this time
his wife and daughter expressed strong feelings to the MICU staff
that no "heroic" measures be undertaken. Thus, serious disagreement arose concerning the appropriate level of supportive care for
this patient. The professional staff of the MICU felt that the medical problems were potentially reversible and that the patient had
both explicitly and implicitly expressed a wish to continue the struggle for life. Because this view conflicted with the family's wishes,
the MICU visiting physician called a meeting of the Terminal Care
Committee (a hospital committee with broad representation that
meets at the request of any physician, nurse, or family member
who would like advice concerning the difficult decision to initiate, continue, stop, or withhold intensive care for critically ill patients). Meeting with the committee were the private physician,
the MICU attending physician, as well as representatives from the
MICU nursing and house-officer teams. The family was given the
opportunity to attend but declined. The committee supported the
judgment of the MICU staff that because of the patient's previously expressed wishes and the medical situation, vigorous supportive
intervention should be continued. A meeting was then held between medical staff and the patient's family, during which it was
agreed by all that appropriate medical intervention should be continued but that the decision would be reviewed on a daily basis. Five days later, the patient contracted a superinfection that
did not respond to maximal antibiotic therapy. He became tran-

siently hypotensive and showed progressive renal failure. In the face of a progressing multilobe pneumonia and sepsis caused by a resistant organism, the decision to support the patient with maximum intervention was reviewed. The family concurred with the professional staff's recommendation that cardiopulmonary resuscitation should not be attempted if the patient suffered a cardiopulmonary arrest. On the eighteenth day in the MICU, the patient died.

Decision-making in this case became more difficult because the patient's deteriorating condition made him unable to participate. The advice of the Terminal Care Committee was critically important in this situation, where the family's perception of death with dignity conflicted not only with the patient's own wishes but also with the professional judgment of the MICU staff.[15]

CASE 11   Misconception by Some of MICU Staff
                                           of Patient's Concept of Death with Dignity

---

A fifty-six-year-old woman was receiving chemotherapy on an outpatient basis for documented bronchogenic carcinoma metastatic to the mediastinal lymph nodes and central nervous system when she had a sudden seizure, followed by cardiorespiratory arrest. Resuscitation was accomplished in the outpatient department, and she was transferred to the MICU. She had been undergoing combination-drug chemotherapy as an outpatient for six months but continued to work regularly.

In the MICU, her immediate management was complicated by "flail chest" and a tension pneumothorax requiring tube drainage of the chest. She was deeply comatose and hypotensive. Several MICU staff members raised questions about the appropriateness of continued intensive care. After initial medical stabilization, including vasopressor therapy and mechanical respiration, her clinical status was reviewed in detail with the family. Because of the patient's ability to continue working until the day of admission, her excellent response to chemotherapy and her family's perception of her often-stated wish to survive to see the birth of her first grandchild (her daughter was seven months pregnant), maximal efforts were continued. She remained deeply comatose for three days. Her course was complicated by recurrent tension pneumothoraces, gram-negative sepsis caused by a urinary-tract infection, and staphylococcal pneumonia. She gradually became more responsive and by the seventh hospital day was able to nod "yes" or "no" to simple questions. Her hospital course was similar to that of many critically ill patients. As soon as one problem began to improve, a major setback occurred in another organ system. With each setback, there was growing dissension among the MICU staff about the appropriate level of supportive care. The vast majority of the MICU staff felt strongly that continued maximum intervention was neither warranted nor humane. A smaller group of staff, supported by the patient's daughter and (once she was able to communicate) the patient herself, felt that as long as there was any chance for the patient to return to the quality of life she had enjoyed before the cardiorespiratory arrest, maximum therapy was indicated.

The patient was the subject of many hours of debate and was a regular topic of conversation at the weekly interdisciplinary conference. She survived all her medical complications and was discharged home after seven weeks in the MICU, aware, alert, and able to walk and engage in daily activities around her home without limitation. She saw the birth of her granddaughter and spent Thanksgiving, Christmas and New Year's Day at home with her family. She died suddenly at home eleven weeks after discharge.[16]

CASE 12   Mr. B.

Mr. B. was a vigorous man of seventy-three who suffered lately of severe vascular problems, such that he could not walk more than a block without getting claudication pains (pains in his legs). He also had almost constant angina that was unstable. He was therefore brought to a major medical center for open-heart surgery. During the surgery, which went "well" as far his heart was concerned, he suffered "shower emboli," a mass of blood clots in his brain. This left him in a persistent vegetative state. He did not recover consciousness at any time after the operation.

His devoted wife of more than fifty years leaned heavily on her husband's two brothers and their wives. One brother for weeks after the surgery felt that a "miracle" would happen and would not participate in the family discussions about possibly withdrawing care. In fact, he was adamant about the others' lack of faith. This wounded

Mr. B.'s wife, who saw herself as having suffered day by day through her husband's gradual demise.

After several stormy sessions with a hospital chaplain, and additional weeks in which no change was observed in Mr. B., the brother "came around" to the view of the rest of the family.

Mrs. B. and her sister-in-law convinced the managing cardiologist on the post-operative cardiology service, the nurses, the patient representative, and the ethicist from an ethics consult service that Mr. B. had stated when visiting friends in nursing homes: "Never let me be so dependent on others. Let me die instead." This was consonant with his generally very independent mind and actions throughout his life.

A plan was formed to (a) introduce no new intervention for any event; (b) make Mr. B. DNR; (c) take him off all antibiotics and cardiac pressor agents; (d) gradually reduce the percentage of his oxygen to 25 percent above room oxygen level through his mask; (e) take him off hyperalimentation.

As part of the plan, the family agreed to continue a sugar water drip (IV D5W) and to continue to permit nurses to suction the respirator so that Mr. B. would not drown in his own secretions.

A month later the family, still very distraught that Mr. B. had not yet died, requested that the doctor "put him out of his suffering." The family refused to consider moving him to a long-term care facility, as his death would be forthcoming soon anyway.

They argued that suctioning should now cease as well, since Mr. B. "could feel no pain."

CASE 13   The Transfused Cat

A seventy-six-year-old widow is in a near brain-dead condition after suffering respiratory arrest on a ventilator. Nine months ago she required open-heart surgery. Since that time she has never left the Medium Intensive Care Unit (MICU) of an acute care facility, suffering one crisis after another due to her underlying atherosclerosis and diabetes. Throughout this stormy course, her only and unmarried daughter, a very obsessive kind of matron, has kept copious notes of what the doctors said, nursing the hurts, angers, and occasional errors. Everyone associated with the widow's care is certain that a lawsuit is pending.

The daughter refuses any discussion of a Do Not Resuscitate status for her mother. Besides suspected reasons of not wanting to "let go," which accompany her personality, she articulates a family tradition of "fighting to the bitter end." This tradition was exemplified during the death of an aunt and the death of her father. The daughter consulted with her mother's oldest sister (age ninety-four), who encouraged her not to give up. "Even our cat got transfusions when it was dying," she says. She has missed only one day of being at her mother's bedside, when she herself was sick.

Her mother has never asked not to be kept alive in this condition. In fact, she has requested throughout her treatment that "everything possible be done." She was alert, but suffering, until one week ago when she suffered the respiratory arrest. The family is wealthy and can pay for the care. The neurologist consultant, and all other physicians, nurses, patient relations coordinators, social workers, and ethicists on the case think it is time to stop prolonging the patient's dying.

CASE 14   Walter Arnold

— Scene 1 —

Walter Arnold is a sixty-eight-year-old man who has been hospitalized for six months at this admission. He has multiple medical problems:

- End-stage renal disease secondary to chronic glomerulonephritis. He has been on maintenance dialysis for ten years. At the initiation of dialysis, he was supervising his own accounting firm and continued in this role until he retired at age sixty-five.

- Mr. Arnold smoked for many years and has developed progressive pulmonary failure over the past four years. Despite intensive treatment of his lung disease, there has been no improvement in pulmonary function.

- Significant hypoxia ($pO_2 = 48$ mm Hg), which could not be treated with oxygen therapy because Mr. Arnold continued to smoke.

- Mr. Arnold had a myocardial infarction two years ago, and since that time his dialysis has been complicated by —

- severe hypotension from decreased cardiac output. His predialysis blood pressure is usually 60/30 mm Hg.

- Over the past year, he has developed intermittent psychotic behavior. Despite intensive inpatient psychiatric care for the past six months, there has been no mental improvement. The psychiatric diagnosis is chronic, psychotic, organic brain syndrome due to cerebral arteriosclerosis, hypoxia, and decreased cardiac output with aggravation by the emotional stresses of chronic hemodialysis. Two psychiatrists nevertheless concluded that Mr. Arnold is competent.

Because of the cumulative effect of multiple organ failures, Mr. Arnold's general condition has been noted to progressively deteriorate. For the past three months, he has been so debilitated that he would crawl down the hall because he didn't have the strength to walk. The nephrologist informed the family that Mr. Arnold would probably expire in three or four months, even with the most aggressive therapy.

On some days during the past year — at times when Mr. Arnold seemed mentally clear — he would privately request his physician and nurses to discontinue dialysis because he was so miserable.

However, on other occasions — and particularly in the presence of his youngest son, Martin (age thirty years) — he expressed a desire to continue dialysis.

On many occasions, the patient was agitated and confused from his organic brain syndrome. At these times, he would hit nursing personnel with his fists. He had damaged dialysis equipment and frightened other patients by throwing large objects. In order to protect other patients and personnel, the nephrologist had ordered sedation to the point of immobility (and incidental noncommunicativeness).

The nephrologist recommended to Mr. Arnold's oldest son, Donald, that dialysis be discontinued. Because his mother was dead, Donald indicated that he wanted to discuss the matter with his younger brother and sister and with his father's one brother and two sisters.

Multiple medical conferences were held to explain the situation to Mr. Arnold and his family.

After weeks of family deliberation, the oldest son indicated that he, his sister, his uncle, and both aunts wanted to stop dialysis because of the magnitude and the prolongation of suffering. They pointed out that Mr. Arnold had once been a respected and proud man.

However, Martin, the youngest son — who, it was revealed, would receive the proceeds of a life insurance policy if his father lived for three more months — was opposed to discontinuing dialysis. He indicated that he would sue the physician and the hospital if dialysis were discontinued.[17]

— Scene 2 —

Frustrated by the family's inability to come to agreement (and more than a bit nervous about the younger son's threat of a lawsuit), the nephrologist called in the unit social worker to meet with the family and help them come to agreement about what to do.

She was unable to bring the family to agreement, but she did explore the family situation in depth and reported the following:

> The youngest son, Martin, has never married. He dropped out of college and broke off an engagement then years ago so he could move back home and care for his mother through a lengthy and progressively disabling course of rheumatoid arthritis.
>
> After her death twenty-one months ago, he remained in the home to care for his father as his condition deteriorated.
>
> The life insurance policy that Martin holds is a high-risk policy, which his father took out immediately following his wife's death. Given his multiple medical problems, the only type of life insurance policy he could qualify for was one that made payment conditional on his surviving at least twenty-four months from the date the policy was issued.
>
> Mr. Arnold did not inform the rest of the family about taking out this insurance policy, but he told the insurance agent — a friend of long standing — that he was doing this in gratitude for Martin's loyal devotion to his mother. He explained that he hoped the proceeds from the policy would enable Martin "to begin to make a life for himself after my death."

CASE 15   The Hotel Guest

A seventy-year-old man found on the floor of a hotel room was brought to the hospital by a paramedic. At the time of admission he was in a stuporous, lethargic state though able to speak. He quickly became comatose. His initial lab results showed low sugar and malnutrition, which was believed to be the result of alcohol abuse. He was placed in the ICU on the remote possibility that the cause was something else. The hope was that his condition would improve in a few days, permitting him to be moved to the ward.

Once in the ICU, he deteriorated quickly. He did not respond to pain, though his EEG test showed some activity. The physician in charge met with the house staff and related the prognosis for the patient. "He will contract an infection, probably pneumonia. There is no family to contact. When the infection takes, no antibiotics will be administered, for the patient has no chance to recover."[18]

CASE 16   Mr. Meissner's Request

Eleven months ago, William Meissner, a sixty-one-year-old business executive with a wife and two adult children, was diagnosed as having head and neck cancer, an extremely painful and disfiguring disorder. At the advice of his personal physician, Dr. Samuel Maxwell, and other specialists, he underwent surgery removing the malignancy and underlying lymph nodes. Subsequently he began radiation therapy. Seven months later the malignancy recurred. A number of chemotherapeutic regimens have been tried to halt the progress of the cancer, but William's condition has continued to deteriorate to the point where he can no longer work and rarely leaves his room. To relieve the pain, Dr. Maxwell has prescribed progressively stronger pain killers, which leave William very lethargic and inactive.

Both William and his wife, Marge, have been informed by Dr. Maxwell that his cancer is terminal and that chemotherapy is merely slowing its progression. William, Marge, their son, and their daughter are quite close, and all have come to accept William's condition and prognosis. During a recent discussion, William expressed his feeling that perhaps a painless death would be preferable to continuing his painful and unpleasant existence. He also expressed his unhappiness that his family and closest friends must see him in such a debilitated state. Additionally, he feels he is cheating his family by using large amounts of family resources to pay for part of his expensive hospital care.

Convinced that his death would reduce emotional drain on his loved ones, William asked Dr. Maxwell during one of their frequent visits about the possibility of euthanasia. After a brief discussion, William offered his plan: "All I want, Doctor, is for you to give me something to end my life quickly — and, hopefully, painlessly. There is almost no point in my living — I can't do any of the things I like to do; I feel miserable because of the treatment; and I seem to always be in pain."

Dr. Maxwell sympathized with William's feelings, but he explained that he could not "kill" his patients, that he (as well as the American Medical Association) held the view that the physician could not intentionally be part of any action that would directly cause his patient to die. "If you wish, however," he offered, "I can discontinue your therapy, which will allow your cancer to progress. If an infection occurs, we could withhold antibiotics; and, in the meantime, I can continue to administer painkillers in the hopes that most of your pain will be relieved."

William was hurt and insulted. "Of all people," he thought, "the one who's supposed to relieve my pain and help me carry out my medical decisions, my doctor, wishes to prolong my pain and refuses to help me!" Dr. Maxwell, of course, did not intend to keep his patient in pain; but, after twenty years of keeping people alive, he simply could not bring about a patient's death. He was certain William was rational and competent to make medical decisions. Although he was willing to withhold treatment, he wasn't comfortable with the idea of committing active euthanasia.

As Dr. Maxwell considered the situation, he wondered if William's solution might not be a better one. A lethal injection would quickly end William's life without pain, and the months ahead might bring even greater misery than William has already experienced. Certainly there was no hope for a cure, or that William would be restored to health.[19]

| CASE 17 | "Feed, but That's All" |

An eighty-year-old man was brought into the hospital in respiratory distress. His medical history indicated that he had suffered two strokes in the past: a partial one on the right side and a later severe one which left him completely paralyzed and aphasic. For the past two years, he has been totally dependent on others for his care. He has been completely noncommunicative, except for partial physical withdrawal from pain stimuli, but it is not clear whether he cannot understand others or cannot express himself.

On admission, the patient was found to be in congestive heart failure, which responded adequately to medical care. The family was contacted for permission to insert a gastrostomy tube for feeding. The house staff wanted the procedure performed because, since he was not in any acute life-threatening distress, they felt constrained to do something for him. The family consented to the feeding procedure, but wished that nothing more be done for him.[20]

CASE 18   Mr. Downmore's Intubation

Paul Downmore is a fifty-four-year-old male who was brought to the hospital emergency room by his stepbrother, Peter Upless.

Mr. Downmore has a medical history of cancer of the rectum, first diagnosed five years ago. Treated with resection, followed by aggressive chemotherapy and radiotherapy, the tumor nevertheless metastasized and is now widely disseminated.

Brain metastases have produced a confused mental state, leading to a court declaration of incompetence and appointment of his stepbrother as official guardian by court process. Mr. Downmore also has a past history of seizures, controlled by antiseizure medication, and an intracranial bleed that had been drained, leaving him with a steel cranial plate.

Mr. Upless was prompted to bring his brother to the hospital on this occasion because he was in severe pain, which could no longer be controlled by the medications being administered at home, and because he was once again showing seizure activity.

On the way to the hospital, the emergency medical technicians intubated Mr. Downmore and instituted ventilator respiratory support.

The physicians who received Mr. Downmore at the hospital considered that the most appropriate course was *not* to institute aggressive treatment or life support measures. Thus, they decided *not* to order a CT scan of the head, even though intracranial bleeding was a likely cause of the seizures. They judged it would be best *not* to admit the patient to an intensive care unit. They did institute medications to make the patient comfortable, and antibiotics to control occurrent infections. A DNR order was written. The guardian was in agreement with all these decisions.

The fact that the patient had already been intubated in transit to the hospital posed a problem, however. To remove the tube might well lead to immediate cessation of breathing. To transfer the patient to a non-intensive-care ward with a tube in place would place an unusual burden on nursing personnel.

CASE 19   Donald C.'s Burns

Two months after being discharged from three years of military service as a jet pilot, the world of Donald C. exploded in a flash of burning gas. He was then twenty-six years old, unmarried, and a college graduate. An athlete in high school, he loved sports and outdoors. Rodeos were his special interest, and he performed in them with skill. Upon leaving the military in May 1973, Donald joined his father's successful real estate business. The two of them had always had a close and warm relationship. On July 25, 1973, they were together, appraising farm land. Without realizing it, they parked their car near a large propane gas transmission line; the line was leaking. Later, when they started their automobile, the ignition of the motor set off a severe and unexpected explosion. Donald, his father, and the surrounding countryside were enveloped in fire. The father died on the way to the hospital, and Donald was admitted in a critical but conscious state. He sustained second- and third-degree burns over 68 percent of his body — mostly third-degree burns. Both eyes were blinded by corneal damage, his ears were mostly destroyed, and he sustained severe burns to his face, upper extremities, body, and legs.

During the next nine months, Donald underwent repeated skin grafting, enucleation of his right eye, and amputation of the distal parts of the fingers on both hands. The left eye was surgically closed in order to protect it from the danger of infection; the cornea was badly scarred and the retina was partially detached. His hands, deformed by contracture, were useless, unsightly stubs. When admitted to the University of Texas Medical Branch Hospitals in April 1974, the patient had many infected areas of his body and legs. He had to be bathed daily in the Hubbard tank to control infection.

From the day of the accident onward, Donald persistently stated that he did not want to live. Nonetheless, he had continued to accept treatment. Two days after admission to the university hospital, however, he refused to give permission for further corrective surgery on his hands. He became adamant in his insistence that he be allowed to leave the hospital and return home to die — a certain consequence of leaving since only daily tanking could prevent overwhelming infection. The tankings were continued despite his protests. His mother, a thoughtful and courageous woman, was frantic; his surgeons were frustrated and perplexed.

Although calm and rational most of the time, the patient had frequent periods of childlike rage, fear, and tearfulness. He engaged his mother by the hour in arguments regarding his demand to leave the hospital — which, of course, he was physically incapable of doing unless she agreed to take him home by ambulance.

At this juncture, Dr. Robert B. White was asked to see the patient as a psychiatric consultant. Prior to seeing the patient he was given the impression that Donald was irrationally depressed and probably needed to be declared mentally incompetent so that a legal guardian could be appointed to give the necessary permission for further surgery and other treatments. The patient's mother was understandably in favor of his remaining in the hospital. She was deeply concerned about her son's welfare, and the prospect of taking him home to die from pus-covered sores on his body was more than she could bear. She was a deeply religious woman and was also concerned lest her son die without reaccepting the church that he had left some time prior to his burns.

Donald was the eldest of three children. By his family's account, he was an active, assertive, and determined person, who since childhood had tended to set his own course in life. What or whom he liked, he stuck to with loyalty and persistence; what or whom he disliked, he opposed with tenacity. His mother stated, "He always wanted to do things for himself and in his own way." Dr. White soon concluded that the mother's summary was apt. In the course of the first few interviews it was apparent that Donald was a very stubborn and determined man; he was also bright, articulate, logical, and coherent — not by any criterion mentally incompetent. He summarized his position with the statement, "I do not want to go on as a blind and crippled person." Arguments that surgery could restore some degree of useful function to his hands, and perhaps some useful vision to his remaining eye, were of no avail. His determination to leave the hospital was unshakable, and he demanded to see his attorney in order to obtain his release by court order if necessary.[21]

CASE 20   Karen Ann Quinlan

Karen Ann Quinlan turned twenty-one (then the age of legal majority in New Jersey) in March 1975. A few months earlier, she had moved out of her adoptive parents' home and into an apartment that she shared with a new friend. She pretty much cut off ties with her high school friends and began running with a new (and "faster") crowd.

She spent the evening of April 15, 1975, with some of these new friends, celebrating the birthday of one of their group at a local tavern. After the first drink at the tavern, she began to act "droopy." It was assumed in the group that she had probably been drinking and/or "popping pills" earlier in the day; and one of the group took her to his apartment nearby to lie down. She went to sleep — and she has never woke up. After awhile, the host checked on her; and he noticed that she had stopped breathing. He initiated artificial respiration and called for paramedics, who took her to the nearest hospital.

There the physician on duty in the emergency room successfully resuscitated her. She could not sustain respiration without assistance, however, so he put her on a ventilator. His basis for this decision was that he had no reliable indication of (a) how long she had been unconscious or of (b) what substances she had taken to induce the cardiac/respiratory arrest.

Later examination revealed that severe brain damage had occurred. One hemisphere of the brain showed no activity, the other hemisphere showed only "disorganized" electrical activity. Neurologists agreed that this situation was incompatible with any form of conscious awareness. They described her condition as a "persistent vegetative state." It was generally believed that she would die within a few minutes or hours if the respirator support were withdrawn (although at least one neurologist who examined her pointed out that she might continue to live without respirator support, since the brain stem appeared to be intact).

Joseph Quinlan, Karen's father, after learning these facts about her condition and talking the situation over with his parish priest, requested that the respirator be removed. The admitting physician was extremely reluctant to comply with this request, citing the following reasons:

- He felt that his professional relationship was with Karen herself, and thus that no one but she herself could release him from a professional duty to maintain her life.

- Since she was legally an adult, her parents had no legal right to make decisions on her behalf.

- He felt that withdrawing a life support measure once it was begun was a much more serious step morally than it would have been not to initiate it.

- He was concerned about his own legal liability if he took this step. By this time, the case had begun to receive some publicity in the local media; and the district attorney had announced publicly that legal action might be brought against the physician if he brought about her death.

Joseph Quinlan and his wife could not bear to see Karen kept in this condition, so he went to court seeking to have himself appointed as Karen's legal guardian for the express purpose of *either* authorizing the admitting physician to withdraw "all extraordinary procedures for sustaining [his] daughter's vital processes" *or*, if this physician continued to feel that he could not do this in good conscience, to transfer her care to another physician who would do so.

The judge who first heard this case — Judge Robert Muir, Jr., of the Superior Court — denied this request. However, Mr. Quinlan appealed the case to the Supreme Court of New Jersey; and, on March 31, 1976, they overturned the lower court ruling and granted the request — with one proviso: consultation with the hospital "Ethics Committee" was mandated to confirm the prognosis that "there is no reasonable possibility of Karen's ever emerging from her present comatose condition to a cognitive, sapient state" and the judgment that "life-support apparatus should be discontinued."

Karen was weaned from the respirator during the third week of May 1976. She did not die as most expected.

She was subsequently transferred to a full care nursing home where she remained alive for more than nine years. She was fed through a nasogastric tube, antibiotics were administered to combat frequent infections, and she was turned regularly to prevent bedsores.

Joseph and Julia Quinlan continued to visit Karen daily, and they claimed that they sometimes detected indications that she was aware of their presence. None of the other staff confirmed this.

The same priest who advised Joseph Quinlan initially told him, after she had remained in this condition for several years, that nutrition and antibiotics could be considered as extraordinary measures, given Karen's overall condition, and thus that he would have legal and moral warrant for authorizing their withdrawal if he chose. Mr. Quinlan's response was: "How can a father not feed his daughter?" He declined to take this step.

Karen remained in the Morris View Nursing Home until June 11, 1985, when she died of "respiratory failure following acute pneumonia on top of a chronic vegetative state." She had contracted the pneumonia five days earlier. No antibiotics were administered, although a nonprescription drug was given to reduce the fever.

CASE 21   Nancy Cruzan

The Supreme Court of the State of Missouri forbade the withdrawal of artificial nutrition and hydration through a gastrostomy in the case of Nancy Cruzan, who has lain in a permanent vegetative state for five years as a result of an automobile accident. She was thirty years old at the time of the accident. If the feeding continues, she might be expected to live another thirty years in this condition. Her parents argued that she did not wish to live in this condition. Their judgment was based on a "somewhat serious conversation" in which Nancy had indicated that if sick or injured she would not want to have her life continued unless she could live "halfway normally." A trial court found this sufficient evidence that she would not want to be maintained on artificial food and hydration, and they ordered the state employees caring for her in the Mount Vernon State Hospital to carry out the request of her parents as her legal guardians to withdraw the fluids and nutrition.

But on appeal, the Supreme Court considered that euphemisms made their way to the fore in cases of this sort, particularly the concept that by withdrawing fluids and nutrition, the patient died of the underlying disease. The majority opinion (4–3) held that neither the constitutional right to privacy nor the common law right to refuse treatment is expansive enough to apply to withdrawing food and fluids. They held that the state's interest in preserving life, which is particularly valid in Cruzan's case because she is not terminally ill, overrides the privacy right of the patient exercised by the family. They judged that the burdens of treatment would not be excessive for her. In their view, other contrary court decisions have been based simply on a desire to interpret the law in favor of one's right to die.

In the course of its opinion, the court also challenged the evidentiary basis of the family's claim that their daughter would not have wanted such care, suggesting that completion of a living will is the clear and convincing evidence that might be required in such cases in the future.[22]

CASE 22   Mary O'Connor

Mary O'Connor was seventy-seven, a widow, with two daughters who were practical nurses. During her later years, she frequently had to confront issues of life-prolongation with relatives and her husband. The daughters and friends were able to testify to her constant and explicit desire never to "be a burden to anyone," "not to lose my dignity"; that it was "monstrous" to keep someone alive using machinery when they are "not going to get any better." She held that people who were suffering very badly should be allowed to die. Several times she told Helen, one of her daughters, that if she became ill and could not take care of herself, she would not want her life to be sustained artificially.[23] All parties agreed that she had never specifically discussed the provision of nutrition and hydration. A trial court approved refusal of the insertion of a nasogastric tube to supply fluids and nutrition after her progressive deterioration following a series of strokes. She was in a geriatric institute at the time and was judged unresponsive. The appellate court affirmed that ruling, but when the institute went to the New York Court of Appeals, it issued a surprise ruling. After affirming that the ideal situation would be to have advance directives from the patient herself, perhaps in the form of a living will (which has no legal backing in New York), and acknowledging that repeated oral expressions are important, the rulings of the lower courts were overturned on the grounds that the patient's statements, as expressed by family and friends, were "not clear" about application for withdrawing fluids and nutrition.[24]

The Society for the Right to Die commented on this case with respect to the role of the family, as follows:

> ...the underlying assumption is that to permit ending treatment without clear and convincing evidence would lead to abuse of the vulnerable elderly. Other courts and authorities...have strongly held that decision-making when the patient is incompetent is best discharged by family members who know and care for the patient, rather than health care providers or courts, to whom she may be a stranger.[25]

The court's position is that there is nothing more than conjecture about whether O'Connor would have wanted the fluids and nutrition withdrawn.[26]

CASE 23   Edward Faulkner

Edward Faulkner was a ninety-year-old man who had moved to Florida with his wife, Grace, twenty-five years earlier upon retirement from his job as a railway-express agent. He was admitted to St. Anthony's Hospital in St. Petersburg by Dr. David Overby with a diagnosis of bronchial pneumonia and a related bacterial infection in the blood, advanced pulmonary emphysema, infection in the urinary tract, and anemia.

At his admission, Mrs. Faulkner made an explicit request, both orally and in writing to Dr. Overby "to spare no expense, to do everything necessary, and to send him to the intensive care unit (ICU) if he should become critical."

With treatment, Mr. Faulkner initially improved, but only slightly. Then he began to do more poorly each day. Dr. Overby did not transfer Mr. Faulkner to ICU. He explains that there were two reasons for his decision. "First, there was a shortage of beds in the unit. Second, although Mr. Faulkner was chronically ill, he didn't seem like he belonged there because he wasn't acute."

On the morning of the fourteenth hospital day, Dr. Overby visited Mr. Faulkner and found his condition essentially unchanged from the day before. At that time, Mr. Faulkner was alert and asked, "Am I all right, Doctor?"

Fifteen minutes later a nurse entered the room. Mr. Faulkner was not breathing and there was no pulse. All vital signs were absent.

She summoned Dr. Overby, who was still in the hospital.

He came immediately to the room. Once he surveyed the situation, he made the decision not to call for the Cardiopulmonary Resuscitation (CPR) team and not to initiate CPR himself.

"When it comes to resuscitating," Dr. Overby explained later, "it's reasonable to revive a man in his fifties or sixties, but criminal to try to resuscitate someone in Faulkner's age group — to prolong life a week at the most, given his condition. Nobody is supposed to live forever. When you get to ninety, you're doing pretty good."

Dr. Overby also noted that in cases like Faulkner's, the patient can end up like a vegetable due to brain damage. "A lot end like that," he said. He pointed out that it was uncertain how many minutes Faulkner had been out when he was found, and he cited medical experts who estimate that significant brain damage occurs within four to ten minutes following an arrest.

Referring to Mrs. Faulkner's earlier request that "everything necessary" be done, Dr. Overby said: "'Everything' in my mind doesn't include CPR. Everything done might mean not doing anything under circumstances like that."

Mrs. Faulkner was angry when she discovered that resuscitation had not been attempted. "'Everything' is the difference between life and death," she said. "He was playing God when he decided he should not try to save my husband. You're not playing God when you've tried everything and exhausted all methods."

"All I wanted was for them to try," she continued. "If they couldn't bring him back, I could accept that. But I cannot accept the fact that they didn't even try to revive him. They think older people don't have a future."

"I don't think the hospitals should allow doctors to do that on their premises. You can't just save the young and not the old. Doctors should be forced to save everybody except those that don't want to be saved."[27]

CASE 24   Mr. McIntyre's Last-Minute Request

James McIntyre, a twenty-eight-year-old diabetic, had been on renal dialysis at the medical center for a number of years. He was legally blind and could not walk because of progressive neuropathy. He had become increasingly disenchanted because of the stress on both his family's finances and his lifestyle created by his need for hemodialysis three times a week. Because of his despair and anger, his wife had ceased to be supportive and did not want to continue to transport him back and forth to the medical center and to attend to his needs between dialysis sessions. Mr. McIntyre came to the conclusion that continued dialysis was unacceptable for him, and, after numerous discussions with Robert Lincoln and other members of the nephrology unit and dialysis staff, he decided to discontinue dialysis. He was fully aware that this would inevitably result in his death. His only concern was that he be kept as comfortable as possible until then. Dr. Lincoln, the nephrologists, and his family accepted his request, feeling that he had made the decision freely and with full awareness of its implications.

Before Mr. McIntyre was taken off dialysis, he and Dr. Lincoln arrived at an agreement about the way in which his final hours would be handled. They decided that Mr. McIntyre would be admitted to the hospital to receive medication, probably morphine sulfate, as needed to control any symptoms that he suffered during this period. In addition, Dr. Lincoln promised to remain with Mr. McIntyre when he returned to the hospital after discontinuing dialysis. Dr. Lincoln also promised that he would, himself, administer the necessary medication to keep Mr. McIntyre comfortable. Further, he agreed not to put Mr. McIntyre back on dialysis should Mr. McIntyre request it under the influence of uremia, morphine sulfate, and ketoacidosis (the last resulting from the cessation of insulin). Mrs. McIntyre concurred with her husband's and Dr. Lincoln's decision.

Mr. McIntyre terminated his dialysis as well as his insulin and was admitted to the hospital some time later in a uremic state.

He had begun to suffer cramps and severe itching, and requested medication, which he was given according to the previous agreement. He slept most of the evening and that night, periodically awakening to request more medication. Dr. Lincoln and Mrs. McIntyre were with him throughout. At approximately 3 a.m. that morning, Mr. McIntyre awoke complaining of pain and, at that point, asked Dr. Lincoln to put him back on dialysis. Dr. Lincoln and Mrs. McIntyre considered this request, but ultimately decided to abide by the original agreement with Mr. McIntyre.

Dr. Lincoln gave him another injection of morphine sulfate. Mr. McIntyre died in his sleep at approximately 7 a.m.[28]

CASE 25   The Quadriplegic Surgeon

A surgeon, thirty-five years old and the single parent of a fourteen-year-old boy, kept himself in great shape, running each morning for ten miles and lifting weights in the evening at his local health club.

One morning while jogging near his own hospital, he was hit from behind by a truck. The force of the impact broke his neck at the C5 disc. He was immediately paralyzed from the jaw down.

After stabilization at the hospital, he was brought to the spinal cord injury service of the V.A. hospital. During a bout with pneumonia, he begged his neurologist not to be treated and be allowed to die. The neurologist refused. This refusal was based in the neurologist's mind on the "ambivalence" expressed by the patient. He did not want to live this way, but when he had difficulty breathing, he wanted help.

The surgeon has allowed only his parents to visit him, but not his son. He constantly claims that he has nothing to live for, and that he particularly does not want his son to see him in this condition.

A second major crisis occurred. After an operation to fuse the discs so that further damage may not happen — an operation agreed to by the patient only after many days discussion — he suffered a respiratory arrest. After resuscitation, the surgeon saw two of his own classmates who now practice at the V.A. Hospital in question and who were involved in the resuscitation attempt. He cried bitterly to them about his status, and begged them not to do it again.

After further stabilization, a more complete discussion with the neurologists took place again. The surgeon's view of his own quality of life included the following features:

- The social position of a surgeon in society, one that he could no longer exercise.
- Fatherhood, which he identified with helping his son with dating, dressing to please and win women, and the like.
- His own sexual prowess, now permanently inoperative. He can no longer have a relationship with a woman, especially with his two girl friends.

The neurologist and other doctors on the case consider these identifications of self-worth to be somewhat superficial. What about the courage he might demonstrate to his son? Wouldn't that be more important than showing his son how to interact with women? And perhaps the patient could learn, too, that he has value simply by being a human being. With his mental ability and medical experience, maybe he could help others who are in a similar condition.

Furthermore, as the physicians caring for one of their own honestly admit, as they look into his eyes and his life, they see themselves. They find there their own ambiguity about self-image and value. It seems important to them to convince him to live, not only for his own growth as a human being, but also for their own. They also admit that their surgeon-patient knows as well as they do that he will eventually die of some pneumonia, since his muscles for breathing are completely dead.

The patient continues to demand no resuscitation or any other measures to prolong his life.

CASE 26   The Insistent Niece

An eighty-five-year-old gentleman lived alone at home. He was doing well until one day when his niece found him unresponsive on the floor when she came by to check on him. She herself had health problems; the worst was arthritis in her knees that limited her own movement. But she found time during the week to see how her uncle was doing.

He was brought by ambulance to the hospital, where it quickly became apparent that he had suffered a very mild stroke. He also had pneumonia and congestive heart failure. No other problem was found except that his niece mentioned he was profoundly deaf. Several months later, the general medicine service thought, with the appropriate consults, that he might be weaned from the respirator upon which he was put when he first entered. Eighty-five-year-old persons have a difficult time regaining their own breathing after so long a time, but he was considered "strong." His other problems had stabilized. But the service did not recommend putting him back on the respirator if his congestive heart failure returned, as it inevitably would, or should he get pneumonia again.

While he was in the process of being aggressively weaned in the ICU where he was transferred for this task, attempts were made to obtain his own wishes. He seemed unable to respond in any but the most elemental, pleasant way, by nodding his head. He was given a writing pad, but did not use it. He could squeeze a nurse's hand, but it quickly became clear that he always answered "yes," even when it was not appropriate.

He was successfully weaned, but was confined to his bed on the ward. In the opinion of the doctors, he would never get out of his bed again.

Throughout the process and later, his niece kept insisting that "everything possible be done to help my uncle." She was told repeatedly by the medical staff, and later by an ethics consultant on the case, that her uncle was in the final stages of his life. To put him on the respirator again would be to condemn him to die on that machine. She could not accept this news. Her vision was that he would soon return home to his own apartment. He had been so independent up to now!

CASE 27   Clarence Herbert

Clarence Herbert, a fifty-five-year-old security guard, was admitted to Kaiser-Permanente Hospital for surgery characterized as "routine" and "elective" (i.e., to remove a colostomy bag inserted a few months before to relieve a bowel obstruction problem).

The surgery, performed by Dr. Robert Nejdl, was uneventful. However, during Mr. Herbert's first hour in the recovery room, he suffered a massive loss of oxygen to his brain. He became comatose and was placed on a respirator.

The neurologist diagnosed severe brain damage due to lack of oxygen. The next morning, Dr. Neil Barber, the attending internist, spoke with Mrs. Herbert, who consented to taking her husband off the respirator.

The following day, Dr. Barber removed Mr. Herbert from the respirator. However, Mr. Herbert did not die when the respirator was disconnected, but unexpectedly began to breathe on his own.

The next day, Mrs. Herbert and other family members signed a consent form, which she wrote out, saying that the family wanted "all machines taken off that are sustaining life."

Thus Dr. Barber ordered all intravenous feeding discontinued: shortly afterwards, Dr. Nejdl ordered the nasogastric tube removed. Mr. Herbert was transferred from intensive care to a private room, where he was turned to avoid bed sores, given alcohol rubs, and checked routinely. Six days later, he died from dehydration and pneumonia.

A nursing supervisor, Sandra Bardenilla, then went to the authorities. Charges of murder were brought against Drs. Nejdl and Barber. These charges were dismissed at one preliminary hearing, reinstated, and then dismissed again at another preliminary hearing.

CASE 28   IV Fluids for the Dying Patient

A man who weighs 70 kg is admitted to the hospital for control of upper thoracic spine-bone pain.

Six months prior to admission, he had a resection of a poorly differentiated squamous cell carcinoma of the soft palate, followed by radiotherapy. Diagnostic studies showed metastatic bone disease. Narcotic analgesia and chemotherapy with methotrexate were instituted with transient benefit. After an initial response, the patient's bone pain worsened. Escalation of narcotic doses led to somnolence and worsening mental status. The patient's performance status declined from being fully ambulatory to being confined in bed. The patient also lost 11.30 kg due to his disease process and had dysphagia as a result of the radiotherapy. Pain control was inadequate because increasing doses of narcotic analgesia resulted in respiratory depression and hypotension.

At this admission, radiotherapy to the thoracic spine and chemotherapy with cisplatin were initiated with palliative intent. A Foley catheter and a peripheral IV were instituted.

On the eighteenth hospital day, the patient is found unresponsive and without vital signs. A "crash cart" is called. Resuscitation is successful, and the patient is placed on a ventilator and transferred to the coronary care unit. Neurologically, the patient is in a flaccid coma with no response to pain. No obvious cause for the cardiac arrest was found.

After discussion with the family the next day, the patient is designated "No Code" and is transferred from the coronary care unit to a private room on a medical-surgical floor. Ventilator, Foley catheter, and peripheral IV are kept in place. He remains in deep coma. Per discussion with the family, no further blood samples are to be drawn, infections will not be treated and roentgenograms will not be taken. Prior to the patient's cardiac arrest, electrolyte levels were normal, as were routine test results of liver and renal function. The patient has virtually no hope of recovery. He is afebrile, and the blood pressure is 120/80 mm Hg. Urine output is 30 ml/hr.[29]

CASE 29   The Wife Has Her Own Ideas

— Scene 1 —

The patient, a sixty-three-year-old dentist, dying of throat cancer, requests that "nothing extraordinary be done" to preserve his life. No attempt was made to become more explicit about his wishes. His wife is distraught and not reconciled to his dying. One evening, he suffers a heart arrest. He is resuscitated in the hospital. The procedure is successful, and he is now alert, on the respirator, and comfortable with pain control medication. A surgical consult is requested by the managing physician for a gastrostomy, as the patient's nutritional and electrolytic status has steadily declined. The wife is behind this request. But the nurses caring for the patient have seen him steadfastly write notes to her that he does not want to "live this way." What should be done?

— Scene 2 —

After some discussion, a decision is reached, with which the patient is comfortable, to proceed with the surgery, but do nothing further for any subsequent events, using DNR orders and other means to withhold any further interventions.

— Scene 3 —

The patient suffers another arrest, but never regains consciousness. He is on a respirator, but is still dying of his underlying cancer. His wife, in this instance, insists that we follow his directives and not do anything further to prolong his life. In fact, she threatens to sue the health professionals for resuscitating her husband and making him subject to the respirator now, against his wishes. She has also threatened not to pay any further bills. Her cousin is a doctor and has agreed to take over the case. His plan is to give the patient a dose of morphine before taking him off the respirator so that "his cousin doesn't have to suffer by watching her husband struggle to breathe." (See our presentation of this scenario in Chapter One, p. 8.)

This complicated scenario is presented with the presumption that the nurses on this service are opposed to such an action, seeing it as very thinly disguised active euthanasia. They argue that the patient's initial request not to have his life unduly prolonged was too vague to cover taking him off the respirator, and especially in this way.

When the ethics committee is called about this case, among the options to consider might be other sorts of withdrawal under a kind of "contract" with the patient's wife, so that the nurses' and the institution's values about the utilization of active euthanasia are not violated, while the wishes of the patient as expressed by his wife are honored. Such a gradual withdrawal of care permits the patient to survive (now painlessly) to the degree of bodily assault he has sustained, rather than through an active intervention to kill him.

CASE 30   R. B.'s Leg Condition

— Scene 1 —

R. B. is a fifteen-year-old boy, the only child of parents now in their fifties. He is a sophomore in high school, academically above average, and interested in sports, having earned positions on both the football and track teams.

His present illness began early in September, when he injured his right leg in football practice. In the next two days after that injury, he continued to have pain just below the knee of the right leg. After two days of continued pain, the coach recommended whirlpool baths but felt that he could continue practice. The pain continued for another week in spite of this program and he mentioned it to his father, who said that he probably had a bruise and that it would improve. However, the pain persisted for still another week and at that time the football coach called the parents and recommended that he be taken to the family physician for further studies. The parents were able to get an appointment toward the end of the next week and the family physician found local tenderness and some swelling. He obtained a roentgenogram at the local hospital and the following day asked the parents to come to his office for a discussion. At that time he told them that it looked as if there was a tumor in the bone just below the right knee. Because of these findings, he referred the patient to the St. Jude Children's Research Hospital.

On further study at this institution, the boy was found, indeed, to have a tumor in the right fibula, which was interpreted as being most likely osteosarcoma. There was no evidence of tumor involvement in the lungs or in other bones. The rest of the physical and laboratory findings supported the impression of clinically localized osteosarcoma. A recommendation of an above-the-knee amputation of the right leg was made, to be followed by a period of adjuvant chemotherapy according to the current protocol study, lasting for a period of ten to twelve months. The protocol study included randomization to receive or not receive immunotherapy with irradiated tumor cells during the course of treatment.

The parents and the boy were understandably upset about this proposal. The boy in particular was concerned about the amputation and asked if there were alternative methods of treatment. He told the parents he did not want to have the leg removed and would refuse treatment. His parents were undecided but finally went along with the boy's wishes. In spite of long conversations, the parents remained adamant.

— Scene 2 —

It was recommended that they return home, talk with their family physician, family, and pastor about this decision. After an additional week of discussion and continued contact with this hospital, the decision was finally made to allow amputation and treatment.

The amputation went without incident, and the boy was fitted immediately with a walking prosthesis. Chemotherapy, according to protocol, was begun after receiving permission from the boy and the parents. After four months, however, the boy decided against any further chemotherapy. He had lost his hair with treatment and had episodes of vomiting, especially in association with the administration of methotrexate. He was missing school and was particularly concerned and distressed about the fact that his friends were beginning practice for track. In talking with both parents, the physicians had been able to convince the father of the need for continued treatment but the mother said that she would not allow any further treatment if the boy did not want it. The boy had expressed to her his conviction that he had been cured and needed no further treatment. The father reluctantly concurred with the mother about this decision, although it was clear that actually he had withdrawn from the situation shortly after the initial surgery and it was the mother who was truly determining the response to the son's decision.[30]

CASE 31   Suicide Attempt and Emergency Room Ethics

After the car that he is driving at high speed hits a telephone pole, Mr. D. is brought to the hospital emergency room in serious condition. The physicians who examine him recommend surgery to repair a major internal hemorrhage. But the sixty-eight-year-old man refuses, saying that he wants to be "left alone to die." The physicians also learn that three weeks earlier Mr. D. was diagnosed as having carcinoma of the tongue. He has refused surgery for the lesion and has asked his own physician not to tell his wife that he has a fatal disease.

The hospital physicians believe that Mr. D. will die without surgery for the hemorrhage, and they call a psychiatric resident to evaluate the patient. Dr. M. interviews Mr. D. and finds him coherent, rational, and alert. Mr. D. describes himself as a man who values independence. He feels he has a good professional life as an engineer, and a good personal life with his wife and two children. He expresses some sadness at his situation, but says, "I have had a good full life and now it's over."

Dr. M. suggests, and Mr. D. does not deny, that the automobile accident was a deliberate suicide attempt. What should Dr. M. recommend? That the patient's treatment refusal for immediate surgery be accepted as the act of a rational person? That the refusal not be honored, and a court order sought on the ground that a presumed suicide attempt is per se evidence of mental illness?[31]

CASE 32   Sharon Rose

— Scene 1 —

Sharon Rose is a fourteen-year-old girl who was initially admitted to Community Hospital nearly two years ago with a three-week history of chest pain and progressive shortness of breath on exertion. It was noted on admission that she appeared thin and undernourished — with height and weight more than two standard deviations below the mean for her age group. A chest x-ray revealed opacification of the right chest and a mediastinal shift to the left. After one liter of serosanguinous fluid was removed from her chest, a large anterior mediastinal mass became evident by X-ray. The fluid drawn from her chest contained lymphoblasts and lymphocytes. After further studies, the following diagnoses were made:

1. malignant lymphoma, lymphoblastic type — involving the mediastinum, right pleural cavity, and right supraclavicular nodes;

2. undernutrition;

3. idiopathic seizure disorder.

Sharon was given chemotherapy and radiation therapy with a rapid and complete regression of tumor. During the next four months, Sharon suffered moderate toxic side effects — including anemia, weight loss, oral ulceration, and radiation pneumonitis — requiring a hospitalization and modification of chemotherapy dosage.

The management of these problems was complicated by the parents' refusal to permit blood transfusions on religious grounds. They were Jehovah's Witnesses. Their wishes in the matter were honored — especially since it was not thought that the blood transfusions were absolutely essential for effective management.

Sharon has remained in initial complete remission for sixteen months now, and she has been treated on an outpatient basis for fourteen of these months.

One week ago, she was admitted to the hospital again for cough, fever, and fatigue. She was found to have diffuse pneumonia of the left lung, for which she has been given antibiotics and supportive measures. Her admission hemoglobin of 7.3 Gm percent has progressively declined to 4.4 Gm percent, however; and her condition is deteriorating rapidly.

The physicians treating Sharon judge that a blood transfusion is now essential if there is to be any hope of saving her life. However, her parents remain adamant in their refusal of transfusion — and Sharon herself indicates that she agrees with their decision.

— Scene 2 —

After lengthy individual interviews with each of the parents and Sharon, the social worker files this report:

Sharon Rose is a fourteen-year-old girl whose cognitive, emotional, and personality development all appear to be within normal limits.

Sharon has had a troubled family situation. When she was two years old, her natural father — Ted Rose — left the home — according to the report of Sharon's mother (whose name is Lilly), this was at Lilly's request. Lilly filed for divorce about a year later, and Ted did not contest the action. Shortly after the divorce was granted (with Lilly given sole guardianship), Ted moved to another state. Lilly reports that Ted has never visited Sharon nor made any direct contact with either of them since that time, although the court-mandated child-support payments are transmitted (sporadically) through Ted's sister who lives in the city.

When Sharon was seven, Lilly married again; but the marriage lasted less than a year and was apparently stormy throughout. At the divorce hearings, Lilly accused her second husband of physical abuse towards both herself and Sharon, as well as sexual abuse of Sharon. However, the judge pointedly commented in the divorce decree that no evidence was introduced to support the latter charge.

Between marriages, Lilly supplemented the meager and sporadic child support payments by working as a waitress at the sandwich counter of a local drug store. She reports that her income was insufficient to provide for the needs of her and her child. "I made just too much to draw welfare, but too little to pay all the bills," she says.

Until she married Bill Stone (her present husband) when Sharon was ten, Lilly recounts that neither she nor Sharon had been active in any church. But Bill has been a Jehovah's Witness all his life; and, since her marriage, both she and Sharon have become extremely active in the local Jehovah's Witness congregation.

Neither Lilly nor Sharon appear to have much understanding of the rationale behind the Jehovah's Witness objection to blood transfusions. One gets the strong impression that the primary interest of both is in honoring Bill's deep convictions — Lilly in order to preserve her marriage and Sharon out of respect and affection for Bill's kindness and warmth as her stepfather.

— Scene 3 —

As they feared, further studies indicate a return of the malignant lymphoma.

Investigational drugs are available that have shown some success in bringing about a second remission with lymphoblastic lymphoma, but no long-term results with these agents have been reported.

However, it is clear that none of these chemotherapy regimens can be started unless Sharon receives blood transfusions.

— Scene 4 —

If they choose to initiate court action, hospital policy dictates that they work with the staff attorney, so they put in a call to him.

The attorney, whose name is Littman Bowers, comes over to the unit at once, listens to the staff's account of the situation, and then responds:

Doctor, I would strongly advise *against* pursuing court action in this case. There is not one chance in a thousand that we will succeed in getting court approval for transfusion in this jurisdiction; and, in the process of trying to get it, we are likely to cause a public scandal which will damage the reputation of this hospital immeasurably and destroy any degree of rapport you have with the patient and her family at present.

I speak from a wealth of frustrating experience. The judge before whom this request would be argued is a religious zealot who would not let anything — not even this child's life — stand in the way of the parents' right to free expression and practice of their religious beliefs. I have argued a number of cases before in the past — including some in which the parents appealed to outlandish religious claims as a cloak for outright child abuse; and he has always ruled on the side of religion.

Furthermore, there are always reporters hanging around this court-room — including some who have a strong track record of attempts to discredit this hospital at every opportunity. If we attempt to get a court order in this case, I have no doubt that they would sensationalize this in the extreme. We would be portrayed as interfering with the internal work-ings of the family and as defaming these honest, hard-working parents by charging them with child neglect (which is the formal, legal charge we would have to bring as part of the request for a court order for transfusion).

If you absolutely insist on it, I will, of course, pursue the court action. But I want you to understand that I would do so only with the greatest reluctance. And you should be prepared for the onslaught of negative publicity to follow.

— Scene 5 —

As if the decision were not difficult enough already, another ele-ment comes into the picture to complicate matters still further.

Ted Rose (Sharon's natural father) telephones. He has heard about her situation through his sister who lives in the city, and he demands that the hospital initiate court proceedings to authorize transfusion.

"Lilly is entitled to adopt some cockeyed religious beliefs if she chooses," he says, "But I'll be damned if she is going to sacrifice my child's life to save her marriage to that jerk."

Ted announces that he is flying to town immediately and plans to contact a lawyer to initiate proceedings to transfer guardianship to him.

"But if you delay in getting authorization for a transfusion and she dies before I get to town," he tells the physician, "I will slap you with a malpractice suit."[32]

CASE 33   M. H.'s GI Bleed

M. H. was a middle-aged man with metastatic carcinoma of the colon. The cancer had been diagnosed two years previously, and de-spite chemotherapy during this time, there was metastasis to the liver. M. H. was told his diagnosis from the outset and informed his private physician and family that he wanted to die at home with no heroic measures.

One week prior to his last hospital admission, M. H. became deeply jaundiced and developed an upper GI bleed. He believed his condition was the result of his cancer and did not want to go to the hospital. He wanted to stay home and die. His family, however, coerced him into going to the hospital. Although it is not clear why they did this, the house staff believe the family panicked when he started bleeding from the rectum and vomiting blood. They had not realized this could happen and that this was how he might die. Throughout all this, the patient was alert and conscious.

Upon arrival at the hospital, it was determined that the upper GI bleed was caused by medication and was not a direct result of the cancer. The patient was treated for approximately one day and then refused all medication. He claimed he wanted to leave the hospital, despite the fact that he was bleeding. He actually took out his IV and signed release papers. Although his private physician was willing to let M. H. die of intestinal bleeding, the house staff was not. Following numerous attempts by the house staff to explain to the patient that the bleeding was probably just intercurrent and would stop in a few days following treatment, M. H. agreed to stay in the hospital. His bleeding finally stopped on the second day, at which time, however, he developed an altered mental status which was believed to be a result of the cancer.

All treatment was then stopped, except analgesics. It was decided not to resume chemotherapy. On the sixth day, the patient died of liver failure.[33]

CASE 34   Pamela Hamilton

Is any among you afflicted? Let him pray. Is any merry? Let him sing psalms. Is any sick among you? Let him call the elders of the church: and let them pray over him. Anointing him with oil in the name of the Lord. And the prayer of faith shall save the sick; and the Lord shall raise him up; and if he have committed sins, they shall be forgiven him.
[James 5:13–15 (King James Version)]

This passage forms the cornerstone of doctrine of the Church of God of the Union Assembly. The organizing tenet of the church appears to be members' opposition to medical treatment. A typical church service includes testimonies by those present of episodes of divine healing. All members are forbidden to use "medication, shots, or injections of any kind," including pain medications. They will accept chiropractic treatments and repairs of cut flesh and broken bones, however, believing that these treatments merely prepare the way for God's healing action.

Other rules of the church include bans on the use of "any adornment" (including makeup, fingernail polish, or jewelry), shaving legs, or cutting of their hair by women. (This last makes it especially difficult for a female member to accept the prospect of the chemotherapy side effect of hair loss.) Women are not permitted to teach or take any leadership role in services in the church.

The church also prohibits tobacco smoking and alcohol, mixed swimming, attendance at movies or ball games, and chewing gum in church.

•

Pamela Hamilton is the twelve-year-old daughter of an ordained minister in this sect. Her father, Larry Hamilton, is pastor of a thirty-eight-member congregation near LaFollette, Tennessee.

Pamela has three brothers, ranging in age from three to fourteen. Their mother was killed in 1981 in an auto-train wreck. Their father remarried within a few months, and he and his new wife are expecting a child in the fall of 1983.

•

In July 1983, Pamela's parents took her to a chiropractor in response to her persistent complaints of a pain in her left leg. He referred her to an orthopedic surgeon, who discovered a tumor as well as a fracture. Biopsy confirmed the diagnosis of Ewing's sarcoma.

Apparently, the Hamiltons did not register any objection to any aspect of the treatment of the broken leg. Installing the pin involved the use of anesthesia and pain medications, and the child was also given sedatives and other medications during her hospitalization. The hospital staff say they were unaware of any religious objections to these medications on the part of the family.

Initial refusal of treatment. Nor, apparently, was anything said about an intention not to bring the child back for the recommended work-up and treatment of the tumor. They merely failed to return for the scheduled follow-up appointment. When the appointment was not kept, the oncologist sent the usual letter of reminder urging the Hamiltons to reschedule the appointment; and, when no response was received to this, he followed up further with a telephone call to Mr. Hamilton.

DHS involvement. It was not until sometime in early August that the oncologist became convinced that his efforts to persuade the father to authorize treatment were not going to succeed. At this point, he contacted officials of the state Department of Human Services (DHS) to notify them of the Hamiltons' intention to refrain from medical treatment for Pamela's tumor.

The state, acting under the ancient legal doctrine of *parens patriae*, assumes final responsibility for the welfare of dependents within its jurisdiction. For example, any child whose "parent, guardian, or custodian neglects or refuses to provide necessary medical... care" may be declared a "dependent and neglected child" and the state may intervene to protect the child's welfare [*Tenn Code Annotated*, Section 37-202(6.iv)].

Court actions. On August 26, the local juvenile court issued an order requiring the Hamiltons to take Pamela to St. Jude Children's Research Hospital for evaluation and treatment. On September 13, after attempts by the family to resist this order, Pamela was taken to St. Jude Hospital by a court-appointed guardian and admitted for a work-up. Mr. Hamilton refused, however, to permit the use of pain medications during any of the diagnostic tests. Pamela voiced agreement with her father's position on this matter. So all of the tests — including a bone marrow aspiration — were performed without anesthesia or painkillers.

Juvenile court hearing. In depositions read at the subsequent court hearing on September 17, St. Jude physicians reported that their medical evaluation confirmed the diagnosis of Ewing's sarcoma. No metastases were detected. They expressed the judgment that, without treatment, Pamela would die within six to nine months, but that there was a chance of "50 percent or better" for a long-term remission with a combination treatment of chemotherapy and radiation therapy. Just under 50 percent of the Ewing's sarcoma patients treated at St. Jude since the early 1960s are still alive; and, the protocol currently being employed appears to have an even higher success rate.

Mr. Hamilton's attorneys argued against treatment, citing the sanctity of the family and the right to religious freedom.

Pamela's wishes. Pamela herself shyly told observers in the crowded judge's chambers that she believed God was more powerful than doctors. "I believe in God, and I believe God can heal me without taking medicine and all that stuff."

Pamela told her court-appointed guardian that she did not believe doctors' prognosis that she would die within six months from the cancer if she did not receive medical treatment. "Do you want to die?" she was asked. "When the Lord gets ready for me," she replied.

The court decision. Juvenile Court Judge Charles Herman issued his decision immediately following the fourteen-hour hearings. Before reading his decision, Judge Herman addressed Pamela directly: "The court is aware of what you have gone through and you have gone through it courageously. You are one of the most courageous people I have ever come in contact with in my life."

Saying that this was "the most difficult decision I have faced on the bench," Judge Herman ruled in favor of treatment. "To allow her to die would constitute a grave public wrong," he stated. Thus, he placed Pamela into custody of the state DHS and ordered medical treatment for the cancer.

Hospitalization. An ambulance was called to the courthouse, and television cameras recorded the scene as Pamela — tearful, reaching out to her father, and making a feeble attempt to resist being parted from him — was strapped to a stretcher for transport to East Tennessee Children's Hospital.

Further court action. However, the Hamiltons' attorneys immediately sought, and received, a stay order from the state Court of Appeals pending their review of the decision; and thus treatment was delayed for four days.

However, after hearing the case, they upheld the lower court ruling, as did the Tennessee Supreme Court.

Sequelae. After six months of treatment by chemotherapy and radiation therapy, an evaluation revealed no signs of tumor cells present. However, nine months later, new tumors were discovered. The oncologist announced that "her condition is not curable" and thus that he would not recommend further treatment.

Pamela was released from the hospital and returned home, where nurses and social workers visited regularly. Her consistent refusal of pain medication was honored, as her condition deteriorated. She slipped into a coma on the morning of March 28, 1985, and died that afternoon.

CASE 35   Respirator — Extraordinary or Routine?

A thirteen-year-old-boy is admitted to the hospital for treatment of severe seizures. This is his thirteenth hospital admission, although all others, some in other cities, related to complications and subsequent surgery for congenital blockage of the kidneys.

Due to the difficult course of the patient over the years, the parents have refused renal transplant because it would simply prolong the agony of their son, whom they apparently love very much. They made this decision five years ago and have been resolute in their decision through subsequent discussion. For a while, during the boy's early years, the mother stopped working and held off having a larger family because of the boy's medical problems. Since then, however, she has had to return to work to cover some expenses. The couple has had no other children, preferring to wait until the boy's condition leads to his eventual death because they want to focus all their attention on him.

The kidney condition is currently considered stable, but the boy's projected life-expectancy is only fifteen years, as his kidneys function with only about 20 percent their normal capacity. The parents now are concerned with their son's loss of affect. He is almost totally unresponsive.

Knowing that the boy's current condition is serious, the parents discuss with the staff of the hospital their concern that no extraordinary means be used to keep their son alive. It is clear that they perceive him to be dying.

A pediatric neurologist is called in on the case and begins a course of treatment to control the seizures, the major agent being valium. The seizures are of unknown origin and may or may not be due to complications from the primary kidney disease.

After the first hospital day, in the evening, after the neurologist has gone home, the boy has a crisis. He alternates rapidly between severe seizures and apneic spells. A family practice resident on call attempts to help in the crisis. The family, standing by, again repeat their desire that no extraordinary means be used on their son. The family practice resident agrees and so writes in the boy's chart. Meanwhile the neurologist returns for evening rounds, and finds the chart with the notation.

He is extremely upset because he views the use of a respirator to be normal and usual for adjusting drug dosages for seizures. It is his opinion that the apneic spells may be due to the drug dosages. Because the family practice resident was not the managing physician, the neurologist demands that his decision to use the respirator be respected despite the parents' request.

CASE 36   "Momma"

A sixty-eight-year-old woman, mother of eight, began having immense pains in the abdomen. She was very obese. She spent most of her married life in the kitchen. She came from Italy when she was a little girl, and married young. She could still not speak English very well. Her husband never involved her in major decisions in the family, nor did the children. She was just "Momma." They all loved her.

The pains turned out to be, as suspected, a cancer that was "bigger than a basketball," according to the surgeon who planned an exploratory operation. Probably cancer of the ovaries originally. "She must have been in a lot of pain lately, and just did not complain," he told the husband and children.

They immediately requested that he not tell her of her diagnosis or prognosis. There was a lot of emotional outburst in the family, much wailing and carrying on. The surgeon, sensitive to their grief, suggested that they go home and think about their approach for a day. Meanwhile, he would honor their request for twenty-four hours, after which he planned to get her involved in the decision to operate and in the details of post-operative care.

The husband immediately shouted at the surgeon that he would sue him if he so much as gave a minor hint to his wife about her illness. When he calmed down, the husband explained that his wife had never been "bothered" by the rest of the family in decisions they had made over the years. He argued that his wife's deathbed was no place to begin this "foreign and communist" idea of wives making decisions in families.

The surgeon was committed to the modern notion in health care of the autonomy of the patient. This was particularly the case in Momma's instance, as he did not feel she would be able to survive for long. He needed to ask her before she became too drugged by painkillers how she wanted her cancer managed. "Is it too late," he thought to himself, "to help her grow through the dying process?"

CASE 37   Billie B.

An eight-year-old Down's syndrome child was swimming in his family's backyard pool when he jumped head-first into the water. He broke his neck at the C2 portion of the spine, but was immediately rescued by his parents, who called the emergency service. The boy could not talk, but was alert.

Seven months later, after several moves from outlying to more progressively intensive hospitals, Billie was still in a pediatric intensive care unit, completely paralyzed, with significant brain damage. He required a succession of shunts to relieve pressure on his brain; he was ventilator dependent, was fed through a gastrostomy, and could not communicate in any way with caregivers or family. A plan was proposed to the parents for yet another shunt operation. They now refused, stating that Billie's progress was nothing of the sort. He had been the recipient of fine care, but this was as far as they were willing to go. They wanted him to remain on the respirator and to be fed, but they wanted him to be DNR and to have no new interventions.

The managing physician, a pediatric neurologist, actually refused to meet with the parents or the rest of the staff (who supported the parents) because his own convictions about preserving the life of this child were at risk. He was afraid they might talk him out of his own values.

When a family conference was finally arranged with caregivers, an ethicist, social workers, and staff, the physician and the ethicist (who had gotten some legal advice before the meeting) argued that not to shunt Billie was to abandon and "abuse" him. It would be murder one. The Department of Children and Family Services would be notified by someone, they feared, and a charge of child abuse would be brought against the physician for neglecting his patient. For the patient would most surely die if he did not get the shunt.

The mother tearfully spoke of her child's values. Although he was retarded, after years of working with him, he had learned to eat by himself and learned to swim in a rudimentary way. She said, "All Billie lived for was to eat and swim. Now he cannot even do that."

CASE 38   Jenny's Heart Condition

Jenny was the product of an uncomplicated pregnancy, labor, and mid-forceps vaginal delivery. She did well until one week of age when she developed a heart murmur that became so intense that she required an oxygen hood at two weeks of age. Jenny was started on digitalis, and a chromosome study was performed. The child was found to have Down's syndrome.

The parents were informed and were asked for consent to place a cardiac catheter in Jenny in order to document her heart disease and thus devise a treatment. The reaction was disbelief, and they demanded another chromosome study, though they reluctantly agreed to the catheterization. They also said that if there was any surgery that could be performed for her benefit, it ought to be done.

The catheter revealed serious heart disease, and Jenny was not responding to the medical management. After considering palliative surgery, the surgeons rejected it, because of the extreme mortality risk and questionable prognosis.

The purpose of such surgery would be to get Jenny to the age (about one to two years) when a definitive, corrective, operative procedure could be performed. If the child made it to this age, the prognosis would be good. If the palliative surgery were not performed, the surgeons believed Jenny would die in a few weeks of congestive heart failure. Corrective surgery was out of the question at her present age.

The repeated chromosome study confirmed Down's syndrome, and the parents were informed of this. The surgeons chose not to inform the parents that they decided against palliative surgery and simply told them that nothing more could be done for their child.[34]

CASE 39   Daniel McKay and Son

Four years after Daniel McKay, a veterinarian, killed his newborn son by smashing his head on the delivery room floor at Ingalls Memorial Hospital in Harvey, Illinois, in the presence of many witnesses, a second mistrial occurred in Illinois because a jury left unresolved the question of whether his actions constituted murder.

The infant, who was to be named John Francis, was born with a hairlip, cleft palate, webbed hands, and heart and lung deformities. McKay did not want his son to suffer. Because he was assisting during natural childbirth, he was present when the baby was born. He was particularly incensed that the doctors involved did not wish his own participation in the ethical decision about what to do with the baby. He picked the baby up from the incubator, walked to a corner of the room, and struck the infant's head to the floor twice.

As soon as the mistrial was declared, the assistant state's attorney announced that the state was going to make a third effort to convict McKay of murder. Some political wrangling took place behind the scenes, since the state's attorney general, Richard Daley, son of the late mayor of Chicago, had a son born with spina bifida; the son spent the two years of his life mostly in a hospital before he died.

Associate Judge Will Gierach, who tried the case, pointed to the problem of considering this act of euthanasia equivalent to murder: "If they [the jury] were dealing with somebody who was going out and committing crimes every week and they felt it was their duty to the citizens to put him away because of his danger to the community, that would be a different question. But here you are not dealing with that question. You are dealing with an isolated event, an event which is as much a tragedy for the accused and his family as it is for society. At some point, you have to temper justice with mercy and with compassion and with humanity."[35]

The crux of the problem was that the jurors, most of whom thought he was guilty, could not reach a unanimous agreement that he was probably not in full control when he did this act. Some wanted a verdict of guilty but mentally ill, others, a verdict of not guilty by reason of insanity. McKay is a prominent member of his community, a volunteer firefighter and the town's only veterinarian. Among letters sent to his attorney in support of his action (or better, in support of understanding his action), came one from a woman who said that she strangled her defective newborn when doctors left her alone in the delivery room. Other issues were whether the hospital was remiss in not removing a distraught father from the delivery room, where he had begged doctors not to use heroic measures to save his son.

CASE 40   "I've Got a Gun!"

On August 8, 1988, seven-month-old Samuel Linares became a
patient in the pediatric intensive care unit at Rush Presbyterian
St. Luke's Hospital on Chicago's West Side. That day, Sammy, at
a birthday party, aspirated an uninflated balloon.

The balloon lodged in his posterior pharynx, blocking the area
around the epiglottis and closing off both the esophagus and the trachea. Sammy's father, Rudy Linares, tried but could not remove the
balloon. Emergency personnel removed it with a laryngoscope. The
medical facts of Sammy's case were clear. Although he had brain
stem reflexes and cortical activity on his EEG, his doctors considered him to be in a permanently unconscious, chronically vegetative
state.

"The parents requested that we do no more for their child," says
Gilbert Goldman, M.D., director of the pediatric intensive care unit
at Rush, "and this seemed reasonable to us at the hospital from an
ethical point of view."

According to Dr. Goldman, they agreed to Do Not Resuscitate orders. No additional levels of care or new therapies were to be added.
Complications were not to be treated. The doctors told the Linares
family that a court order permitting the life-support equipment to be
disconnected would be supported by the hospital.

Four months later, in December 1988, Dr. Goldman says the
parents had shown no interest in following that course of action.
Sammy's condition remained unchanged. His father, Rudy Linares,
made an unsuccessful attempt to disconnect the life-support equipment. Sammy did not suffer any complications as a result of his
father's action. The doctors once again told the parents that the
hospital would cooperate with any attempt to obtain a court order
permitting disconnection of the life-support equipment.

On Wednesday, April 26, at one a.m., this time with a gun in his
hand, Rudy Linares again disconnected the equipment. The child
died and the father was arrested by Chicago police. Murder charges
against him were dropped by May 18.

"In cases like Sammy's where the medical personnel and the legal
guardians are in agreement on what should be done," says Dr. Goldman, "we need a clarification of the legal standing of the child. The
major dilemma for us is that we have no judicial precedents or legal
statutes in Illinois which allow us to withdraw life-support therapy

when we know it will lead immediately to the death of the child. If anything positive was going to come out of this controversy, it would be to spur the legislature or the courts to develop clearer guidelines for us."

Richard Epstein, senior fellow at the Center for Clinical Medical Ethics at the University of Chicago, does not agree. "Until now, cases like this have been decided between the parents and the hospital. Customary practice is often times better than legislation," he said. "I almost hope that legislation will not be passed as a result of this."

Ethicist Kenneth Vaux, Ph.D., professor of medical ethics at the University of Illinois–Chicago, also thinks that cases like this should be decided among parents and medical teams. While he does not want to see the Linares case become a precedent, he states that "when a human being is irretrievably brain dead it's wrong to keep him alive, a punishment to keep forcing breathing into lungs that no longer function on their own."[36]

CASE 41   Baby Boy Miller

Baby Boy Miller is a four-day-old infant in the intensive care nursery (ICN) who is being maintained on a respirator due to severe respiratory deficiency. A chromosomal analysis by karyotype has been ordered, but the report will not be available for a week to ten days. However, clinical evidence points to a diagnosis of Trisomy 18 — a genetic disorder leading to severe mental retardation, growth failure, and numerous anatomical abnormalities. The full extent of B.B.M.'s abnormalities have not been determined. While there have been scattered reports of patients with Trisomy 18 living to adulthood, 87 percent die within the first year of life, most of the rest die in childhood, and those few who survive childhood are severely retarded and physically disabled.

— Scene 1 —

A conference is being held by the ICN staff to decide what to do with Baby Boy Miller.

The *chief of pediatrics* reports several conversations with Mr. Miller, the baby's father. Mr. Miller said: "If you cannot guarantee that my child will be normal, I don't want you to do anything for it." The chief says that he shares the sympathies of the father and has told him: "I promise to do everything in my power to see that your wishes are carried out."

A *staff psychiatrist* in the hospital also has had several conversations with the father, and he feels that Mr. Miller is presently in a state of acute denial. However, his judgment is that, if the respirator were turned off at the father's initiative, later guilt feelings could create psychiatric problems for him. The psychiatrist also notes that parents who bring a retarded child home only to have it die later might well suffer guilt over that also.

The *psychiatric social worker* disagrees with the psychiatrist's evaluation of Mr. Miller's decision. She feels that Mr. Miller is facing the reality of his child's condition and has made his decision after thinking about what the baby's life and the family's life would be like if they tried to take the baby home. She feels that the family would, indeed, be put under extreme stress if the infant were taken home.

At this point, a *medical student* who has been assisting with the care of B.B.M. interrupts with an obvious sense of outrage. He insists that the infant has every right to live and should not be allowed to die by the hand of man. In fact, he says that, if necessary, he is willing to try to adopt the infant, and he and his wife would care for it themselves.

•

Options include:

1. Turn off the respirator immediately and allow Baby Boy Miller to die within a few hours.

2. Inject a lethal drug so the baby will die within minutes and without suffering.

3. Keep B.B.M. on the respirator until the report of the karyotype is received in a week or so, and then:

   a. turn off the respirator at that time if the diagnosis of Trisomy 18 is confirmed.

   b. let the parents make the decision at that time.

4. Commit yourselves to keeping him on the respirator and providing all other necessary care indefinitely — even if the diagnosis of Trisomy 18 is confirmed by karyotype. Inform Mr. Miller of this decision.

— Scene 2 —

It is decided to take B. B. Miller off the respirator immediately.

The members of the group are slowly and somberly getting up from the conference table in order to carry out this decision when an *obstetrics resident* enters the room and announces a new development in the case. Mrs. Miller, the baby's mother, has been comatose since the delivery due to complications of labor, which she was not expected to survive. While the group was meeting, Mrs. Miller died.

Upon being informed of his wife's death, Mr. Miller said: "Now we must save the baby — in her memory."

The group sits down at the conference table again to discuss this new development.

The *pediatrician* argues that the respirator should still be turned off immediately, and the father should be told: "We did all we could, but the baby died anyway." He explains: "This will spare the father the burden of carrying through on this rash decision he has just made."

The *psychiatrist* agrees in part — but he suggests that the respirator be maintained until the karyotype report is received. "This will give the father a chance to adjust to the initial shock of the loss of his wife, and we can begin to prepare him gently for the loss of his son."

The *psychiatric social worker* argues that the respirator should be maintained until the karyotype report is received, the results should be presented to Mr. Miller, and he should be permitted to make the decision about continuing treatment at that time. "He will have had some time by then to rethink today's decision," she explains.

The *medical student* is still adamant about maintaining the baby indefinitely.

— Scene 3 —

The group decides to keep B. B. Miller on the respirator, at least until the report of the karyotype is received. The members of the group are just getting up from the conference table when a *pediatrics resident* enters the room. She informs the group that a patient of hers in the newborn nursery has developed a moderate respiratory distress but cannot be put on a respirator because all the machines in the hospital are in use. She has been told that Baby Boy Miller is the most likely candidate for removal from a machine to make room for her patient, given the seriousness of his medical condition.

Melissa Stanton (the other infant) is otherwise healthy, but she will run a 50 percent risk of significant brain damage unless she is put on a respirator immediately and kept on it for several days — until her temporary respiratory insufficiency has cleared.

The group sits down at the conference table again to discuss this new development.[37]

CASE 42   Grandma or the House

A seventy-six-year-old woman was admitted to the hospital on January 8, 1985, with a diagnosis of respiratory failure, felt related to congestive heart failure and pneumonia. Her medical history was significant for congestive heart failure, atrial fibrillation, and a stroke in the past.

Despite these problems, up until a couple of days prior to admission, she had almost normal function, was mentally alert, and had largely recovered from the stroke. The patient's admitting physician diagnosed rapidly progressing respiratory insufficiency, evidence of pneumonia (by history, exam, chest x-ray, and white cell count), and perirenal insufficiency.

The patient was intubated and admitted to the ICU. Antibiotics were begun. The following day, the attending physician found the patient much more stable, awake, alert, and apparently oriented, responding appropriately to questions. Over the next few days, the patient became slowly more obtunded, and remained ventilator-dependent, despite efforts of the pulmonary service to wean her. By two weeks after admission, no real progress had been made.

In the evening of January 22, 1985, the patient extubated herself and suffered a cardiopulmonary arrest. She was resuscitated and placed back on the ventilator. There was marked decrease in her neurologic status following this arrest, and her course was further complicated by worsening gastrointestinal bleeding, requiring transfusions. However, over the next few days she gradually became more alert mentally.

She was seen in consultation by cardiology because of persistent heart problems. The cardiology consultant felt that the patient had mild to moderate aortic stenosis and possible mitral stenosis, and suggested that a cardiac catheterization might be appropriate if her mental status improved. Over the next few days her mental status did improve, and on January 29, 1985, a cardiac catheterization was done. This revealed significant three-vessel coronary artery disease (CAD), and mild to moderate mitral stenosis. However, the mitral stenosis was not felt to be severe enough to explain her persistent respiratory insufficiency. It was also felt that the patient may well have a hypertrophic cardiomyopathy.

About this time, the patient's husband began to question the extent of the care. He did not want to abandon his wife, but did not want her to suffer needlessly, either. The staff told him that in their opinion it was too early to abandon intensive care efforts. The patient began to become more agitated and required some sedation.

On February 6, 1985, a family conference was held with the patient's husband and son. The staff discussed her poor prognosis, and the probability that she would never be weaned. All parties agreed that the patient would not be resuscitated in the event of a cardiac arrest. A tracheostomy was scheduled, although the husband objected to this because he did not feel that his wife would want to go on living on a ventilator. The medical ethics department was consulted.

Dr. T. (staff medical ethicist) spoke with the patient concerning her present condition and asked her if she agreed with discontinuing the ventilator as her husband desired. She shook her head "yes." However, she was apparently unable to shake her head "no"; and she was also sedated with Haldol and Ativan, so it was difficult to know exactly what her degree of mental awareness was.

On February 8, 1985, the attending physician had a long discussion with the family. By this time, the husband was adamant about discontinuing the ventilator. He could not understand why he should not be allowed to make that decision. He felt that the patient was clearly suffering unnecessarily, and this is not what she would want. He was not a man of means, and continuing this hopeless but expensive care would likely cost him his house. He loved his wife deeply and could not bear to see her suffer. However, he thought it was very cruel and inappropriate to discuss things with his wife in her present condition; and, when taken into the room to discuss the situation with the family and the physician both present at the patient's bedside, the husband became extremely agitated when the attending physician asked the patient if she wanted the ventilator discontinued and if she understood that discontinuing the ventilator might result in her death.

The patient was transferred out to a private room, and the ventilator was continued. The patient's husband and son became more agitated daily. They stated that they felt betrayed by the patient's attending physician because he had won their confidence early but now would not discontinue the ventilator. Slow progress was made in continuing efforts to wean the patient, and on February 22, 1985, the patient was finally extubated. By that time her mental status had slowly deteriorated to the point where she was able to do little more than nod her head. Over the next few days, she slowly declined; and on February 26, she died.

In addition to the obvious ethical issues of *what* should be decided, this case also raises the issue of *who* should decide. The typical patient in intensive care units who dies this sort of high tech death dies in bits and pieces, and there is a long period of deepening mental twilight before it becomes obvious that the *patient* can no longer decide.

CASE 43   Bobby Nourse

The patient we shall call Bobby Nourse is a forty-eight-year-old male whose mental status is essentially a vegetative state (although his reaction to painful stimuli gives some indication that he may be capable of experiencing pain). Mr. Nourse has a long-term history of alcoholism; as a result, he has been estranged from his family for many years and has no enduring relationship with any physician.

His family consists of two adult children: a daughter who lives in town and a son who lives out of state. The daughter has been the contact for the physician; the son has been heard from only via his sister's reports. The daughter is not readily available — she visits the hospital infrequently, and she does not have a phone at home. She can be reached only through her husband's work telephone.

Mr. Nourse's present troubles began when he extracted two of his own teeth with a pair of pliers. Infection ensued, which necessitated surgery. On the way to the operating room, Mr. Nourse suffered a cardiac arrest; by the time he could be resuscitated, severe brain damage had occurred.

He was subsequently admitted to a skilled care nursing home, where he was managed on a ventilator with a permanent tracheostomy and an NG tube. His mental status showed no improvement over the next three months, and he had intermittent fevers and other complications.

He was brought to the teaching hospital because of a report that he was "bleeding from his trach" and had paled to an "ashen color," neither of which was observed on admission. However, admission x-rays revealed a mass in the right lung. When the daughter was consulted about further studies to investigate the nature of the lung lesion, she indicated that she herself might prefer to forego aggressive diagnostic tests for her father, but that her brother had said to her over the phone that he would consider it "murder" unless "everything possible" were done to extend his father's life. He indicated that this view on his part was linked to religious beliefs, but he was not specific about theological details. When pressed for a specific decision, she insisted on a delay in order to think the matter through and consult her brother.

Meanwhile, Mr. Nourse's physician of record released him to the care of a family practice resident and the nursing home discharged him. Nursing home placement is complicated by the reluctance of long-term care facilities to accept a patient with bacterial infection at the NG tube site.

During the weekend following admission, while a decision was being made about diagnostic work-up for the lung mass, Mr. Nourse began to experience internal bleeding. His hematocrit dropped to 14.5; his pulse increased to 150. Unable to reach the daughter for consultation, the attending physician responded to this crisis by ordering transfusions. Four units of packed red cells were administered.

CASE 44   When Did Billy Die?

The patient was an eleven-year-old male who was brought to the hospital by his adult uncle after having been shot in the head by his eight-year-old brother. The two boys had been exploring the uncle's house, which they were visiting; and they discovered a hand gun which they apparently assumed was not loaded.

Day 1. The patient was taken to the Pediatric Intensive Care Unit (PICU). Shortly after his arrival there, he suffered a cardiac arrest. He was promptly resuscitated.

The initial x-rays were mislabeled and thus read as indicating a bullet entrance on the left side of the head, with a visible exit wound on the right. Upon closer examination in the PICU and with new x-rays, it was determined that both entry and exit wound were on the right side. An implication of the first interpretation would have been that the bullet had cornered the midbrain, possibly causing significant irreversible brain damage.

The patient was intubated and placed on a respirator. An intravenous line was started with D5 solution with electrolytes.

A cerebral angiogram was taken to assess the extent and location of brain damage. It revealed no hematoma at this time. The overall assessment was that there was extensive damage to the right temporal and parietal lobes of a sort that was not incompatible with survival, but would undoubtedly lead to severe (though not necessarily irreversible) neurological impairment. The location and extent of the damage made surgical repair contraindicated.

There was a marked improvement in his condition during the first day — with growing response to verbal commands, half-open eyes, response to deep pain, and leg raising motor control exhibited in response to commands. An intracranial screw was inserted to measure the intracranial pressure (ICP), which was at first markedly elevated, but began to drop toward the normal range during the second day.

Day 2. On the second day, the patient was removed from the respirator.

By the end of the day, however, respiratory difficulties required support of a respirator again. The patient then began to show increased intracranial pressure and a lack of responses to any stimuli except deep pain.

Day 4. On the fourth day, the patient was taken for a CT scan. During the procedure, he suffered cardiorespiratory arrest and was resuscitated.

The CT scan revealed distortion of the brainstem, due to extensive hemorrhage, which appeared to be expanding toward the midbrain. Neurosurgeons were consulted; but they indicated that the lesions were not amenable to surgical resolution.

Day 5. There was no improvement in response; and, on the fifth day, he exhibited hypothermy (i.e., low temperature), no neurological signs, and flat EEG in two readings. The residents, in consultation with the neurologists, decided that the patient's brain had failed, assuming midbrain damage due to cerebral edema and the high intracranial pressure. The ICP screw was removed.

Day 6. On the sixth day, the parents were reached by telephone for consent to do an EEG and cerebral bloodflow study to determine brain death. The parents requested that respirator support be maintained until they could consult with their pastor.

Support was maintained during the next several days, although the ICP screw was not replaced. There was no ICP monitoring and therefore no care for further deterioration of ICP.

During this period, a resident approached the mother to discuss the possibility of donating kidneys for transplant. The mother became very angry and insisted on the maintenance of her son.

On the eleventh day, the patient suffered a cardiac arrest with a flat EKG and was declared dead.[38]

CASE 45   Grandpa's Grandpa

Grandpa's Grandpa was scheduled to die tomorrow, but three members of the family said they positively couldn't get away for his funeral any time soon, so the demise of Grandpa's Grandpa was postponed again, giving him his sixth new lease on life.

He's a very old man now and a lot of grandpas have come and gone in our family in his time. That's why we call him GG for short, to tell him apart from the others.

GG died once, but at the time he was in the hospital having surgery for a hernia. When his failing heart stopped, they hooked him up to an artificial heart and restored his life. That was more than fifty years ago, when GG was about seventy-five, and the doctors and nurses who performed that hook-up are now gone.

What with Social Security, Medicare, and his annuity, GG has always had good care and has never really been an invalid. He has had a couple of leg fractures and an occasional bout of asthma or indigestion, but on the whole his health is good, considering his 125 years. He weighs only ninety pounds, so it doesn't cost much to keep him — two small meals a day and a bit of wine. He doesn't smoke and he sits so still that his clothing lasts for years, although it does get somewhat unfashionable.

The consensus seems to be that GG has a good disposition, otherwise the family would have let him die long ago — by just stealing the battery that runs his heart, for instance, or simply failing to replace it with a new one in June, causing a sure summer funeral.

About the time I was born, GG turned a hundred. That was the year when the family first decided that they should let GG pass away, a decision that, I understand, didn't come easily, but took the best part of an afternoon.

There was considerable opposition to letting GG die, mainly because he was not really in poor health for a man his age. But it was admitted that, although he had a heart in good working order, his brain was badly run down.

By a slim majority, GG was doomed. And then he was resurrected. Someone, who had reached a pretty high station in life by living by the rules, noted that a quorum was not present.

After that first meeting, the subject of GG's funeral didn't come up again for years, possibly because his health seemed to be getting even better, but probably because GG was becoming an asset while his heirs became fewer and fewer.

A small sum of money he had once invested had grown quite large over the years because he used little of the income and the rest just kept accumulating and compounding.

In the summer of his 110th year GG's fate was again discussed at a family meeting. No one mentioned it openly, I've been told, but everyone knew that if GG was allowed to die then, a no-good grandnephew would get a sizeable portion of the estate.

The vote was in favor of keeping GG with us, and a farsighted vote it was because the no-good heir passed on within the year.

With the no-gooder gone, there seemed little reason to prolong the old gentleman's life, so a special session was called. It was noted at the meeting that GG was becoming more forgetful and he sometimes refused to eat. But before the matter came to a vote, a couple of juniors enrolled in premed at one of the universities spoke up and said GG was becoming a valuable research specimen.

The logic of their arguments won over the rest of the family, and GG's funeral was put off for the third time.

At times though, it almost seemed as if the decision had not been a wise one. During the following winter, GG fell and broke his right leg. Later he fell and broke his left leg. Each time he was hospitalized for six weeks before returning home.

While in the hospital, the artificial prolongation of his life, which everybody agreed was really quite useless, became the subject of widespread debate among doctors, nurses, medical students, and orderlies.

Merely removing the stimulus to the artificial heart could not be considered murder, the argument went. After all, God had created GG with a heart and the heart was still present in the body. If the heart machine were turned off, then it was God's decision whether GG's human heart would function.

A meeting of the clan was called to discuss the wisdom of keeping GG alive, especially in the light of community pressure and gossip. But the family closed ranks — no outsiders were going to tell them what to do with their poor old Grandpa's Grandpa.

The fifth "make-the-decision" session, the first that I've attended, was rather serious because the nature of the problem had changed.

A miraculous device had been invented which, if installed, would prolong GG's life indefinitely, possibly for hundreds of years.

Many problems had been created by the invention of that device, not the least of which was how to justify *not* using the machine. When Grandpa, at age seventy-five, had become the recipient of an artificial heart, his existence had been presented to a future generation, to prolong or end as it thought best.

This new twist to the GG problem completely broke down the decisionmaking process. No decision was made — as I said before, three members of the family ended the discussion when they said they couldn't make it to a funeral, although we all knew that they really could.

So GG is 125 today, and I couldn't help thinking during the meeting...

> The surgeon put a ticker in
> To keep our Gramp alive.
> But who will turn the gadget off
> At a hundred twenty-five?
> We often call a problem solved
> Because it goes away.
> And then we find to our chagrin
> The same one's there next day.
> But progress is our way of life,
> So why should it seem strange.
> If the questions must remain the same,
> It's the answers that we'll change.[39]

CASE 46   Mr. Burntree's Lady Friend

Mr. Burntree, sixty-five years old, was admitted by his internist to the medical-surgical unit with the diagnosis of probable bowel obstruction. Mr. Burntree had a history of two myocardial infarctions, chronic obstructive pulmonary disease (COPD), and arteriosclerotic heart disease (ASHD). A surgeon was consulted, and Mr. Burntree underwent surgery in the late afternoon. A cancerous growth was removed from his colon, and a permanent colostomy was performed. He returned to the unit several days later (a Friday afternoon), alert, oriented, and aware of his condition. He was receiving IV fluids at the rate of 125 ml/hr and had a Foley catheter in place. His urinary output for the previous eight hours had been only 200 cc. Both the internist and surgeon were made aware of this fact.

During visiting hours, Mr. Burntree was visited by Ms. Scanlon, a friend with whom he had made his home for the past ten years, after having been divorced for about six years previously to moving in with her. Ms. Scanlon was very attentive to Mr. Burntree and appeared quite concerned about him. Later in the afternoon, Mr. Burntree's daughters (from his marriage) called the nurse's station. They talked with Liz Holden, the evening charge nurse. The daughters were calling from a city several hours distant (where both lived), and were requesting information about their father's condition. Both seemed unaware of their father's post-operative diagnosis. Ms. Holden advised the daughters that his condition was stable and that they could talk with their father on his room telephone.

By the end of the 3 to 11 shift, Mr. Burntree's urinary output was a total of 85 cc. Ms. Holden contacted the surgeon on call (both internist and surgeon were signed out to their respective partners for the weekend) and received orders to give Mr. Burntree Lasix IV and to increase his IV fluids to 166 ml/hr.

By the next afternoon, Mr. Burntree's condition had deteriorated significantly. His urinary output had failed to increase during the night. The surgeon on call was notified during the day, and he ordered Lasix IV, as well as blood albumin, O_2 per NP, and the insertion of an NG tube to allow suction. Given the patient's diagnosis and condition, the day nurse requested a DNR order. The physician on call refused, citing his unfamiliarity with the patient and his family. By early evening, Mr. Burntree was extremely restless and confused. He was pulling off his O_2 cannula and tried to climb out of bed, necessitating the use of a Posey restraint. Within an hour, the patient was diaphoretic and extremely lethargic with Cheyne-Stokes respirations. The surgeon on call was notified, but no additional orders were given, and he did not come to visit Mr. Burntree. At this time, Mr. Burntree's daughters called again for a report on their father's condition. They were informed of his deteriorating condition. The daughters were adamant that they wanted everything done for their father and announced that they would arrive at the hospital within three to four hours.

Mr. Burntree's friend, Ms. Scanlon, who had been visiting him all afternoon and evening, approached Ms. Holden and stated that she just wanted Mr. Burntree kept comfortable. She did not want any heroic measures taken. Mr. Burntree had apparently shared his diagnosis with her; and, since he had COPD, he had asked that he not be kept alive "hooked up to any machines" in order to live. Ms. Holden assured Ms. Scanlon that she would record this information and notify the physician on call.

Before she could reach the physician by telephone, Mr. Burntree suffered a cardiac arrest.[40]

CASE 47   Kenneth Wright

Kenneth Wright, a former high school football star, was twenty-four years old. He had broken his neck in June 1979 and had been confined to a wheelchair ever since. Before this confinement he was very active, enjoying such activities as football, hunting, skin diving, and wrestling.

It seemed that he could not cope with his paralysis. On September 27, 1980, Wright was allegedly carried by two of his friends, William King and Brian Taylor, into the woods. After his friends had left, Wright killed himself with a shotgun.

The laws of Connecticut (the state in which this occurred) forbid one to aid another person to commit suicide. Thus Harold Dean, the assistant state's attorney, charged King and Taylor with second-degree manslaughter.

CASE 48   "Please, Please Kill Me!"

Jamie Lou Martin was a vivacious and happy twenty-six-year-old who worked as a waitress. Driving home from work one evening, she suddenly lost control of her car, veered across seven lanes of traffic, and flipped over. She awoke after two months in a coma to find herself paralyzed from the lips down. Jamie needed a feeding tube, a respirator, a catheter, and a special mattress to regulate her body temperature. Worse, she was in constant, excruciating pain, and the doctors told her they didn't expect it to go away. Because they didn't want her to become addicted, the doctors prescribed only mild painkillers on a four-hour schedule. She had an ulcer, a hernia, blood clots in her legs, even an impacted tooth that no one could fix because her jaw couldn't be pried open. She could think and reason, but she was unable to speak, so she had to communicate by blinking her eyelids. Tediously, with the help of an alphabet board, she told her family repeatedly that she didn't want to live like this. Sometimes she would blink out the words, "Please kill me." Other times it was, "Pull the plug," or, merely, "Die." The family steadfastly refused to honor these requests. They insisted that God must have spared her life for a purpose.

Thirteen months after the accident, Jamie was released from the hospital and went "home" to a fully-equipped long-term-care wing that had been added to the house by the insurance company. Home-coming did not cheer Jamie up as expected. She continued to repeat her request to die over and over.

Gary Weidner, a next-door neighbor in his fifties, had a habit of "hanging around" Jamie's home even before her accident, but now he spent far more time with her than with his wife and two children next door. He intensively explored rehabilitation possibilities and outfitted his van to accommodate her special wheelchair so he could take her on occasional outings. She persuaded him to contact a lawyer on her behalf who arranged for her to execute a living will. Since she was unable to move her hands, Weidner signed it in her name.

When she tried to refuse her food tube on the basis of the living will, the family would not allow this. Finally, she asked Weidner: "Will you help me die?" He finally agreed and devised a plan to kill both her and himself the first time they were left alone by cutting their wrists and throats.

He succeeded in killing Jamie, but he survived and was charged with first-degree murder. The situation has torn the family apart. Jamie's sister devoted herself actively to Weidner's defense (and eventually moved in with him); Jamie's grandmother wrote a letter to the judge asking for a lenient sentence for Weidner; Jamie's parents remain bitterly angry at him for his act.[41]

CASE 49   Elizabeth Thomas's Leukemia

Elizabeth Thomas is a two-and-one-half-year-old girl who was referred to a regional pediatric hospital. She had experienced two weeks of hemorrhagic and infectious insect bites, bleeding skin lesions, paleness, and intermittent fever. Antibiotics were first prescribed following an original diagnosis of tonsillitis, but this treatment only arrested the condition for several days. Subsequent blood counts revealed she had acute lymphocytic leukemia (A.L.L.), and her parents were advised to seek treatment at the regional hospital.

Physical examinations and laboratory results determined that Elizabeth was a standard risk patient, and she was thus enrolled on a Total 10 Standard Risk Protocol. During Stage I of the treatment, she, like all patients on this protocol, received a drug regimen of Prednisone and Vincristine. She had to be hospitalized several days longer than most patients because of throat and skin infections, as well as some hyperglycemic problems. However, a standard bone marrow remission was attained one month and two days following induction to therapy.

The first part of Stage II treatment seeks to prevent later inception of leukemia to the brain and central nervous system. The most established prophylactic regimen is 2,400 rads of radiotherapy to the brain and spinal column. Research has shown that this therapy causes children to be shorter in stature than would normally be expected and it possibly causes learning disabilities in some patients. Thus, the radiation is no longer given to the spine, and the dosage has been reduced to 1,800 rads. The first research goal of this protocol is to measure the therapeutic and side-effect results of the new level of radiation. In addition, certain drug regimens seemingly prevent central nervous system and brain leukemia as effectively as the radiotherapy; however, the comparative effectiveness of these two treatments has never been scientifically established. Thus, the initial part of Stage II treatment randomizes the patients either into Group A for chemical prophylaxis or into Group B for radiation prophylaxis. After Part I of Stage II, both groups receive identical chemotherapeutic regimens. Elizabeth was randomized into Group B on the day of her bone marrow remission, and her treatment thus included a twofold research component.

Throughout Elizabeth's treatment, both Mr. and Mrs. Thomas had adamantly opposed radiotherapy for their daughter. In many conversations with various staff members, the parents had expressed four objections. First, they feared that Elizabeth would suffer permanent brain damage. Second, Elizabeth displayed several behavioral problems, which the parents felt would be increased by the therapy. Third, the daily round trip of 120 miles for radiotherapy would create management problems in relation to the other three children in the family. Fourth, the parents were concerned about sibling reaction to the dye utilized to mark the radiation field and the hair loss experienced during this type of treatment. On the day Elizabeth was randomized to

Group B, the parents stated, "We don't want her to have radiation. Radiation to her brain cannot be good for her. If it were any part of her body besides her brain, the radiation would not be so bad. Why can't she have the drug therapy instead?"

The attending physician and the nurse practitioner once again explained Part I of Stage II treatment and sought to assist the parents in comprehending the research component of Elizabeth's treatment. During this session, two items of misinformation were resolved. First, Elizabeth would receive only twelve days of radiotherapy rather than six weeks as her parents had originally thought. Second, they learned that only part of the brain, rather than the whole, would be irradiated. However the parents stated that none of their concerns were adequately answered or resolved. Even though they still objected to the therapy, Mr. and Mrs. Thomas did sign the consent form for radiation.

CASE 50   Claire Conroy

Claire Conroy was an eighty-three-year-old woman who had been admitted to a nursing home three years previously with "organic brain syndrome." Her mental condition probably approximated that of many patients in nursing homes: she was neither competent nor comatose, and could communicate only on a very primitive level.

Except for minor movements of her head, neck, arms, and hands, [Claire Conroy] is unable to move. She does not speak. She lies in bed in a fetal position. She sometimes follows people with her eyes, but often simply stares blankly ahead....She has no cognitive or volitional functioning.

Medical testimony as to whether she was capable of experiencing pain was ruled as "inconclusive."

Ms. Conroy developed necrotic ulcers on her left foot as a result of diabetes. She was transferred to a hospital where doctors recommended that her left leg be amputated above the knee.

Her guardian (a young nephew) refused permission and later also demanded that Ms. Conroy's nasogastric tube be removed. Her physician would not remove the tube, and so her guardian petitioned the court for authority to order it removed.

After a hearing (and also a personal visit to the hospital to view

Ms. Conroy's condition for himself), Judge Stanton ordered removal on February 2, 1983. His decision was stayed pending appeal.

On February 15, Ms. Conroy died with the tube still in place. On July 8, 1983, an appeals court reversed the lower court's decision. Late in October, the New Jersey Supreme Court agreed to review the case.

CASE 51   Elizabeth Bouvia

Elizabeth Bouvia is a twenty-six-year-old woman suffering from cerebral palsy. She is a wheelchair-bound quadriplegic with almost no motor control, who also suffers from painful arthritis.

Described by her friends as "a fighter, a survivor," she moved into her own apartment at the age of eighteen. She has been married (and separated) and has undergone a pregnancy terminating in miscarriage. She went on to earn a bachelor's degree in social work and credit toward a master's degree.

The dean of her graduate school reportedly told her that because of her handicap, she probably would never find work in her field.

Ms. Bouvia was admitted at her own request to the psychiatric ward of a community hospital, claiming that she was suffering from depression. Once admitted, she announced that her real purpose in entering the hospital was to be provided with painkillers and nursing care as she starved herself to death. She explained that she did not want to live "trapped in a useless body" and dependent on others.

The hospital refused to comply with her request. Ms. Bouvia went to court seeking an injunction preventing hospital staff from giving her anything but painkillers.

The court denied this petition. Pointing out that she was not terminally ill, the judge ruled that society's interest in preserving life and the medical profession's obligation to do so outweighed her right to self-determination in this situation.

The hospital announced plans to continue to provide her with liquid nutrition as long as she remained a patient, although they were willing to discharge her in the care of any person she chose — including any of the several volunteers who came forward offering to support her in her plan.

CASE 52   Family vs. Caregivers

A seventy-two-year-old lady, with a large family, suffered a massive stroke that left her paralyzed on both sides. Further, blindness from an unknown cause set in. Her family pleaded with the managing physician at a large teaching hospital to withdraw the respirator, IV fluids, and antibiotics that now kept her alive. He was uncertain, however, that she was really dying. Her stroke had now stabilized. She was partially alert, such that she could mouth words appropriately. Furthermore, her family struck the ethics consultant on the case, the neurology consultant, and a nurse specialist as being somewhat selfish. They were not certain that the family properly represented the patient's current wishes.

When the family was rebuffed by the health care team now taking care of the woman (it was their view that she could be transferred to a nursing home on a respirator and live quite comfortably), they called in the original physician who took care of her at a community hospital. He had privileges at the university hospital. The current physician agreed to transfer her back to the referring physician, transfer her out of the ICU, and put her on an entirely different floor in the hospital. It was the original physician's view that the university hospital hopelessly garbled the case, and that if she were at the community hospital, he could have withdrawn the care easily as per the family's request.

He ordered no further treatments, including pain control medications. Then he later gave her a shot of morphine to control the discomfort of trying to breathe before he took her off the respirator. Most thinkers would regard the shot as a form of active euthanasia, since morphine depresses respiration. The shot insures that the patient would not be able to breathe on her own, in the unlikely event that she could otherwise have done so.

CASE 53   Death in Transit

An eighty-one-year-old woman, dying of disseminated breast cancer, had exhausted the reimbursements from both her insurance company and, later, her Medicare policy. The family began pleading with the doctor to transfer her to a critical care nursing facility, but even that proved too expensive. Eventually, a full discussion about lack of reimbursement led to a decision to transfer the patient, on IV pain control only, to her home to die. She died, in fact, in transit in an ambulance. The intention was that she would die either in transit or at home. How does this differ from what is called "direct" action in killing someone? Can this be called only indirect action?

CASE 54   Phenobarbital Overdose

A thirty-two-year-old mother from the West Side of Chicago administered an overdose of phenobarbital to her teenage son who suffered from cerebral palsy. She then took an overdose of the same drug herself. She survived, and said that the reason she gave her son and herself the overdose was frustration because she could not find a babysitter and therefore could not get a job. Phenobarbital is an antidepressant used to control seizures.[42] Since the boy survived, albeit in serious condition after his father, the evening of the overdose, took him to St. Anne's Hospital, the mother was charged with aggravated battery, and not intent to murder. But how does this case differ from a more sophisticated attempt to deny care to a person judged "assaulted" by nature?

CASE 55   Connie Evans's First Nursing Position

Connie Evans's first nursing position was on a medical unit in a large city hospital. After she had been there about six months, just as she was gaining confidence in her nursing abilities, she was ordered to give a dose of morphine that she considered unsafe.

The patient, Mrs. Johnson, had terminal cancer. She had been on smaller doses of morphine that seemed to control her pain well; however, her respirations were becoming depressed. During the past two days Mrs. Johnson had begun to talk about death. She told her family the hymns she wanted sung at her funeral and mentioned that she was looking forward to seeing Jesus and her husband, who had died previously. Her son and daughter became anxious whenever

Mrs. Johnson began to talk about death. They requested a conference with the attending physician. After talking with the family and checking Mrs. Johnson, the attending physician doubled Mrs. Johnson's morphine dosage and increased its frequency. He handed Connie the chart after writing the order and said, "Here, I want this to begin *now*."

Connie was shocked. She considered Mrs. Johnson's talk of death to be a positive growth experience for her and her family, even though it made the family uncomfortable. She had encouraged Mrs. Johnson to verbalize her feelings about death and was attempting to support the son and daughter in the process. The increased dosage of morphine would mean imminent and, most likely, premature death.

As Connie stood holding the chart, trying to decide what to do, the physician roared, "I said give it to her *now!*"

"Her respirations are only six per minute," Connie replied. "It might kill her."

"Young lady," the physician answered, as he squinted at Connie's name tag and wrote her name on a slip of paper, "I've been on the staff here for twenty-eight years, and the custom has always been that I write the orders and the nurses carry them out. Are you going to give that morphine, or do I have to call your supervisor?

CASE 56   Tom Wirth

Tom Wirth, forty-seven, had been diagnosed as having AIDS related complex (ARC) before he was admitted to Bellevue Hospital on July 6, 1987. His admitting diagnosis was toxoplasmosis, a parasitic infection found in patients with ARC, which is potentially reversible. On April 13, 1987, he had executed a living will and a medical power of attorney appointing his friend of twenty-two years, John Evans, as his agent to make all decisions relating to his medical care and treatment. The living will stated:

> I direct that life-sustaining procedures should be withheld or withdrawn if I have illness, disease, or injury, or experience extreme mental deterioration, such that there is no reasonable expectation of recovering or regaining a meaningful quality of life. These life-sustaining procedures that may be withheld or withdrawn include, but are not limited to: surgery, antibiotics, cardiac resuscitation, respiratory support, artificially administered feeding and fluids.

On arrival at Bellevue Hospital, Tom Wirth was stuporous and unable to communicate. Medical tests showed that he had multiple brain lesions, which were probably attributable to toxoplasmosis. Toxoplasmosis frequently responds to treatment with antibiotics, but these were included in the list of possible treatments to be withheld in the living will. John Evans maintained that Tom Wirth would not want antibiotic treatment or artificially administered feeding and fluids in this circumstance. All parties agree that the patient was currently unable to make medical decisions.

The hospital acknowledged that a living will was a valid instrument to express a patient's wishes, but contended that it did not clearly apply to the facts of this case: there was a reasonable likelihood that Tom Wirth could "recover" from the toxoplasmosis to a "meaningful quality of life." The hospital also questioned whether Evans was the appropriate person to interpret the living will and its phrases.

Therefore the hospital began life-sustaining treatment on July 10, 1987. On the same day, John Evans petitioned the court to enjoin the hospital from providing the medical treatment. After Tom Wirth had received antibiotics for over two weeks, he had still not improved to a status in which he could express his own wishes.

NOTES

1. *Journal of the American Medical Association* 259, no. 2 (January 8, 1988), 272.

2. Glenn C. Graber, "Some Questions About the Double Effect," *Ethics in Science and Medicine* 6 (1979), 65–84. Richard McCormick, *Ambiguity in Moral Choice* (Milwaukee: Marquette University Press, 1973).

3. One of us (Graber) said: "There can be cases where this kind of action might be justified. I don't think this is one of them" (*Knoxville Journal*, February 29, 1988, A2). Graber holds that the patient's wishes come first. On this basis it may, at times, be appropriate to help a patient die. He prefers using the principle of double effect when considering the relief of suffering: "If the physician's intent is to relieve suffering with a morphine injection, Graber said it is justified, even if death comes as a side effect of the injection" (ibid., A3).

4. As quoted in "Letter from Dying Woman's Killer Draws Legal, Ethical Fire," *Knoxville Journal*, February 29, 1988, A2.

5. See James Walter, "The Meaning of Quality of Life Judgments in Contemporary Roman Catholic Medical Ethics," *Louvain Studies* 13 (1988), 195–208.

"Quality of Life Judgments...," *op. cit.* Yet Walter would not support killing Debbie, because he would proscribe killing on other grounds, e.g., on the commandment "Thou shalt not kill."

6. Robert Barry, O.P., "Book Review: *By No Extraordinary Means,*" *Linacre Quarterly* 54 (November 1987), 87–90.

7. "Euthanasia in Practice: The Dutch Model," *Frontlines* 6, no. 2 (August 1989), 7; also see Carla Carwile and Kristy Anderson, "Euthanasia: America Reexamines Its Position, Its Philosophies," *Frontiers* 6, no. 2 (August 1989), 1, 4–6.

8. "When the Doctor Gives a Deadly Dose," *Hastings Center Report* 17, no. 6 (December 1987), 33.

9. From "In the Matter of Shirley Dinnerstein," Supreme Court of Massachusetts, 1978 — Mass. App. — 380 N.E. 2nd 134.

10. Adapted From: W. St. C. Symmers, Sr., "Not Allowed to Die," *British Medical Journal* 1 (1968), 442.

11. From David L. Jackson and Stuart Youngner, "Patient Autonomy and 'Death with Dignity': Some Clinical Caveats," *New England Journal of Medicine* 301, no. 8 (August 23, 1979), 404–408.

12. Ibid.

13. Ibid.

14. Ibid.

15. Ibid.

16. Ibid.

17. Adapted from Case 13 in Tom L. Beauchamp and James F. Childress, *Principles of Biomedical Ethics* (New York: Oxford University Press, 1979).

18. Case 21 from Natalie Abrams and Michael D. Buckner, *Medical Ethics: A Clinical Textbook and Reference for the Health Care Professions* (Cambridge, Mass.: M.I.T. Press, 1983), p. 603.

19. Case prepared by Daniel Merrick.

20. Case 19 from Natalie Abrams and Michael D. Buckner, *Medical Ethics,* p. 602.

21. *Hastings Center Report.*

22. *Cruzan v. Harmon,* 760 S.W.2d 408 (Mo. Sup. Ct. 1988); *Cruzan v. Director, Missouri Dept. of Health,* no. 88–1503, *cert. granted,* 109 S. Ct. 3240 (1989).

23. "O'Connor Case Highlights Problem of Incompetent Patient with No Living Will," *Medical Ethics Advisor* 5, no. 1 (January 1989), 13–16.

24. Ibid., 15.

25. As quoted in ibid., 15–16.

26. *In the Matter of Mary O'Connor,* 72 N.Y.2d 517, 531 N.E.2d 607, 534 N.Y.S.2d 886 (Ct. App. 1988, amended, 1989).

27. Adapted from the *St. Petersburg Times,* January 5, 1981, pp. 1-D, 5-D.

28. Case 11 from James F. Childress, *Who Should Decide? Paternalism in Health Care* (Oxford, 1982), 212–213.

CASES

29. Kenneth C. Micetich, M.D., Patricia H. Steinecke,
Thomasma, Ph.D., "Are Intravenous Fluids Morally Requir
Patient?" *Archives of Internal Medicine* 143 (May 1983), 975–9,

30. Case 17 from Natalie Abrams and Michael D. Buckner,
Ethics, pp. 599–600.

31. Michael Jellinek, "A Suicide Attempt and Emergency Room Ethic.
Hastings Center Report, August 1979.

32. Adapted from David C. Thomasma, Ph.D., "Training in Medical
Ethics: An Ethical Work-Up," *Forum on Medicine* 1 (December 1978), 33–36.

33. Case 33 from Natalie Abrams and Michael D. Buckner, *Medical
Ethics*, pp. 610–611.

34. Case 27 from ibid., p. 606.

35. Andrew Fegelman, "2d Mistrial for Dad in Newborn's Death," *Chicago Tribune*, October 10, 1987, sec. 1, 1, 7.

36. *Illinois Medicine*, May 26, 1989, p. 8.

37. This case is adapted from Robert M. Veatch, *Case Studies in Medical Ethics* (Cambridge: Harvard University Press, 1977), pp. 36–37.

38. Case 32 from Natalie Abrams and Michael Buckner, *Medical Ethics*.

39. W. C. Bornemeier, "Grandpa's Grandpa: A Scenario for Tomorrow," *Chicago Tribune Magazine*, June 26, 1966.

40. Adapted from Robert M. Veatch and Sara T. Fry, *Case Studies in Nursing Ethics* (Philadelphia: J. B. Lippincott Co., 1987), pp. 294–295 (Case 112).

41. Rachael Migler, "Please, Please Kill Me!" *Good Housekeeping* (November 1988), 160, 274–277.

42. "Mother Charged in Son's Overdose," *Chicago Tribune*, October 19, 1987, sec. 2, 2.

Appendix II ———————————————————————

VARIETIES OF HARM

INTRINSIC, INTENDED, INCIDENTAL EFFECTS

The difference between *causing* harm or injury and *doing* or *inflicting* it is tied up with the distinction between intrinsic effects, intended effects, and incidental effects. Consider the following cases:

> *Edgar* is a wartime secret agent who is captured by the enemy. Knowing that he will be tortured mercilessly to the death, he takes a cyanide capsule from a hidden compartment in his shoe, bites into it, and dies.

> *Francine* is another wartime secret agent who is captured. She has heard about these particular captors before and knows that they always torture to the death any agent who refuses to divulge the information they are after. Nevertheless, she refuses to tell them anything. After three painful days, she dies from their tortures.[1]

To get at the difference between these two cases, we must notice some preliminary points about the nature of action.

1. *Actions have effects.* The actions of Edgar and Francine, although very different in themselves, both have the same effect in the end — bringing about the death of the agent.

2. *A single action has multiple effects.* For example, Edgar's action not only has the consequence of bringing about his death, but it has the additional effects (a) of guaranteeing that he does not divulge whatever strategic information he knows ("dead men tell no tales") and (b) of sparing him the pain of the tortures that would otherwise be inflicted upon him. His action may have still other effects, as well. If we suppose (as is not unlikely) that one of Edgar's captors had been assigned the responsibility of searching captured agents in order to find concealed poisons, and if the commanding officer is as ruthless as his procedures for treatment of captives suggests, then Edgar's action of taking the poison may have the additional consequence of (c) prompting the execution of this one of his captors.

3. *However, these effects relate to the action in different ways.* Edgar's death is an *intrinsic* effect of taking the poison; Francine's

death is a remote effect of her refusal to reveal information. In contrast, for Francine the effect of not revealing secrets is an *intrinsic* effect of not talking; whereas, for Edgar, protecting secrets is a remote effect of the action of taking the cyanide capsule.

4. Next are some points about the interrelationships between these different effects of the same action. *Some effects are effects of other effects.* For example, Edgar's death is an effect of his initial act of swallowing the cyanide. Further, his guaranteeing his silence is an effect of his death — hence, it is a sort of causal grandchild of the initial act of swallowing the poison.

Notice that, in claiming these causal relationships, we are not denying that these same effects *could* have been brought about by other means. Edgar *might* have brought about his death by accidentally setting off an explosive device in the prison camp. We are interested in the actual causal relationships between events as they actually happened.

5. *Some effects are causally independent of other effects.* For example, consider the two consequences: (a) Edgar's guaranteeing the protection of his secrets and (c) his bringing about the execution of the one of his captors who failed to find the poison. Neither of these is directly causally related to the other. The captor was executed, not because the secrets were successfully protected, but because he failed to carry out an assigned responsibility. Imagine that Edgar had *not* succeeded in guaranteeing the protection of his secrets. Imagine, for example, that he had inadvertently left a written statement of them intact in his pocket. The chances are good that his captor would still have been executed. The fact that the soldier had failed to do his assigned duty would remain as the basis for punishment. Thus these two consequences are both effects of Edgar's swallowing the poison, but they are causally independent of each other.

6. Now we must consider the element of *intention* in action. *Some of the effects of a given action are intended.*

7. More specifically, *whatever goals the agent hoped or planned to achieve by performing the action are intended effects of the action.* It is reasonable to assume that both Edgar and Francine had the same ultimate goal in mind in doing what they did: both wanted to protect the secret information in their possession. Thus this is clearly an intended effect of their respective actions. In addition, it is likely that Edgar was also influenced by the realization that death from the poison would spare him the pain of torture. Hence this can plausibly be interpreted as a second, coordinate goal of his action, and thus another intended effect of it.

8. *Some effects of an action are* not *intended effects.* To see this, consider the consequence of the execution of the one of Edgar's captors who failed to find the concealed poison. Surely this was *not* an intended effect of Edgar's action. He was probably not even aware that this would result. Of course, it is possible that he *knew* beyond reasonable doubt that this would follow. (Perhaps he had obtained reliable information from a double agent about the practices of this particular commanding officer.) But, even if he *knew* what would happen, it would still seem a mistake to say that he *intended* for it to happen. Awareness of this consequence played no role at all in his decision to act as he did. His interest was in protecting his secret information in the best way he knew how. The realization that this enemy soldier would die as a result of his action made him neither more nor less inclined to perform it. It was, then, a *by-product* or a *side effect* or an *incidental effect* of his action — a consequence that was perhaps foreseen but not intended.

9. This brings us to our next point about action: *Some of the effects of an action that are foreseen are nevertheless not intended effects.*

10. *Some means can be distinguished from others in a parallel way.* For Edgar, death was a *chosen means* to his goal of containing his secrets. He might have chosen to behave as Francine did. Since he deliberately selected the poison-capsule route, it becomes a chosen means for him.

WAYS OF HARMING

If a certain harm or injury (e.g., the death of Edgar's captor) is an incidental effect of one's action, he would be said to have caused it but not to have done injury or to have inflicted it. In contrast, if the harm is either an intrinsic effect of the action or its intended effect, then we would say that he had done injury or inflicted harm and not merely caused harm. For a concrete example of this distinction, consider the following set of cases:

> A. A person digs a large hole in his front yard in order to install an elaborate decorative fountain. Carelessly, he fails to mark the danger with warning signals. You happen to pass by the spot one dark night, and you fall into the hole.

Here the harm (i.e., your falling into the hole) is clearly an incidental effect of the agent's actions. You would have the right to say that he has caused harm to you through his carelessness (and you could sue him for damages on that basis). But it would be too strong to say that he had done you an injury or inflicted harm upon you.

> B. A person digs a large hole in her front yard, directly in the path along which you regularly come jogging late at night. The hole is intended as a trap for you to fall into. You do.

Here the harm to you is the whole point of the action (i.e., its intended effect). In this case, it is not strong enough to say that the person has caused you harm. She has done more than this. She has deliberately inflicted harm and done injury. (In this situation, you will undoubtedly want to do more than file suit for damages. You will look for criminal charges to bring against her.)

> C. A person digs a large hole in his front yard; and, when you come over to complain about how unsightly it is, he pushes you into it.

Here your falling into the hole is an intrinsic effect of his pushing you into it. Even more clearly than in the previous case, the person has done you injury and not merely caused you harm.

> D. A person digs a large hole in her front yard for the purpose of installing a decorative fountain. But, as she digs, the thought occurs to her that the hole happens to be directly in your jogging path and thus that you might fall into it. With a vile chuckle, she deliberately refrains from putting up warning signals to mark the danger. You fall in.

This case is considerably more complicated than the other three. We include it to illustrate some of the complexities that can arise in connection with these distinctions. In these circumstances, your falling into the hole seems to be more than an incidental effect but somewhat less than an intended effect.

Classification would be more clear-cut if the circumstances were different. If, for example, it was discovered that the person had deliberately chosen the location of the fountain so that the hole would coincide with your jogging route, then we would not hesitate to say that the harm to you was *one* intended effect of her action (with the installation of the fountain being another intended effect).

One reason we bring up this possible additional motivating factor is that we have encountered cynical readers who automatically postulate that the fountain-planner must have engaged in this sort of calculation subconsciously. (Needless to say, we are disappointed in them for assuming that our friend would stoop this low.) But we do not want this to be a feature of case D; this would make it no more than a variation of case B, robbing it of its most interesting features.

To rule out any such suggestion firmly, let us suppose that the location for the fountain was chosen entirely by a landscape architect, who knows nothing about your jogging routine and has no ill feelings at all toward you.

The first step toward a clearer analysis of this case is to separate out several distinct actions that occur within it: the landscape architect's action of choosing the location of the hole, the property-owner's action of digging it (which is actually a series of positive actions — i.e., lifting this spadeful of dirt, lifting that one, etc.), and her negative action or omission in failing to put up warning signals. Part of our confusion in determining whether the harm to you is intended or incidental is that it has each of these relationships to different ones of these actions. Your fall is an incidental effect of the architect's choosing the location and of the property-owner's digging the hole, but it is one of the intended effects of her failing to put up warning signals.

However, even though the harm to you was intended, it does not seem fully appropriate to say that she inflicted injury or did harm. These expressions imply not only the intention that you suffer harm but also that this intention is expressed in a positive action like digging a trap (case B above) or pushing you into it (case C above), whereas in the present case your neighbor expresses her intention in a negative action or omission.

On the other hand, it seems too mild to say merely that she caused harm to you. This sort of case requires a special, intermediate category. We could say either that she *willfully caused* the harm or that she *virtually inflicted* it.

The point of distinguishing these general ways of bringing about harm is to mark important normative differences between them. We have a duty to avoid bringing about harm in any of these ways, but violation of this duty is a more serious matter in some cases than in others. For example, inflicting injury (i.e., bringing it about deliberately by means of positive action) is, in general, a much more serious wrong than causing harm through carelessness or lack of foresight. This can be confirmed by comparing case B or C above with case A. We must include the qualification "in general" in this judgment because the scales may shift in the opposite direction if a substantial discrepancy exists between the two acts with regard to the *amount* of harm that could result. Thus to be careless with a loaded gun is a more serious wrong than deliberately hitting someone with a loosely-packed snowball.

Inflicting injury is also more serious than willfully causing it (assuming, here again, that there is not a substantial discrepancy with regard to the amount of harm in each case). The normative difference is a reflection of general tendencies of actions of these kinds. Although in the situation at hand B, C, and D (and A as well, for that matter) all have the same result (i.e., your falling into the hole), it does not follow that the four patterns of action represented here are equally likely to bring about harm in all circumstances.

Even if the neighbor is always equally as careless as in case A above, this might not often result in harm to others — especially if the other parties exercise due caution.

However, it would take a much more watchful eye to avoid the effects of calculated omissions of the sort represented in case D. Since the neighbor *hopes* the other parties will come to harm, she will undoubtedly select for her negligence the source of danger that she thinks they are least likely to detect.

Further, if one takes positive action to design and create a source of harm (as in case B above), then it would be still less likely that the intended victims could avoid the harm merely by exercising an ordinary level of caution. The perpetrator will probably take steps to disguise the danger — for example, by covering the hole with sticks and grass.

Finally, if one engages in direct and overt aggression (as in case C above), then caution on the victim's part will not begin to be sufficient to avoid the injury. Their only hope would lie in active measures of self-defense.

Thus the reason one pattern of action is a more serious wrong than another is that it is more dangerous — that is, more likely to result in harm under ordinary circumstances. This criterion yields an ordered series of patterns of action in terms of degree of danger (and hence of seriousness): direct aggression (as in case C); overt action designed to produce harm indirectly (as in case B); willfully causing harm (as in case D); and, finally the least serious of all of these, carelessness (as in case A).

These four patterns of action do not exhaust the possibilities for ways of bringing about harm. For example, none of them really fits the situation of active euthanasia that we considered in Chapter Three. Closer to it would be the following case:

E. A water main bursts, and the resulting flooding threatens to undermine the foundations of your house — but not, let us suppose, of your neighbor's. (Imagine that your house is downhill from his.) You are not available to do anything about it, so (being a good neighbor — unlike the nasty person of cases A through D) he immediately begins to dig a large hole in his front yard at the site of the break in order to repair it and stop the flooding. He recognizes that the hole is directly in your jogging path and that there is a chance you will fall into it, but there is no time for him to stop and put up warning signals without jeopardizing your house by this delay. He figures you would rather suffer the indignity and (probably slight) bodily injury from falling into the hole than to lose your beloved and expensive house. Sure enough, you come jogging along and tumble into the hole.

Here the harm to you is clearly an incidental effect of his action. It is not inappropriate to say that he caused the harm to you; but this would not be said in an accusatory way — at least, not once you had heard his explanation for what he was doing. His actions were compelled by the urgent necessity of saving your house — a fact which we would indicate by saying that these events themselves created the danger. (We might say this either *in addition to* saying that he created the danger, in order to moderate his responsibility, or else *instead of* commenting upon his role, in order to effectively relieve him altogether of responsibility for the harm.)

The chief difference between case E and the other four cases of hole-digging is that in this situation creating the danger is an aspect that cannot be eliminated of the neighbor's attempt to bring about a genuine and substantial benefit to you. In contrast, the corresponding benefits involved in the other cases (i.e., the added beauty contributed to the neighbor's home by the decorative fountain and/or the cruel pleasure the neighbor receives from your being injured) either are not genuine values or are not inseparably linked to the harm in question. Beauty is a not-unreasonable value; but it is obviously far less weighty than the urgent need that is involved in case E, and, furthermore, it was not essential to have created the danger in order to have achieved the goal of a beautiful fountain. The neighbor could have located the fountain away from your jogging route and/or have posted warning signals. The danger does have to be created in order to achieve the pleasure of having you injured, but the value of this kind of evil pleasure must be seriously disputed on moral grounds. Finally, it is significant that, in case E, the benefit as well as the danger accrue to the same person: you; whereas in the other cases it is primarily the neighbor who benefits, but at your expense.

These same features that distinguish case E from the other four cases also provide a moral justification for the actions in case E. We would still say, even here, that there is a duty not to bring about this harm. This is important in order to remind the agent that she ought to make an effort to avoid the harm (by hastily rigging up some sort of warning signal, for example) if this is at all possible without jeopardizing her urgent goal. But this duty is outweighed by the urgency and importance of the task. In the final analysis, surely we would say that the action was morally justified in spite of the element of danger it creates. As we argued in Chapter Three, Case 16 (p. 226) is parallel to case E in all these respects.

EXPECTATIONS

There may be an additional element of wrongness in stopping ongoing treatment that cannot be expressed in terms of the usual (essentially consequentialist) calculations. To get at this element, consider the following case:

At a time when kidney dialysis units are in short supply, Bert presents himself at a dialysis center suffering from renal failure. He is accepted for treatment and scheduled on the dialysis machine. At the end of the first month of treatment, he is doing well medically — with no serious physical complications of treatment.

However, he is experiencing a severe emotional reaction to his therapy (something that is not uncommon in dialysis patients). He is deeply depressed — so much so that he has been unable to work or to take an active part in the life of his family. He spends most of his time sitting alone in his room. He is hostile and abusive toward the medical personnel who supervise his therapy. Further, he has begun to violate some of the dietary restrictions that accompany dialysis treatment, which is likely to lead to some troublesome (though probably not life-threatening) complications in the future. A psychiatrist who examines him (with his reluctant consent) concludes that this situation will moderate somewhat in time, but that he will continue to experience strong depression as long as he is dependent on the machine for life.

At about this time, Ernie — another patient in renal failure — is referred to the center. Among his records is a psychiatric evaluation that expresses confidence that his personality strength is such that he would not develop any significant emotional disturbance as a result of dialysis therapy.

The dialysis machine is operating at full capacity. It is not possible to schedule Ernie for treatment unless someone presently being served is removed from treatment. (No vacancies due to death are imminent.)

On the basis of consequentialist reasoning, it is possible to construct a moral justification for stopping ongoing treatment for Bert and giving his place on the machine to Ernie. To see this, let us pretend that we can quantify values with numerical precision. (Some consequentialists believe this is really possible, in principle.) Then the relative plights of Bert and Ernie can be represented in Table 9.

TABLE 9
Bert and Ernie

x	=	net contribution of Bert's life to *himself* (that is, the sum of all the positive values he is likely to experience if his life is sustained *minus* the sum of all expected negative values)
x^*	=	net contribution of Ernie's life to *himself*
y	=	net contribution of Bert's life to all other people whom he affects in any way
y^*	=	net contribution of Ernie's life *to others*
z	=	net dismay Bert and others would feel if he were allowed to die — discounting any hopes and expectations that have been raised as a result of his having been accepted for treatment
z^*	=	net dismay Ernie and others would feel if he were allowed to die
w	=	net value of the disappointment of hopes and expectations formed by Bert and others as a result of his having been accepted for treatment
w^*	=	zero, since Ernie has not yet been accepted for treatment

In one respect, Bert clearly has a stronger claim to treatment than Ernie. The symbol w represents a sum of disvalue that would result from stopping treatment for Bert, for which there is no equivalent disvalue in Ernie's case.

However, given Bert's emotional problems and Ernie's freedom from them, it is possible that this quantity of disvalue will be more than matched by the difference between x and x^*. And, further, considering the difficulties that Bert's problems cause for other people, it is even more likely that the initial discrepancy in Bert's favor will be more than overcome if we add in the difference between y and y^*. (We separate these two elements in this way in order to make our example compelling both for utilitarians, who hold that such decisions ought to take into account the consequences for all who are affected, and for those who hold that one ought to focus exclusively on the patient's own interests. Further we assume — largely for the sake of simplicity — that z and z^* are roughly equal.)

The point is that, on the basis of the consequentialist line of reasoning, there would be moral justification for withdrawing treatment from Bert and giving his place on the machine to Ernie if w were outweighed by differences in the appropriate other elements — even if the resulting discrepancy in favor of Ernie were a very small quantity.

This conclusion does not square with moral intuition — not *ours*, at any rate. We find ourselves saying: "But surely Bert has a special claim to this treatment, which goes beyond any and all calculations of the quantity of disappointment he and others would feel at having treatment withdrawn." This sort of reaction finds natural expression in the terminology of *rights*. We want to say that Bert has a right to continuation of dialysis therapy once it is begun. We may even want to say that *every* patient has a right to the continuation of *any* given therapy once it is begun. This furnishes a reason against stopping ongoing therapy that is much stronger than the reason based on quantity of disappointment. The purpose of invoking a rights-claim is precisely to rule out the sort of calculational comparisons that we went through in the foregoing discussion of Bert and Ernie. If Bert has a right to a place on the dialysis machine, then it does not really *matter* that Ernie would profit from it more.* The space is Bert's, by right, even if he would not profit from it most.

What is the *basis* of this right? Several explanations have been suggested by various people, but we find most of these inadequate.

1. Some claim that it stems from an implicit *promise* to continue therapy as long as necessary, which is somehow presupposed in the act of initiating treatment. But if this were the whole basis of the right, then it would be possible to avoid creating any right by explicitly disavowing such a promise at the time treatment is begun. ("I am scheduling you on the machine for now, but don't get the idea that you have a right to continued therapy. If somebody comes along who would profit from treatment more than you, I plan to remove you from treatment and give your space to him.") However, we are not at all convinced that this sort of statement would avoid creating a right. Our reaction to this statement is to say that Bert has a right not to be put in this tenuous position — and this is merely another expression of the right to continued therapy. Thus we must look elsewhere for the true basis of this right.

2. Another suggestion is that the right expresses a demand of justice: "First come, first served." However, this would establish too much. By this principle, a right to a vacancy on the dialysis machine would automatically go to the first person who applied — even if there were serious medical questions about whether he could be helped by it. But we do not think any such right as this exists. We see nothing wrong with the actual practice of surveying a number of candidates for the vacancy and choosing the one likely to benefit most from the treatment. However, once this selection has been

---

*Obviously, this statement is subject to qualification. If the benefit to Ernie were dramatically greater than that to Bert (for example, if Bert were irreversibly comatose and Ernie were conscious and active), this might override the force of Bert's right to treatment.

made, the person chosen has a right to continued treatment even if a still stronger candidate shows up at a later time.

3. Some might argue that Bert's right to treatment stems from the difference between a "positive" duty to render aid (which is supposed to be a weaker principle, applying toward Ernie) and a "negative" duty *not* to harm (which is supposed to be a much stronger principle applying toward Bert).

We agree that the negative duty not to harm is a great deal stronger than the positive duty to render aid. This is why it would be wrong, for example, to kill a healthy person in order to save the lives of several others by distributing various of his organs for transplantation into them. To kill a person deliberately has the intrinsic effect of harming her; thus it violates the negative duty not to harm. On the other hand, to allow the others to die for want of an organ transplant is not to harm them directly, but merely to fail to render aid — which is a violation of the weaker, positive duty. Thus, even though several lives would be lost by refusal to kill the one person, the strength of the negative duty is such that this should be allowed to happen.[2]

However, although it is valid in itself, this normative distinction cannot serve as the basis of Bert's right to continued treatment. The problem is that, unless the prior existence of this right is presupposed, there is no basis for classifying withdrawing treatment from him as a *harm* as opposed to a failure to render (further) aid. The only way in which Bert is harmed that Ernie is not is by having his right to continued treatment violated.

By our hypothesis, failure to receive care will cause as much and more unhappiness to Ernie (and, perhaps, to others) and will deprive him of as much and more of positive value as it will for Bert. But these negative consequences would not be classified as *direct* harms, since in neither case are they either intended or intrinsic effects of the action. In both cases, the disvalue to one person is an incidental effect of the decision to supply the treatment to the other person. Hence in neither case would bringing about these negative effects count as violating the negative duty not to harm. (This point is related to the distinction between *doing* harm and *causing* harm, discussed above, p. 284).

4. Perhaps the right to ongoing care is rooted in the highly individualized and personal nature of the doctor-patient relationship. Charles Fried indicates this in the following:

> the relationship of assisting a person in need is an action and a relationship that have a special integrity of their own.... And so when a doctor does

less than he is able for his patient, albeit in the name of...the welfare of larger numbers of persons, this is disquieting because it does violence to the integrity of a relationship which the patient assumes he is in, and which doctors have traditionally stated they were in.[3]

This image of the doctor-patient relationship is extremely attractive as an ideal, but we see serious drawbacks to making it the basis of a right to continued treatment. In the first place, this ideal could not be realized intact in presently existing structures of health care delivery. Even a physician in private practice must compromise her all-out efforts to serve the needs of any one patient in order to meet the demands of her other patients. An institutional setting, such as a welfare clinic or a dialysis center, requires still further compromise of this ideal. And it is not clear that enough of this ideal will remain after these compromises are made to ground a strong right to ongoing treatment.

In the second place, it is not clear that this ideal gets at the basic foundation of the right. We find ourselves asking: "Why do we find ourselves drawn to this image of the doctor-patient relationship? Why do we need to feel that our doctor is related to us in this special way?" The answer to these questions will reveal the basis of the right to continued treatment.

5. We think the fundamental source of the right to continued treatment lies in a recognition of the disastrous consequences that would follow from the alternative policy. Can you imagine what Bert's emotional state would be like if he had no assurance of continued therapy? He would not know from day to day whether he was to be treated or replaced on the machine by someone else. This uncertainty would undoubtedly cause tremendous anxiety. Further, his relationship with his doctor would degenerate into one of extreme fear and mistrust. Instead of telling the doctor the truth about his physical condition, he would be motivated to tell him facts that would ensure continuation of therapy — keeping secret symptoms that he feared would count against him and fabricating (or unwittingly imagining) symptoms that he thought would strengthen his position. And, since the patient is unlikely to have an entirely accurate picture of which symptoms count each way (especially since the physician would have reason not to share this information with patients), the result is likely to be total confusion on all sides about the patient's real condition. To avoid this outcome, there must be a basis for trust in and honesty with one's doctor; and this requires, in turn, the strong assurance provided by a claim of a *right* to continued treatment.

What, then, are the limits of this right? For one thing, it would seem to be the sort of right that the patient could waive or transfer if he determined that the life being sustained by means of the treatment was more a burden than a benefit. There would be no basis for unusual anxiety or mistrust if the physician was acting at the request of the patient in stopping treatment. The only basis for mistrust here would be a suspicion that the physician would *not* honor his request and would, instead, continue to prolong his life against his will.

There is also a second source of limitation on the right to continued treatment. A right gains its effectiveness by imposing a corresponding obligation on some one or more other parties. Thus if Bert has a right to continued treatment, then some one or more persons have an obligation to provide that therapy. But circumstances may arise in which this obligation imposes a grave burden on the providers, and if this happens they will no longer be morally required to fulfill this obligation.[4] This provides a justification for involuntary euthanasia within the boundaries in which we defended it above (see Chapter Three, p. 54).

SOCIAL EUTHANASIA

The category of "social euthanasia" discussed in Chapter Six (p. 174) requires further analysis in terms of the distinctions we have been working out here. Case 53 is explicit about the intention of the decision-makers: "The intention was that she would die either in transit or at home." Since the transfer was a positive action that was taken to implement this decision, we should have to describe it as *killing* the patient. To take action to put a person in a position expected to be fatal and to do so for the purpose of bringing about death is to kill that person. A similar analysis would apply to a decision, made with the intention of bringing about the patient's death, to perform surgery on a patient whose condition was so moribund that the patient could not be expected to survive the surgical procedure. Most of the Nazi euthanasia decisions follow a similar pattern.

A negative action or omission taken with the intention of bringing about death would be a case of *virtually killing* or *willfully allowing to die*. For example, if a pharmacist deliberately refrained from stocking the drug needed to save the life of his worst enemy precisely in order that it would be unavailable when the enemy next suffered a health crisis, this would be a case of virtually killing him.

However, this is not the motive from which "social euthanasia" decisions are typically made. Even his sharpest critics do not suggest that Daniel Callahan offered his proposals to limit medical treatment for patients above a certain age *in order to* bring about their deaths.[5] His goals are, rather, (a) economizing on health care expenditures and (b) justice. His proposals would have the effect that some people would die as a result of denial of treatment. But the most that can be said of him is that he would *allow them to die*, since the action he proposes is a passive one (refraining from treating these patients) and the resulting deaths would be incidental effects of implementing the policy he recommends.

One might argue that to withdraw coverage that these people currently enjoy is an *active* measure rather than a passive one. (After all, it is likely to take quite vigorous lobbying efforts to pass such legislation — and legislating itself is an activity.) But recall our discussion in Chapter Three (pp. 63–66) about the distinction between stopping ongoing treatment and not starting it in the first place. From the points we made there, it is clear that withdrawing treatment or the right to treatment is to be classified as a passive measure.

Hence, the various social euthanasia measures described in Chapter Six (p. 174) are forms of negligence or allowing harm rather than killing or willfully allowing to die. As such, they may be deplorable — especially for those who believe that we have a duty to care for these vulnerable members of our society and/or those who are not convinced that denial of treatment to them is just. But these should not be conflated with the active euthanasia measures employed by the Nazis.

NOTES

1. These two cases and much of the analysis that follows are taken from Glenn C. Graber, "The Rationality of Suicide," in Samuel E. Wallace and Alben Eser, eds., *Suicide and Euthanasia: The Rights of Personhood* (Knoxville: University of Tennessee Press, 1981), pp. 53ff.

2. For a discussion and defense of this distinction, see Philippa Foot, "The Problem of Abortion and the Doctrine of the Double Effect," *Oxford Review*, no. 5 (1967), 5–15; reprinted in Samuel Gorovitz, et al., eds., *Moral Problems in Medicine* (Englewood Cliffs, N.J.: Prentice-Hall, 1976), pp. 267–276.

3. Charles Fried, *Medical Experimentation: Personal Integrity and Social Policy* (New York: American Elsevier, 1974), pp. 69, 74.

4. This conclusion could also be defended on the basis of principle 2 in the statement by Pope Pius XII quoted in Chapter Three, p. 59.

5. Daniel Callahan, *Setting Limits: Medical Goals in an Aging Society* (New York: Simon and Schuster, 1987).

Appendix III —————————————————————————

COURT CASES

Quinlan   1976   A father withdraws the respirator from his permanently comatose daughter.
In re Quinlan, Supreme Court of New Jersey, 1976. 70 N.J. 10, 355 A.2d 647.

Saikewicz   1977   Nontreatment of acute myeloblastic monocytic leukemia in a sixty-seven-year-old man who had been profoundly retarded since birth. *Superintendent of Belchertown State School v. Saikewicz*, 373 Mass. 728, 370 N.E.2d 417

Candura   1978   Refusal of treatment by patients of questionable competence.
Northern   1978   *Lane v. Candura*, Mass. Adv. Sh. 588 N.E.2d 1232 (1978); Department of Human Services v. Northern, 563 S.W.2d 197 (Tenn. Ct. of Appeals, 1978)

Dinnerstein   1978   Do Not Resuscitate order for patient in terminal stages, agreed to by family.
In the Matter of Dinnerstein, Mass. App, 380 N.E.2d 134 (1978).

Chad Green   1978   Three-year-old boy with acute lymphocytic leukemia whose parents refuse chemotherapy in favor of an approach combining megavitamins, diet, and laetrile.
Custody of a Minor, 379 N.E.2d 1053 (Mass 1978), reviewed and aff'd, Mass Adv. Sht. 2124 (1979).

Phillip Becker   1979   Eleven-year-old boy with Down's syndrome and ventral aeptal defect whose parents refuse cardiac surgery.
In re Phillip B., 92 Cal. App. 3d 796, 156 Cal. Rptr. 48 (1979).

Cf. *Guardianship of Phillip Becker*, Superior Court, Santa Clara County, Cal., No. 10198 (August 7, 1981)

Eichner v. Dillon   1980

Withdrawal of ventilator from an eighty-three-year-old monk with massive brain damage following routine surgery. The religious leader of the order made the decision, acting on prior remarks by the patient about cases of this sort.

Eichner v. Dillon, 73 A.D.2d 431, 426 N.Y.S.2d 517 (1980), reviewed and aff'd, N.Y. Ct. of Appeals–420 N.E.2d 64 (1981).

Earle Spring   1980

Discontinuation of dialysis for a seventy-eight-year-old, senile man at the request of his wife and adult son.

In re Spring, 405 N.E.2d 115 (Mass 1980)

John Storar   1981

Fifty-two-year-old profoundly retarded man with cancer of the bladder whose mother requested discontinuation of life-sustaining blood transfusions.

In the Matter of John Storar, 52 N.Y.2d 363, 420 N.E.2d 64, 438 N.Y.S.2d 266 (1981).

Stephen Dawson   1983

Severely retarded child whose parents refused permission for surgery to replace cranial shunt (Canada).

Pamela Hamilton   1983

Twelve-year-old girl with Ewing's sarcoma whose father refuses chemotherapy and radiotherapy on religious grounds (Tennessee).

Conroy   1983

An eighty-four-year-old woman with organic brain syndrome whose nephew (and guardian) requests removal of a feeding tube.

In re Conroy, 190 NJ Super 453, 464 A2d 303 (NJ App 1983) appeal docketed, No. 21, 642 (NJ Sup Ct); 98 N.J. 321, 486 A. 2d 1209 (1985).

Barber and Nedjl v. Calif.   1983

Physician charged with manslaughter for withdrawing nutrition from a brain-damaged patient.

		Barber & Nedjl v. Calif., Sup. Ct., 2 Civil No. 69350, 69351, Ct. of App. 2d Dist, Div. 2, Oct. 12, 1983.
Elizabeth Bouvia	1984	Twenty-seven-year-old quadriplegic who requests hospital's assistance as she starves to death; contrast with New York case in which force-feeding was not authorized. *Bouvia v. Superior Court*, No. 4 Civ. 33225 (cal Ct App 1983), cert denied (Cal 1984); *Bouvia v. County of Riverside* 159780 (Riverside Co, Calif Sup Ct 1984); *Bouvia v. Superior Court* 179 Cal. App. 3d 1127 [1986].
Bartling	1984	Conscious patient asks to have ventilator removed. Refused by lower court, but overturned (after his death). *Bartling v. Superior Court*, 163 Cal. App. 3d 186 [1984].
Estate of Leach	1984	Appeals court rules that "a cause of action exists for wrongfully placing and maintaining a patient on life-support systems." *Leach v. Akron General Medical Center*, 68 Ohio Misc. 1, 426 N.E.2d 809; *Estate of Leach v. Shapiro* 469 N.E.2d 1047 (Ohio App. 1984).
Brophy	1985	Probate Court declines to authorize removing gastrostomy tube in permanently comatose patient. The family is appealing the ruling. *Patricia Brophy v. New England Sinai Hospital* (Norfolk Probate Ct., No. 85 E0009-GI); *Brophy v. New England Hospital* 497 N.E.2d 626 [Mass., 1986].
Cruzan	1988	*Cruzan v. Harmon*, 760 S.W.2d 408 (Mo. Sup. Ct. 1988); *Cruzan v. Director, Missouri Dept. of Health*, no. 88–1503, *cert. granted*, 109 S.Ct. 3240 (1989)
O'Connor	1988	*In the Matter of Mary O'Connor*, 72 N.Y.2d 517, 531 N.E.2d 607, 534 N.Y.S.2d 886 (Ct. App. 1988, amended, 1989).

INDEX

299